Secrets

ANGUS MACKENZIE

Secrets

The CIA's War at Home

With a Foreword by David Weir

UNIVERSITY OF CALIFORNIA PRESS

BERKELEY   LOS ANGELES   LONDON

University of California Press
Berkeley and Los Angeles, California

University of California Press, Ltd.
London, England

First Paperback Printing 1999

Library of Congress Cataloging-in-Publication Data

Mackenzie, Angus.
    Secrets : the CIA's war at home / Angus Mackenzie.
        p.   cm.
    Includes bibliographic references and index.
    ISBN 0 520 21955 4 (pbk. : alk. paper)
    1. Government information—United States.
    2. Freedom of Information—United States.
    I. Title.
    JK468.S4M33   1997
    323.44'5'0973-dc20   96 22685

Printed in the United States of America
9   8   7   6   5   4   3   2   1

The paper used in this publication meets the minimum
requirements of American National Standard for
Information Sciences—Permanence of Paper for Printed
Library Materials, ANSI Z39.48-1984. ∞

*To the great journalists of my generation
whose writings were discouraged by the secret efforts
of the U.S. government to put their publications
out of business, with hopes that they pick up their
pens again. And to my daughter, Kate, with wishes
that her generation may have the unfettered
First Amendment to enjoy.*

CONTENTS

Illustrations follow p. 121

FOREWORD

THIS BOOK IS THE FINAL WORK AND LEGACY of Angus Mackenzie, a fierce advocate and practitioner of freedom of speech, of the press, and of the spirit. Since his untimely death in 1994, a determined group of people has worked to ensure that this book, which he almost completed before he died, would find its way to print. Thanks to the University of California Press, that project is now coming to fruition.

The story Mackenzie tells is distressing on many levels. It is the story of a government so obsessed with keeping secrets from its own people that it waged a form of war against those who, like Angus Mackenzie, sought to expose its actions. As the twentieth century approaches its end, it is fitting to reflect on the damage this kind of official secrecy and suppression of controversial ideas and information can do to a democracy.

The ideal of free speech, fundamental to our society, has differentiated the United States from much of the rest of the world. Yet this basic freedom has been achieved only partially. What success we have had in attaining the ideal is due largely to a ragtag succession of rugged advocates who keep appearing in the land—from the irrepressible pamphleteer Tom Paine at the founding of the republic to the muckrakers at the turn of the last century to modern-day journalists like Angus Mackenzie.

Angus was born right at this century's midpoint, on New Year's Eve, 1950. He grew into an activist child of the 1960s, part of the generation that perhaps more than any other challenged America to live up to its founding principles. He also inherited a proud family's journalistic tradition, from his great-grandfather, the publisher S. S. McClure, whose magazine carried articles by muckrakers like Ida Tarbel and Lincoln Steffens, through his parents, the journalists Cameron Mackenzie and Anna DeCormis (Mackenzie).

Angus was a protester, an underground publisher, a plaintiff, an investigative reporter. He was irascible, determined, and relentless. He had a particular skill for making people angry. Those of us who worked with him at the Center for Investigative Reporting from the late seventies to the early nineties marveled at his energy and commitment to press his First Amendment rights to the limit. He was, without a doubt, one of the most determined, unapologetic First Amendment freedom fighters of this generation. He also was a generous and deeply kind friend and a doting father.

From his work on the Vietnam-era underground paper *The People's Dreadnaught,* which he helped organize, to his landmark lawsuit under the Freedom of Information Act (FOIA) against the CIA, Angus personified the spirit of the independent watchdog journalist. Suspicious of power, uncompromising in the face of official stonewalling, he pursued his stories with a singularity of purpose. That he ultimately prevailed over the CIA in his lawsuit is a testament to his perseverance as well as to his personal commitment to digging out secrets the public has the right to know. The benefits of gaining access to those secret files are shared with the rest of us in the pages that follow.

After years of award-winning reporting in newspapers and magazines, Angus decided it was time he set down what he'd discovered at greater length for a broader audience; and so he started this volume. As he wrote the book, he saw that he had uncovered an important story that has been virtually ignored by the major media to date. He also discovered that he was dying of brain cancer.

Angus knew about government suppression of unpopular opinions firsthand, and he used that knowledge to track down the experiences of many others. As he built his trail of evidence, piece by piece, in the best tradition of investigative reporters, he exposed a pattern of an official effort to suppress unpopular and unconventional opinions.

It is sad and ironic that in the final years of the century, as the formerly closed societies of the Eastern Bloc have opened their borders and exhumed the secrets of the cold war era, the United States has been unwilling to examine the damage a half century of official secrecy has done to our society. No one can read Angus Mackenzie's book without worrying about how to repair that damage.

It is the sign of a healthy, strong society that such questions can be raised and openly debated and that structural reforms can be found and implemented. Another, less enviable type of society, however, avoids such discussion and ignores these critical questions. Which kind of society is ours? This question looms large as the century draws to its close. It has been brought into sharp focus by Angus Mackenzie in his final work. The vitality of America as a democratic society in the coming century will depend on the answer.

It took Angus Mackenzie to marshal the evidence to raise this vital question. It is up to the rest of us to supply the right answer.

David Weir
San Francisco
May 1996

EDITORS' PREFACE

AFTER A DECADE OF WORK and at least two drafts, *Secrets* was headed for publication when, on Christmas Eve 1992, Angus Mackenzie had a grand mal seizure. A few days later he learned he had brain cancer. Despite the diagnosis, he continued to work on the manuscript until the progress of the tumor dictated brain surgery in April 1993 at the Stanford University Medical Center. Although he was never able to work again, Mackenzie's spirits received a tremendous boost when the University of California Press committed to the book's publication that November. Mackenzie died at the age of 43 at his home in the Mission district of San Francisco on Friday, May 13, 1994.

In the two and a half years since the author's death, his family has assembled the work in progress—from the dedication and acknowledgments through the chapters to the only partially completed epilogue and endnotes. Howard Kohn, Mackenzie's longtime friend and mentor, wrote the first draft of the epilogue in 1994, incorporating as much of the original manuscript as he could. The complete appendix was discovered on a computer disk. The illustrations, largely photographs by the author, along with their captions were delivered to the press before the author's death.

The laborious task of fact checking the manuscript was started in earnest the winter following Mackenzie's death by his mother, Anna, his brother, Jim, and his sister-in-law, Mary Wommack. This job was made immeasurably easier by the assembled source materials, mostly contained in a four-drawer fireproof file cabinet, that the author had gathered while writing the manuscript. Jane Hundertmark, his wife, retrieved and organized materials from other files for additional documentation. The Center for Investigative Reporting (CIR) housed the fact-checking project under the watchful eye of Director Dan Noyes. The CIR staff as well as the dedicated, patient, and understanding editorial staff at the University of California Press helped carry the manuscript to its completion.

Mackenzie arranged for the National Security Archive (NSA) in Washington, D.C., to house his research materials and to make them available to the public according to NSA policy. Regrettably, as indicated in the notes, a few of the documents could not be located.

James Mackenzie
Anna DeCormis Mackenzie
November 1996

ACKNOWLEDGMENTS

Howard kohn, author of *WHO KILLED KAREN SILKWOOD?* nurtured the manuscript. Jane Hundertmark edited it brilliantly, as did my father, Cameron Mackenzie. My brother, James, was behind this project from day one, as was Anna DeCormis Mackenzie. Attorney Stuart Richter successfully and on contingency sued Beloit, Wisconsin, police who raided our newspaper offices. The Dade County, Wisconsin, jury that convicted those police of falsely arresting me during the raid on our newsroom reaffirmed my belief that people love our Bill of Rights and, given a chance, will defend it. Scott Chrichton told the *Quicksilver* story before we dreamed that the CIA was involved. Cary Ritter provided couch space. Howard Bray provided support and connections to editors James Boylan, Jon Swan, and Spencer Klaw at the *Columbia Journalism Review,* who encouraged research into the FBI-CIA-army suppression of the underground press. The Newspaper Guild backed my testimony on Capitol Hill against the CIA Information Act, and the Guild's *Madison Press Connection* sponsored my Freedom of Information Act request for CIA documents on U.S. newspapers.

Jack C. Landau and Tonda Rush, then of the Reporters Committee for Freedom of the Press, arranged pro bono services of Steptoe and

Johnson attorney Kevin Brosch. Richard O. Cunningham and Diane L. Silberstein, of the same firm, sued the CIA for documents on U.S. newspapers. Kevin's wife, Patricia, and their kids did without Kevin while he gave weekends to the case and won the release of many documents used herein. Poet-fundraiser Viola Weinberg and Cynthia Elliott kept the project in beans and travel money, and a cast of a thousand helping hands included Charles Garry and Pat Richards, Nancy Clegg, Frank Speltz, Terri Shuck; Scott Armstrong, founder and executive director, and Tom Blanton, director of the National Security Archive; Seth Rosenfeld, Monica Andres, Marion Edey, and Chicago's Heartland Cafe; John Kelly, Bud Fensterwald, James H. Lesar, Sheila O'Donnell, Abe Peck, Cleo Wilson, G. Flint Taylor, Kevin T. Knobloch, Rebecca Perl, John Crewdson, Bernard Ohanian, Marty Teitel, Raymond Mungo, David Armstrong, Micha X. Peled, Daniel Ben-Horin, C-Cubed, Frank Donner, and Danny Schechter; the news dissector, Robert Scheer, Jay Peterzell, Jane Lehman, Harvey Kahn, Norman Lear, Victor Navasky, Paul Hoffman, Tom Goldstein, John Raymond, Mary Stake Hawker, Ann Marie Buitrago, Lindsay Webb, John Hanrahan, Conrad Martin, and agent Ellen Levine, who kept the orphan housed; and Jon Dann, Bill Willson, Todd Gitlin, Herb Chao Gunther, David Hunter, Patricia Hewitt, Linda Jue, Mark Knops, Naomi Marcus, Lance Lindblom, Joe Spear, Michael Orrfelt, Adam Diamant, Mae Churchill, Andy Marx, Floyd Abrams, the Center for National Security Studies, the American Civil Liberties Union, the Mudd Library at Princeton, James R. Wheaton, Jeremy and Carole Smith, Seamus Mackenzie, the Congressional Research Service, Fred Kaiser, Graham Bush, Linda Healey, Mick Long, Rocky Kistner, Barbara Koh, Barbara Grob, Abe Peck, Rob Warden, the San Francisco Public Library, and Andrea L. Sevetson of the Government Documents Room at the University of California Berkeley Library.

The Freedom of Information Project of the San Francisco–based Media Alliance and the Center for Investigative Reporting sponsored this book. The research, writing, and fact checking were made possible by generous donations from the Arca Foundation, C. S. Fund, J. Roderick MacArthur Foundation, Joint Foundation Support, Deer Creek Foundation, Tides Foundation, Fund for Constitutional Government, Public Concern Foundation, Samuel Rubin Fund, Field Foundation, Fund for Investigative Journalism, and W. H. Ferry and Carol Bernstein Ferry.

The Center for Investigative Reporting provided a home for this project in the early days, and later a seat and phone in Washington, and for that special thanks go to David Weir, Dan Noyes, Lowell Bergman, and its staff, including Stephen Levine.

INTRODUCTION

If there be time to expose through discussion the falsehood and fallacies,
to avert the evil by the processes of education, the remedy to be applied
is more speech, not enforced silence.

JUSTICE LOUIS BRANDEIS, 1927

MY EARLIEST MEMORY OF THE FIRST AMENDMENT dates back to my boyhood town of Westport, Connecticut. The fervor of the American Revolution was kept alive in Westport by old Connecticut Yankees, and there was no one more fervent than the very old proprietor of the general store where I picked up the bundles of newspapers for my paper route. The old man had been impressed by the battles of the American Revolution that had been fought in our town, and he took it as his duty to impress them in turn on the minds of the youngsters of Westport.

On cold winter afternoons we warmed ourselves by a woodstove and listened to his lectures about how the American revolutionaries had died for freedom on Compo Hill. It didn't require a great leap of imagination for an eighth grader like myself to visualize being in the thick of battle. On my paper route every day I passed by a big-bore memorial cannon and a worn green statue of a gallant Minute Man standing where the volunteer soldiers stood on April 25, 1777, the day three thousand British troops landed on the beach and then marched inland to raid a colonial armory. Nervous farmers and store clerks, carpenters and militia men from nearby towns crouched behind stone walls, waiting until the king's men were a stone's throw away. I can still remember the old man's words: "Our boys were out-numbered three to one, but they didn't sneak away to fight another day. No sir, they let the redcoats have it right between the eyes."

The thrill for the old man, though, was not just in the heroic stand of the young volunteers but in the whole idea of sacrificing your all for the freedoms that distinguish Americans. "You know why our boys fought that war?" he would say to us. "It was so Americans can say any damn thing they please!"

Many people who grew up in America tell similar stories. One of the fundamental lessons passed on from generation to generation is that Americans have the greatest of all freedoms, the freedom to express ourselves in open and public debate. Imagine my surprise, then, a few years later, when I found myself in trouble with the law for publishing a newspaper.

The year was 1970, and I was nineteen. Two friends had driven with me in a 1954 Cadillac to Beloit, Wisconsin, where my brother, James, a Vietnam veteran, was attending college on the GI Bill. All four of us were disillusioned with U.S. policies in Vietnam, so we decided to launch our own newspaper, *The People's Dreadnaught*. It was one of more than five hundred periodicals that popped into existence all over the country in the Vietnam era to give voice to the antiwar movement. During the next several months, I learned the hard way that suppression of free speech and the free press did not end with the defeat of the redcoats.

One memorable incident occurred across the state line in Loves Park, Illinois, where I was hawking copies of the *Dreadnaught*. I walked into an auto parts store, and, while I was handing a copy to the man at the counter, three men sitting on crates gave me the hard eye. I left the store and was half a block up the street when the three men caught up with me. They identified themselves as police officers and asked me if I had the police chief's permission to sell newspapers. Politely I told them about the First Amendment. The next thing I knew a blue Plymouth swooshed to the curb, and I was hustled into the back seat. At the police station, after the chief interrogated me in front of a semicircle of officers, he began flipping through the code book, trying to find a violation of the law with which to charge me.

Disorderly conduct? Disturbing the peace? Finally he settled on selling obscene materials. I almost laughed. "Do you know that grandmothers are buying our paper?" I told him. Obscenity was an interesting charge, though, given that particular issue of the *Dreadnaught*. It contained an article about the massacre of Vietnamese civilians in the village of My Lai and another article about the binding and gagging of Black Panther leader Bobby Seale at a Chicago trial of antiwar activists. Was it possible that my conduct as a purveyor of news was somehow more obscene than the conduct of trigger-happy soldiers or the conduct of a dictatorial judge?

The charges were dropped, but soon I was arrested again, this time at our newspaper office in Beloit. A raiding party of ten police officers tried to pry open the front door with a tire iron, and when that failed they kicked it open. Ostensibly they were looking for an AWOL soldier, but it was me they took downtown and booked. Although the charges again were dropped, this pattern of harassment by the police continued. In addition, I was approached by young longhaired strangers who tried to insinuate themselves into my life and encouraged me to commit crimes—buy drugs, vandalize government buildings, and so forth. That I did not fall for these ploys has to be attributed to a little good sense and a lot of good luck, because it was not until later, after my brother and I had filed a lawsuit against the authorities in Beloit, that I came to understand that these indeed were traps, set by undercover police officers.

The lawsuit accused the police of violating our civil rights "under the color of law." It would take five years for a jury to be impaneled, by which time we had long since been forced by the police onslaught to fold the *Dreadnaught*. During the course of the lawsuit, however, I got an education far different from the one I had received back in Westport. I learned that editors at scores of other underground newspapers had experienced similar treatment at the hands of local and state authorities. I learned that local cops who proved themselves effective tormentors of underground editors were rewarded by federal authorities. The police captain who led the raid on our office was promoted to a position with the intelligence unit of the Internal Revenue Service. I learned that this IRS unit was specifically assigned to target the dissident antiwar press and furthermore that the IRS was connected to two larger surreptitious operations, one run out of the Central Intelligence Agency (code-named MHCHAOS) and the other out of the Federal Bureau of Investigation (code-named COINTELPRO).

The jury awarded us $2,500, but our lawsuit was most valuable for what I learned about the cynical contempt in which some agents of the government hold the First Amendment. In the process I also learned about the Freedom of Information Act (FOIA), a law enacted to open up the tax-supported activities of federal agencies and departments to better scrutiny. The attorneys who had handled my case (from the Madison firm of Greenberg, Karp, and Heitzman) happened to be among the early FOIA experts because of their work with Les Aspin, then a Wisconsin congressman. Through them I picked up several pointers, and I soon realized the FOIA might provide a way for me to learn more about the attempts to sabotage not only the *Dreadnaught* but all the underground papers. In short order I filed FOIA requests for documents from the CIA, the FBI, and various other agencies.

————

While the concept of this book can be traced to my days in Westport, it is more precise to say that the book itself began with those FOIA requests. Federal government lawyers contested the requests through more than a decade of litigation, but the information that I eventually obtained is the underpinning for much of this text. The harassing, delaying, and stonewalling tactics of the government were also instructive. I did not expect to receive carte blanche access to the most sensitive internal workings of government operations, since the FOIA does not entitle anyone without a security clearance to have such access, but the lengths to which CIA and FBI lawyers went to impede my requests were so beyond the pale as to constitute of themselves a form of suppression. To start with, I was told I had to pay an advance deposit of $30,000 to the CIA and $1,100 to the FBI for search fees, even though I had supplied file numbers (obtained from heavily censored files previously released) for many of the periodicals in question.

This outlandish set of fees was just the beginning: clearly I was being told to get lost. However, the treatment of my FOIA requests only served to further convince me that the government had something to hide. This indeed proved to be the case.

Along with finding out all I could about the CIA's and FBI's domestic espionage operations, it became my goal to face down the counterintelligence men who carried them out. Crisscrossing the country, traveling at times with only a bag and my thumb, I did manage to talk to some of them. These interviews are also part of this book, as well as an unusual series of interviews of a CIA records officer that I was allowed to conduct at the Agency's headquarters. These interviews came about as a result of a court order. In 1979, while investigating the disruption of the dissident press during the Vietnam War—citing the Freedom of Information Act—I requested documents from the CIA on its operations affecting some five hundred antiwar newspapers. When this request was refused, I sued (*Mackenzie v. Central Intelligence Agency,* No. 82 1676 [D.D.C. 1982]). In an attempt to settle the dispute, Judge John H. Pratt ordered the Vaughn procedure. In these oral sessions, Louis Dube, information officer of the CIA Directorate of Operations, read aloud or paraphrased a stack of unexpurgated CIA reports, in the presence of other witnesses. I took shorthand notes, as I was not allowed to inspect the documents myself. It cannot be known what elements of the documents Dube omitted, but the quotation marks enclose the precise language he used in the Vaughn interviews. All information attributed to Dube was obtained in this manner; most of these CIA documents have not been published before. As for documents not directly produced through the FOIA litigation, many thousands of pages—for instance, a number of classified government papers and a sealed court transcript never before published—were turned over to me by other researchers. The accumulated store of documents has filled up a large portion of my garage.

By the time I embarked on this investigation I was already so disillusioned that it never occurred to me I could be taken by surprise again. Yet it soon became clear that the suppression of antiwar newspapers undertaken by government authorities in the late 1960s and early 1970s could not be dismissed as isolated, aberrant cases of cops and spies run amok. Rather, it revealed a fundamental and radical change in the relationship between the American government and the American people. The government-sanctioned suppression of dissent, even after it became the subject of scandalous headlines and of special congressional inquiries, even after it was officially called off, had an afterlife whose consequences to the First Amendment were just as dire. Suppression was being replaced by censorship.

Suppression and censorship are flip sides of the same coin, of course, and perhaps it was predictable that one would lead to the other. Not only is suppression unappealing to the American sensibility, but it often crosses the line into criminality, and the natural instinct of the counterintelligence officers associated with Operations MHCHAOS and COINTELPRO was to try to cover their tracks. They had every incentive to devise new methods of hiding their misdeeds. What surprised me, though, was the extent to which many other federal officials were dedicated to the proposition that censorship is an American virtue. It is one thing for professionals trained in skulduggery to prefer the secret life; it is quite another for people high up in policy positions in government to do so. Somehow they had missed out on the lesson taught by the old Connecticut Yankee.

The major villains of the censorship story are a succession of policymakers from the Johnson administration through the Nixon and Bush periods and on into the Clinton era, including several of the presidents themselves. In a sense, theirs is a spy story—not action-packed, like in the movies, but featuring sleight of hand and subterfuge and far truer to reality. Incrementally over the years they expanded a policy of censorship to the point that today it pervades every agency and department of the federal government. So gradual was the change that most guardians of the First Amendment—working members of the fourth estate and dues-paying members of the civil liberties community—scarcely noticed. Some journalists and some civil libertarians who were aware of the seismic shifts chose—for reasons difficult to comprehend—not to stand up in opposition and thus by their silence became complicitous.

If I sound judgmental, it is because of the Battle of Compo Hill. The volunteer infantrymen who freed us from British tyranny knew instinctively that the freedoms of speech and press are necessary for the people to be sovereign. Those who control information can control debate and by controlling debate can force policies upon us. The free exchange of ideas must be preserved if Americans are to be able to choose those policies for themselves.

It is in the spirit of the freedom-loving Minute Men that this book is written.

San Francisco
1993

The CIA and the Origins
of the Freedom of Information Act

Congressman Clare E. Hoffman's first reaction to the National Security Act of 1947 was exceedingly positive. Indeed, Hoffman, a conservative Michigan Republican who chaired the House Committee on Government Operations, agreed to introduce the legislation in the U.S. House of Representatives.[1] The surprise Japanese bombing of Pearl Harbor in 1941 had profoundly shaken American intelligence officials, and it was generally agreed that the absence of a centralized intelligence authority was at least partly to blame. Once the war was over, Army Major General Lauris Norstad and Navy Vice Admiral Forrest Sherman laid out a plan for the consolidation of command and intelligence. The Joint Chiefs of Staff would oversee military planning at the Pentagon; a National Security Council would coordinate the conduct of foreign affairs and national security matters at the White House; and, most important, a Central Intelligence Agency, independent of both the Pentagon and the White House, would function as a neutral repository of military intelligence.

Norstad and Sherman's plan was incorporated in the National Security Act, and with Hoffman's support it was expected to sail smoothly through Congress. The more Hoffman studied the legislation, however, the more it troubled him. The proposed CIA was to advise the National Security Council in matters concerning intelligence, to make recommendations for the coordination of spying, to disseminate intelligence, and to perform "other functions and duties related to intelligence affecting the national security as the National Security Council may from time to time direct."[2] Hoffman feared this open-ended authority.

Hoffman's concerns were shared by a fellow Midwestern conservative Republican, Clarence J. Brown of Ohio, who also worried about the seemingly unlimited power of the proposed director of Central Intelligence. In open hearings, Brown confronted Secretary of the Navy James Forrestal, a key advocate of the plan. "I am not sure that I want to trust, unless it is just absolutely necessary, any one individual or any one group with all-out power over citizens of the United States," Brown remarked. "How far does this central intelligence agency go in its authority and scope?" He posed a hypothetical question: "Should [the CIA director] decide he wants to go into my income tax reports, I presume he could do so, could he not?"

"No, I do not assume he could," Forrestal replied.

Brown pressed on. "I am not interested in setting up here, in the United States, any particular central policy agency under any president, and I do not care what his name may be, and just allowing him to have a Gestapo of his own if he wants to have it." Forrestal argued that the CIA's authority would be "limited definitely to purposes outside this country." But when asked a key question—"Is that stated in the law?"—Forrestal was stymied: "It is not; no sir."[3]

Without protections for domestic liberties written into the law, it was easy to imagine any number of situations in which the power of the proposed CIA or its director could go unchecked: the president could use the CIA to spy on Congress, could secretly manipulate elections, or could undermine political opponents. The greatest danger was that, once created, the CIA would be hard to contain. Should Congress try in the future to legislate a change, the president could veto such legislation and attack members of Congress for being weak on national security. Hoffman said, "If we are going to fix anything we had better do it now before we turn over any blanket authority to anyone because we can never get it back."

Admiral Sherman suggested a compromise. The CIA would not have "police, law enforcement, or internal security functions," and it would be prohibited from "investigations inside the continental limits of the United States and its possessions." Once this bargain was struck, most opposition to the CIA faded away. Little attention was given to a seemingly innocuous sentence buried in the proposal: "The Director of Central Intelligence shall be responsible for protecting sources and methods from unauthorized disclosure."[4]

Almost no one foresaw the sweeping secrecy powers that would emanate from those few words. Almost no one had a hint that these words would be taken by courts, twenty-five years later, as congressional authorization for peacetime censorship in a nation that had been free of such censorship for nearly two hundred years. Almost no one, that is, except Hoffman, who had become convinced that the new CIA was anathema to a democracy. Although he had introduced the bill in the House, Hoffman at the end was speaking sharply but unsuccessfully against it—virtually a solitary voice in the wilderness.[5]

In the decades that followed the passage of the 1947 National Security Act, the CIA would become increasingly involved in domestic politics, abridging the First Amendment guarantees of free speech and press; it would spy on law-abiding American dissidents, tell the Internal Revenue Service to investigate political "enemies" of the Agency, and attempt to silence news reporters and news publications in order to keep the American public from learning that the 1947 law was being systematically violated. Moreover, more than four million employees and contractors of the United States government would be prevented from disclosing matters of wrongdoing, large or small, because the 1947 act would be interpreted as an endorsement of widespread censorship.

In 1954 Congressman John Emerson Moss, a Democrat from California, tried to find out if supervisors at federal agencies were using allegations of security violations as an excuse to fire federal employees who were not well liked or who had contrary political views. Moss wrote to the Civil Service Commission, asking for a review of dozens of firings, but he was not afforded even the courtesy of a reply. "No response, no letter, no nothing," he said.[6] Moss realized that certain members of the executive branch had little more than contempt for congressional prerogatives. His response was to introduce the Freedom of Information Act, known as the FOIA. The FOIA was designed as a legal means of access for members of Congress, as well as for citizens at large, to obtain a wide array of documentary information from inside the executive branch.

At earlier times in American history not only would the FOIA have been enacted as a matter of course by Congress, it would have been perceived as part of mainstream political tradition. The American government's dedication to a policy of openness had been one of its hallmarks since the War of Independence. In the panic and self-doubt that followed the catastrophe at Pearl Harbor, however, a different attitude had begun to prevail in the corridors of government. During World War II new regulations were instituted, imposing an unprecedented regime of secrecy in Washington, and with the onset of the cold war many high-ranking government officials believed that the wartime rules should continue in force.

As the Eisenhower administration gave way to the Kennedy administration and in turn to the Johnson administration, Moss still did not have enough votes in Congress for his bill to pass. Even though by no stretch of the imagination would the FOIA have caused the release of legitimate secrets—plans for nuclear weaponry, for instance, or private communiqués between heads of state—it was construed as a threat by a new school of political thought. For the first time in American history, the combined wisdom of official Washington leaned toward advocating secrecy and restricting openness as much as possible. This school of thought, which had been codified in the 1947 National Security Act, ran counter to the very foundation of American democracy, and yet in the atmosphere of the cold war it passed for patriotism.

In 1966 Moss achieved a political breakthrough, and the FOIA became law.[7] The essential conflict, however, was far from resolved. In fact, the conflict was merely formalized. The Freedom of Information

Act's requirements of openness placed it on a collision course with the National Security Act and its provisions for secrecy. For the next three decades there would be a series of confrontations between those devoted to reducing governmental secrecy and those bent on adding more layers to it.

ONE

Conservatives Worry and the Cover-up Begins

LATE AT NIGHT IN THE WATERING HOLES of American intelligence agents, the mention of Stanley K. Sheinbaum's name can still arouse a muttering of anger. Sheinbaum was the first person to go public with his experience of CIA activity in the United States—a story about the Agency's infiltration of a legitimate civilian institution. Sheinbaum so embarrassed senior officials of the CIA that they set in motion an elaborate internal operation intended to prevent anyone else from ever doing what he had done.

Sheinbaum's connection with the CIA began in the 1950s, a period when security officers at the rapidly expanding Agency were sometimes overworked. On occasion they neglected to ask someone to sign a secrecy contract, which was normally a prerequisite of employment. Once signed, it committed a CIA agent to complete secrecy, beginning with the first day on the job and continuing until death. But Sheinbaum's association with the CIA was indirect, through a university that turned out to be working under contract with the Agency. He was never a CIA employee and, as far as he can remember, was never asked to sign a secrecy agreement.[1] During his days as a doctoral student at Stanford University and as a Fulbright fellow in Paris, Sheinbaum developed a strong interest in helping the economies of underdeveloped nations expand. When his Fulbright ran out in the summer of 1955, he landed a position at Michigan State University, working on a $25 million government project to advise South Vietnamese President Ngo Dinh Diem. By 1957, Sheinbaum was coordinator of the project.[2]

His new responsibilities included inspecting work in Vietnam. Before he went on a trip there in 1957, university officials told him about the general CIA connection; once there, Vietnamese officials informed him that his project staff included CIA officers. The revelation bothered him. He thought it inappropriate that he and other legitimate academic advisers were being used as cover for U.S. government manipulation. Sheinbaum left Vietnam feeling that his work and his program had been compromised. Upon his return to the United States, he was further entangled when he was called upon to meet with four top South Vietnamese officials in San Francisco. "Within an hour of their arrival," Sheinbaum later recalled, "the youngest, a nephew of Ngo Dinh Diem, conspiratorially drew me aside and informed me that one of the others was going to kill the eldest of the group."[3] While taking steps to thwart the plot, Sheinbaum realized that his original goal, the economic improvement of impoverished nations, was getting lost in his administrative work as coordinator. His growing dismay—at what he later called the "unhealthy" CIA component and "the general U.S. policy . . . in Vietnam"[4]—led him to resign from the project in 1959.

By this stage, however, Sheinbaum had information that was confidential. Following the buildup of U.S. troops in Vietnam and the assassination of Diem, Sheinbaum decided it was his patriotic duty to publicize information that he hoped might put the brakes on U.S. involvement. Writing about the connections between Michigan State University, the CIA, and the Saigon police (with the help of Robert Scheer, a young investigative reporter), the Sheinbaum story was to appear in the June 1966 issue of *Ramparts* magazine. The article disclosed that Michigan State University had been secretly used by the CIA to train Saigon police and to keep an inventory of ammunition for grenade launchers, Browning automatic rifles, and .50 caliber machine guns, as well as to write the South Vietnamese constitution.

The problem, in Sheinbaum's view, was that such secret funding of academics to execute government programs undercut scholarly integrity. When scholars are forced into a conflict of interest, he wrote, "where is the source of serious intellectual criticism that would help us avoid future Vietnams?"[5]

Word of Sheinbaum's forthcoming article caused consternation on the seventh floor of CIA headquarters. On April 18, 1966, Director of Central Intelligence William F. Raborn Jr. notified his director of security that he wanted a "run down" on *Ramparts* magazine on a "high priority basis."[6] This strongly worded order would prove to be a turning point for the Agency. To "run down" a domestic news publication because it had exposed questionable practices of the CIA was clearly in violation of the 1947 National Security Act's prohibition on domestic operations and meant the CIA eventually would have to engage in a cover-up. The CIA director of security, Howard J. Osborn, was also told: "The Director [Raborn] is particularly interested in the authors of the article, namely, Stanley Sheinbaum and Robert Scheer. He is also interested in any other individuals who worked for the magazine."[7]

Osborn's deputies had just two days to prepare a special briefing on *Ramparts* for the director. By searching existing CIA files they were able to assemble dossiers on approximately twenty-two of the fifty-five *Ramparts* writers and editors, which itself indicates the Agency's penchant for collecting information on American critics of government policies. Osborn was able to tell Raborn that *Ramparts* had grown from a Catholic lay journal into a publication with a staff of more than fifty people in New York, Paris, and Munich, including two active members of the U.S. Communist Party. The most outspoken of the CIA critics at the magazine was not a Communist but a former Green Beret veteran, Donald Duncan. Duncan had written, according to then CIA Deputy Director Richard Helms, "We will continue to be in danger as long as the CIA is deciding policy and manipulating nations."[8] Of immediate concern to Raborn, however, was Osborn's finding that Sheinbaum was in the process of exposing more CIA domestic organizations. The investigation of *Ramparts* was to be intensified, Raborn told Osborn.

At the same time, Helms passed information to President Lyndon Johnson's aide, William D. Moyers, about the plans of two *Ramparts* editors to run for Congress on an antiwar platform. Within days, the CIA had progressed from investigating a news publication to sending domestic political intelligence to the White House, just as a few members of Congress had feared nineteen years earlier.

Upon publication, Sheinbaum's article triggered a storm of protests from academicians and legislators across the country who saw the CIA's infiltration of a college campus as a threat to academic freedom. The outcry grew so loud that President Johnson felt he had to make a reassuring public statement and establish a task force to review any government activities that might endanger the integrity of the educational community. The task force was a collection of political statesmen—such as Attorney General Nicholas Katzenbach and Secretary of Health, Education, and Welfare John Gardner—but also included Richard Helms, the CIA official who himself had been dealing in political espionage. The purpose of the task force, it soon became clear, was to forestall further embarrassment and preclude any congressional investigation of CIA operations. Helms, furthermore, organized an internal task force of directorate chiefs to examine all CIA relationships with academic institutions—but that review, from all appearances, was designed only to ensure that these operations remained secret.

Meanwhile, CIA officers spent April and May of 1966 identifying the source of *Ramparts*'s money. Their target was executive editor Warren Hinckle, the magazine's chief fund-raiser and a man easy to track. He wore a black patch over one eye and made no secret of the difficult state of the magazine's finances as he continually begged a network of rich donors for operating funds. The agents also reported that Hinckle had launched a $2.5 million lawsuit against Alabama Governor George Wallace for calling the magazine pro-Communist (information that Osborn dutifully passed on to Raborn). The real point of the CIA investigation, however, was to place *Ramparts* reporters under such close surveillance that any CIA officials involved in domestic operations would have time to rehearse cover stories before the reporters arrived to question them.

Next, Raborn broadened the scope of his investigation of *Ramparts*'s staff by recruiting help from other agencies. On June 16, 1966, he ordered Osborn to "urge" the FBI to "investigate these people as a subversive unit." Osborn forwarded this request to the FBI, expressing the CIA's interest in anything the FBI might develop "of a derogatory nature."[9] One CIA officer, who later inspected the CIA file of the *Ramparts* investigation, said that the Agency was trying to find a way of shutting down the magazine that would stand up in court, notwithstanding the constraints of the First Amendment.

In January 1967, in the dining room of the Algonquin Hotel in New York City, Hinckle met Michael Wood, a former employee of a CIA contractor like Sheinbaum. Wood, twenty-four years old, was nervous. A Pomona College dropout, he had been a fund-raiser for the National Student Association, whose representatives attended a variety of international meetings on behalf of three million American college students. In the course of his work, Wood learned that money for the student association was coming from the CIA Covert Action Division No. Five. The CIA was funding the association in order to counter the Moscow-dominated student groups around the world and to assist with recruiting foreign students. Having financed a large segment of the association's budget, the CIA had effectively made agents out of many of the association's senior officers. Wood told Hinckle that the CIA had required most officers of the student association to sign secrecy oaths, leading the students to believe they would be imprisoned if they violated the oath. Wood was one of the very few students who both knew about the CIA connection and had not signed a secrecy contract. He had in his possession copies of the association's financial records, which he turned over to Hinckle.

Hinckle was wary. "Wood's story was not one calculated to instill faith in the skeptic," he wrote later.[10] Hinckle told his reporters to check Wood's story. They found that several years earlier, Texas Congressman Wright Patman had openly identified eight philanthropic foundations serving as undercover financial conduits for the CIA.

Obtaining publicly available IRS records on the tax-exempt foundations, Hinckle's reporters cross-referenced them with the financial records that Wood had provided. To their astonishment, they discovered that the foundations named by Congressman Patman had funded the National Student Association. Wood was telling the truth. Hinckle could scarcely believe the CIA's poor spycraft: even after the CIA conduits had been exposed, the Agency had continued to use them. The *Ramparts* reporters soon ran into obstacles, however. "The CIA knew we were onto their game before we had time to discover what it really was. Doors slammed in the faces of our inquiring reporters. . . . The blank walls were impressive," Hinckle recalled.[11]

Meanwhile, President Johnson had replaced Raborn as CIA director with Helms, who immediately made a crucial decision. He transferred responsibility for the *Ramparts* operation away from Osborn to a key CIA operative whose identity would not be known for years. Richard Ober's name is curiously absent from indexes of books about political spying of his era. Ober managed to keep in the shadows—a force behind the scenes, a man careful to say nothing that would reveal his true role. Few of his associates would even admit to knowing him. It was a breach of the code when one associate gave me a rough description of Ober as a big man with reddish skin and hair.

Ober was a counterintelligence specialist in the Directorate of Plans, sometimes known as the dirty tricks department. He had joined the Agency in 1948 and had a background that CIA directors trusted—Harvard class of 1943, army experience, graduate study in international affairs at Columbia University. At the CIA, Ober had completed two tours of duty abroad, returning to run clandestine operations from a desk and to study at the National War College before becoming the elite of the elite: a counterintelligence officer.[12] Ober and his fellow counterintelligence agents worked in isolation from the rest of the Agency, in the most secret of the Agency's secret compartments. Counterintelligence involves destroying the effectiveness of foreign intelligence services and protecting one's own spies from exposure and subversion. During the 1950s and early 1960s counterintelligence had been widely expanded to all manner of internal police jobs, which now included stopping American publications from printing articles about questionable CIA operations.

As Ober studied the legal options for getting the courts to prevent *Ramparts* from printing a story about the National Student Association, he found that none existed. There simply was no legal precedent for stopping publication. Instead a decision was reached to try to achieve "damage control." A press conference was planned before *Ramparts* was due to break the story. Leaders of the National Student Association were to admit to their CIA relationship and were to say it had been ended at their insistence. The plan was to steal the thunder from the *Ramparts* story, limiting its impact by making it old news.

However, Hinckle discovered the plan before the press conference could be held. "I was damned if I was going to let the CIA scoop me," recalled Hinckle. "I bought full-page advertisements in *The New York Times* and *Washington Post* to scoop myself, which seemed the preferable alternative."[13] Hinckle's ad read, "In its March issue, *Ramparts* magazine will document how the CIA has infiltrated and subverted the world of American student leaders over the past fifteen years." On February 13, 1967, the day before Hinckle's advertisements appeared, the news that they were forthcoming panicked the CIA, the State Department, and the White House. The acting secretary of state drafted a secret memorandum for President Johnson suggesting a Plan B for handling this fiasco. The State Department, making a "bare bones" admission, would claim that the student operation was "tapering off" and would soon come to a complete halt.

Even as the fallback plan was being developed, a new surprise was in the works. Although CIA officers had already told the students not to talk, one of the student leaders confirmed to reporters the accuracy of the *Ramparts* allegations. Hinckle was astounded yet again: "It is a rare thing in this business when you say bang and somebody says I'm dead."[14]

In short order, eight influential congressmen—California Democrats George E. Brown Jr., Phillip Burton, and Don Edwards, plus Democrats John G. Dow, Benjamin S. Rosenthal, and William F. Ryan of New York, Robert W. Kastenmeier of Wisconsin, and John Conyers Jr. of Michigan—signed a letter of protest to President Johnson. It arrived at the White House the same evening the *Ramparts* advertisements were printed. "We were appalled to learn today that the Central Intelligence Agency has been subsidizing the National Student Association for more than a decade," the letter said. "It represents an unconscionable extension of power by an agency of government over institutions outside its jurisdiction. This disclosure leads us and many others here and abroad to believe that the CIA can be as much a threat to American as to foreign democratic institutions."

The day after the ads appeared, the IRS acted on a request from the CIA by providing copies of *Ramparts*'s tax returns to Ober. It turned out that the IRS had audited the magazine's corporate returns, as well as the personal returns of publisher Edward Keating, for the tax years 1960–64.[15] Keating, a philanthropist in the 70 percent tax bracket, had been deducting the magazine's annual deficit from his personal taxes. A CIA officer analyzed the tax data and noticed an apparent discrepancy overlooked by the IRS. While Keating was claiming all of the losses, which were in the range of $450,000 a year, five others, including Hinckle, also owned stock in the magazine. The IRS advised the CIA it intended to check out this discrepancy. Ober by now had a fairly clear picture of the financial situation at *Ramparts*. One of Ober's men had filed the following report: "Keating's wife, the former Helen English, had a substantial personal estate (derived from family interests in U.S. Gypsum) from which came the capital funds which provided the wherewithal for the operations of *Ramparts*. They have been liquidating this estate steadily over the years and by 1965, it was completely gone. Examination of bank statements and capital transactions confirmed this source of funds."

The bad news for Ober was that none of his men could turn up any foreign funding of *Ramparts*. Without any evidence of foreign influence over the magazine, Ober was legally barred by the 1947 National Security Act from further pursuit of the *Ramparts* staff. Instead of halting the operation against *Ramparts,* however, Ober went on the offensive. On the same day he got the IRS tax data on *Ramparts,* Ober circulated a memo discussing "certain operational recommendations." While the CIA continues to withhold the full story of what Ober had in mind, this much has been discovered: news stories meant to discredit *Ramparts* were to be planted. CIA officer Louis Dube would later admit, somewhat cryptically, that Ober's operational recommendations involved "articles that would appear in other media." In fact, Ober planned a propaganda campaign against *Ramparts*.

Ten days later, the campaign began. A story presumably planted by the CIA was widely syndicated in newspapers such as the *Washington Star*. The story was written by Carl Rowan, former director of the United States Information Agency. Now a national columnist, Rowan implied that *Ramparts*'s exposés were Communist-inspired:

> A few days ago a brief, cryptic report out of Prague, Czechoslovakia, was passed among a handful of top officials in Washington. It said that an editor of *Ramparts* magazine had come to Prague and held a long, secret session with officers of the Communist-controlled International Union of Students.
>
> *Ramparts* is the magazine that exposed the fact that the Central Intelligence Agency has been financing the National Student Association, which in turn has worked for several years to prevent the International Union of Students from dominating the youth of the world.
>
> The Prague report aroused deep suspicions here among officials who are privately shocked and dismayed at the damage to the CIA and to U.S. foreign policy interests caused by the needless series of busted intelligence "covers" that has resulted from the *Ramparts* exposé.
>
> What, if any, relationship does *Ramparts* have to the IUS?[16]

At Langley, a CIA officer summarized Rowan's article in a memo. That memo is still secret. To release it, the CIA contends, would reveal a CIA "method." Rowan refused to discuss the matter at the time.

On March 4, 1967, Richard Ober got a report from a person who attended a *Ramparts* staff meeting at which magazine reporters had discussed their interviews of high executive branch government officials and their attempts to meet with White House staff members. Now Ober knew who was saying what to whom.[17] Three days later, Ober's task force found out that a *Ramparts* reporter was going to interview a CIA "asset": that is, someone under CIA control. In preparation, CIA officers told the asset how to handle the reporter, and after the interview the asset reported back to the CIA.[18]

On March 16, two of Ober's men drove from CIA headquarters to a nearby airport to pick up a CIA agent who was a good friend of a *Ramparts* reporter. They went to a hotel, where the CIA agent was debriefed. Then the agent and his case officers reviewed his cover story, which he went on to tell his *Ramparts* contact as a means of obtaining more information. During the same period Ober was trying to recruit five former *Ramparts* employees as informants. "Maybe they were unhappy," a CIA agent would later explain.[19] On April 4, Ober completed a status report on his *Ramparts* task force. His men had identified and investigated 127 *Ramparts* writers and researchers, as well as nearly 200 other American civilians with some link to the magazine.

Three more CIA officers joined Ober's team, bringing to twelve the number of full-time or part-time officers coordinating intelligence and operations on *Ramparts* at the headquarters level.[20] On April 5, 1967, the task force completed its tentative assessment and recommendations, setting forth future actions—which, the CIA was still insisting in 1994, cannot be released under the Freedom of Information Act. CIA officer Louis Dube described the recommendations as "heady shit" but refused to be more specific.

It is known that Ober became fascinated with *Ramparts* advertisers. "One of our officers was in contact with a source who provided us with information about *Ramparts*'s advertising," Dube admitted.[21] On April 28, a CIA analyst working for Ober tried to learn if the CIA had any friends who might have influence with *Ramparts* advertisers,[22] apparently with the intention of getting them to drop their accounts.

––––––––

Richard Ober, acutely aware that the scandals exposed by *Ramparts* were symptoms of a leaky secrecy system, took pains to protect his own operation from similar leaks. Indeed, Ober knew that any publicity about his work would generate a much bigger scandal. The twelve men working with him on the operation were his primary concern. Even though he expected them to maintain their silence, he reinforced this expectation by relying heavily on secrecy contracts. In secret testimony Ober would later explain, "Those [secrecy] agreements were signed by everybody exposed to my project at headquarters."[23]

Eventually, the failure to have Michael Wood sign a secrecy agreement meant the CIA had to sever its ties to the National Student Association. The instrument of this divorce was a settlement drafted by the CIA chief counsel. On August 11, 1967, the CIA signed over to the student association the title to a building at 2115 and 2117 S Street, N.W., Washington, D.C., which the CIA had owned. However, the building was heavily mortgaged, and after the CIA stopped paying the debt, the payments bled the student treasury for many years. The National Student Association changed its name to the United States Student Association but never fully recovered its reputation.[24] American students, unlike their European counterparts, are for the most part still without an effective organization to lobby their national legislature, the Congress.

TWO

You Expose Us, We Spy on You

IN RESPONSE TO PRESIDENT JOHNSON'S rising anxiety about Vietnam, CIA interest in the dissident press dramatically expanded in the summer of 1967. In July, Director Helms appointed Thomas H. Karamessines, an admirer of Helms, one of four deputy directors in the Agency. As deputy director of operations, Karamessines was in charge of all espionage, counterespionage, and covert action worldwide—including, of course, such activities within the United States.

Karamessines's twenty-three years in the CIA had included, most recently, the top job in foreign intelligence. He began as a desk officer in Greece at the end of World War II, when Greece was a focal point in the developing cold war. He did similar duty in Vienna and Rome, attended the prestigious National War College in the mid-1950s, and later was deeply involved in often deadly operations to bring down nationalist leaders such as Salvador Allende, Che Guevara, Fidel Castro, and Patrice Lumumba.[1]

Less than a month after Karamessines was promoted, he started an operation to handle the antiwar press. The new campaign was evidently sprung on August 4, 1967, when a "telegram [went out] to a great many field stations talking about high level interest in this activity," according to Richard Ober, in testimony before the Rockefeller Commission years later. The new operation, called Special Operations Group (SOG), was to be part of counterintelligence, and as such in the domain of the counterintelligence chief, James Jesus Angleton, then working under Karamessines. When Angleton learned of the new group, he was also given the names of two candidates to head it. He chose Ober.[2]

On or about August 15, Angleton called a small meeting to announce Ober's new title and responsibilities. Ober's job was to coordinate SOG and expand his *Ramparts* investigation to encompass the entire antiwar underground press, numbering some five hundred newspapers. He was to use the same plausible denial—"foreign funding"—that was used to justify the *Ramparts* operation. The special operation was later designated MHCHAOS: "MH" for the worldwide area of operations, "CHAOS" for, well, chaos. The *Ramparts* Task Force had been "high priority." MHCHAOS was above that: "operational priority in the field is in the highest category, ranking with Soviet and Chinese" operations.[3] In twenty years, from 1947 to 1967, the CIA had moved from forswearing internal security functions to assigning domestic political espionage the highest level of priority.

Ober was stunned. He left Angleton's office and proceeded down the waxed hallways of CIA headquarters. "I can still vividly remember saying to myself at that moment, as I walked back to my office, that I had a bear by the tail. I was convinced then that the project would ultimately leak with explosive results," Ober told the Rockefeller Commission later.[4]

The need to hide MHCHAOS was overwhelming. Discovery would mean congressional inquiries, the end of careers, and perhaps even prison. Those most likely to leak MHCHAOS to the press would be the CIA's own officers. Ober, therefore, had a dilemma of the first order. He would need to keep MHCHAOS secret from as many CIA officers as possible, and yet the operation was of such a high priority that he would be forced to rely on other Agency personnel for help. During the *Ramparts* operation, the CIA Domestic Contact Service office in San Francisco had supplied Ober with dossiers on San Francisco–based writers, and now Ober needed that sort of assistance from virtually every CIA bureau. Even with a counterintelligence staff that would grow to more than sixty field agents, he would have to involve other CIA compartments.

Ober's strategy, therefore, was the same as in the *Ramparts* operation. He would be certain that no Sheinbaums or Woods would slip through a crack in his security system. Everyone involved in MHCHAOS would have to sign a secrecy contract. Also, Ober would use a cover story with any agents brought in from other compartments. They would be told the underground newspapers had "foreign connections," even if there was little, if any, evidence to that effect. Ober had to realize that the better sleuths within the CIA would suspect he was trying to conceal a domestic spying operation. When any agent voiced suspicions or raised complaints, Ober took him aside and ordered him to sign the secrecy agreement. Once the secrecy contract was signed, Ober gave the agent the cover story about investigating foreign connections. Even if the agent did not buy the story, the contract silenced him.

As a further security precaution, Ober moved his operation inside the specially shielded vaults in the basement of CIA headquarters, where he was safe from electronic eavesdropping. Electric typewriters and computer keyboards give off electronic signals that can be intercepted and deciphered, and the vaults were designed to prevent such penetrations. No one was allowed into Ober's vaults except members of his team. Ober said his security system was based on a British model. He kept a list of everyone who had been given access to MHCHAOS, and everyone had to sign the secrecy contract, which said, in part: "I recognize that this project is particularly sensitive, and I will not reveal it to anyone who is not also known to me to be cleared for this information, and I will call this [telephone] extension to find out if he is cleared, if I have any doubt."[5] Whether the secrecy contract would stand up in court was untested. Nevertheless, Ober's oaths were the initiation rite into an ultrasecret club.

Down in his vaults, Ober began receiving a tremendous volume of reports and names. To sort them out and keep track of them, Ober turned to several computer programs. "This allowed efficient record keeping and checking with a minimum of manpower," he later said. "The computer system was totally isolated from outside access and it was consulted through computer terminals which were installed in my office. I believe this was the first time this was done in the operational components of the Agency."[6] Ober was so proud of his computer system that he suggested to Helms that it be adopted by the entire counterintelligence unit.

Ober's reports on domestic dissent were sent on to President Johnson and later to President Richard Nixon. According to one CIA source, Ober sometimes carried his reports personally to the White House, in the fashion of a presidential political police chief—just as had been feared by congressional critics back in 1947. Originally, the CIA targeted *Ramparts* because it had embarrassed the Agency. Now, these widely scattered antiwar newspapers were embarrassing the whole Johnson administration. The Ober counterintelligence operation's basic job was to disrupt the enemy, and, his team staffed with ten officers, that is what Ober set out to accomplish.

The underground press was the spinal column of the antiwar movement. In California, Max Scheer had founded the *Berkeley Barb* on Friday, August 13, 1965. The front page of the *Barb's* first issue had a report on antiwar demonstrators attempting to stop a troop train carrying soldiers to a deployment point for Vietnam. Subsequent issues contained regular reports from the front lines of the movement. *Barb* staffers left their offices on Friday afternoons to hawk papers on street corners. Circulation grew to 85,000 copies a week. In Washington, D.C., the *Washington Free Press* distributed antiwar polemics on the streets outside the White House and the State Department. One of the *Free Press* editors was Frank Speltz, a white student at predominantly black Howard University. He had started the paper as a newsletter meant to carry civil rights news to nearby white campuses, but he then broadened its focus to include reporting on antiwar demonstrations. In Chicago, Los Angeles, Atlanta, San Francisco, and New York, similar papers sold for twenty-five cents a copy. By 1967, there were hundreds of antiwar, counterculture newspapers—some of them in towns as small as Grinnell, Iowa, and Lubbock, Texas. They had their own news service, the equivalent of an underground Associated Press. Their combined circulation would peak at seven million a month. In conjunction with the campus press, the underground press was a mighty antiwar propaganda machine.

The CIA was not alone in its mission. Ober coordinated efforts with agents of the army, the local police, and the FBI.[7] At the U.S.

Army Intelligence Command, Ralph Stein was assigned to a similar underground newspaper desk. Stein soon figured out that antiwar publications were being financed by change collected on the street, not by the KGB or the Chinese secret service. When Stein was called from his office to brief Ober's team at CIA headquarters, he was shocked to find that the CIA officers had knowledge about the lives of underground editors so intimate that it could only have come from infiltrators. Concerned that Ober's task force was operating in violation of the 1947 National Security Act, Stein returned to his office and registered an official objection with his commanders. The next thing he knew, he had been relieved of his liaison duties with the CIA.

In some respects Ober was a fugitive within his own agency, but the very illegality of MHCHAOS gave him power. Because he had been ordered to carry out an illegal mission, he had certain leverage over his bosses, as long as he kept his operation secret. Indeed, he had leverage over not only Karamessines but also CIA Director Helms, as well as anyone at the White House and the National Security Council who received his domestic intelligence reports. In time these would include Henry Kissinger and Nixon's counsel, John Dean. Ober was a man walking on the edge of a razor. As long as everything remained secret, he was not only safe but powerful: he had the ear of presidents.

With Richard Nixon in the White House, the demands on Ober for more political espionage became louder and clearer. Ober's sixty agents became the Nixon administration's primary source of intelligence about the antiwar leadership. As far as Ober was concerned, infiltration of antiwar periodicals had become a highly useful modus operandi to accomplish this.

———————

One of Ober's top agents, who excelled at analyzing divisions between political camps, was Chicago-born Salvatore John Ferrera, a diminutive young man with black hair, black eyes, and (according to his girlfriend of the time) a frightfully nervous stomach. He was recruited by the CIA while studying political science at Loyola University in Chicago. From his studies, he developed an ability to navigate the ideological, strategic, and tactical differences of the antiwar groups in the United States and abroad. Only a few bare facts of Ferrera's story as a domestic spy have surfaced, lines here and there in scattered news reports. The full story is still classified as secret, but what is now known provides a noteworthy illustration of Ober's operation at work.

Ferrera's first assignment was to infiltrate a group of antiwar activists who were setting out to publish a tabloid newspaper in Washington, D.C. Their leader was Terrence "Terry" Becker Jr., a former college newspaper editor and former Newhouse News Service reporter. Becker was struggling to assemble the first issue of *Quicksilver Times* when Ferrera walked up the stairs of a recently rented white clapboard house that was to serve the group as both home and office. With Ferrera was a friend, William Blum, who introduced Ferrera to Becker. Blum was an old hand in Washington's dissident circles. He had recently resigned from the State Department and in 1967 helped found the *Washington Free Press*.[8] Becker welcomed Ferrera as Blum's buddy, and Ferrera offered to help Becker with the task at hand: building frames for light tables. Once finished, they inserted the bulbs and got down to the business of pasting together the first issue of *Quicksilver Times*.

Ober was kept well informed about *Quicksilver* and hundreds of newspapers like it. According to CIA officer Louis Dube, Ober soon learned that *Quicksilver* was "just making it financially" and that the newspaper "was not receiving outside financial help, foreign or domestic."[9] Again, however, despite the lack of any evidence of foreign funding, Ober kept investigating. At *Quicksilver,* Ferrera made himself indispensable as a writer and photographer. His articles and photographs appeared in nearly every issue, in more than thirty issues altogether. After writing one piece under his own name—on June 16, 1969, in the first issue of the paper—he assumed a pseudonym, Sal Torey.

Ferrera made an ideal domestic CIA operative: young and hip-looking, with a working vocabulary of the Left. Born January 5, 1945, to immigrant parents who owned a Chicago restaurant/bar, Ferrera was raised in a four-story brick house on a tree-lined street, to which he would return on holidays between CIA assignments. His appearance was reasonably modish, with a Beatles-style haircut. After earning a master's degree at Loyola University, he had moved to Washington as a doctoral candidate in political science at George Washington University. At Loyola, Ferrera had written his master's thesis on Marxism, with particular emphasis on the conflict between orthodox Marxists and the upstarts Fidel Castro, Che Guevera, and Regis Debray, who had advocated a leap into guerrilla struggle.[10] Ferrera had read Marx on economics, Castro on revolution, and North Vietnamese General Vo Nguyen Giap on military tactics and strategy. Probably he was more widely read in the literature of the Left than were many of the dissident writers he was spying on. Ferrera's studies also gave him a fairly astute understanding of ideological divisions within the antiwar movement, divisions that other agents would later exploit to weaken the movement.

One of Ferrera's early targets was Karl Hess. An influential conservative Republican, Hess had headed the party's platform committee in 1960 and 1964 for Barry Goldwater, but by the late 1960s he had strayed from his party into the ranks of antiwar radicalism. He was editing a libertarian-anarchist newsletter, *The Libertarian,* and was about to launch a new publication, *Repress,* intended to document the growing repression of liberty in the United States. Hess was especially interested in uncovering police espionage and surveillance. *Repress* was never published, but Ferrera spent quite a lot of time working on it, all the while reporting back to Ober about Hess's activities.

Ferrera also sent Ober reports on the Youth International Party, better known as the Yippies. When the U.S. Justice Department indicted Yippie leaders Jerry Rubin and Abbie Hoffman and other antiwar activists for conspiring to cross state lines to incite riots at the 1968 Democratic National Convention in Chicago, the *Quicksilver* staff got parade permits for a protest march in front of the Justice Department. The subsequent "Chicago Eight" trial turned into a major courtroom confrontation between the Nixon administration and the antiwar movement. (The case became known as the "Chicago Seven" after defendant Bobby Seale was removed and tried separately.) Ferrera befriended the defendants and interviewed their lawyers, William

Kunstler and Leonard Weinglass, providing the CIA with inside intelligence about the most important political trial of the era. Ferrera's pose as a newsman allowed him to ask questions, take notes, and photograph his targets, and his pose as a friend of the movement let him insinuate himself into meetings where antiwar actions and legal strategies were planned.

Ober and FBI counterintelligence chief William Sullivan employed one special agent, Samuel Papich, just to carry thousands of daily reports by hand between FBI and CIA headquarters, and at least seven FBI informants were deployed around Becker, Ferrera, and Blum at *Quicksilver.* New volunteers at *Quicksilver's* staff meetings sowed opposition to the paper's founders, which led to a shutdown of the newspaper at a critical moment. Several of the supermilitant newcomers took control of the *Quicksilver* office and literally hurled Becker's allies out the door and down the stairs. A white female supporter of Becker was called a white racist by the black leader among the newcomers, who threw her to the floor and hit her in the face. Becker's allies did manage to get some of their production equipment out of the building, including their homemade light tables, and moved everything to another apartment building, but publication had to be suspended just as Nixon announced the invasion of Cambodia. The answering protests were a high-water mark of the antiwar movement. College students conducted a nationwide strike at more than three hundred campuses, but *Quicksilver* was unable to print one word on the action.

In an FBI report about *Quicksilver,* since declassified, the FBI special agent in charge assured headquarters that he was continuing to use his agents to create dissension within protest groups. In his words, he was "continuing attempts to develop plans to utilize sources to promote political differences in New Left organizations." He also reported that he was planning to produce a newsletter to counter *Quicksilver.*[11]

On May 8, 1970, *Quicksilver Times* resumed publishing and Salvatore Ferrera sent Ober several reports on the reconstituted newspaper commune. Terry Becker had been shaken by the earlier influx of disruptive volunteers. Because of the democratic form of *Quicksilver* meetings, the newcomers had each been accorded one vote and so were able to overthrow him. But now Becker was beginning to suspect this had been a government-directed coup, and he took steps to tighten his control of the paper and keep out dissenters. Becker would no longer accept people who simply showed up on his doorstep, posing as helpers. As it turned out, Ferrera also was eased out, even though Becker had no inkling that Ferrera was a CIA agent. "We collectivized at that point," Becker says. "If you worked on the paper, you had to live in the house. No outside income. If you had outside income, you pooled it. No outside jobs. The paper paid everybody's bills. We were criticized for being too closed, but it was the only way to avoid a repetition of what had happened."[12]

Ferrera wrote that the collective was so tense and introspective he found it difficult to tolerate: "No male or female chauvinism is tolerated. Both sexes at the *Quicksilver* collective assist in all aspects of the commune. There is . . . plenty of sex and this causes problems." Ferrera reported that one woman was spending less time with the father of her child and more with another man. Ferrera told Ober that he could not imagine living so close to the people he was spying on, day in and day out. "He wouldn't even consider staying there," a CIA agent later reported.

———

At CIA headquarters, the controversial nature of MHCHAOS, together with the popularity and power of the antiwar movement, meant Ober was overworked. After being able to rely initially on the Domestic Contact Service (DCS) of the CIA, whose normal function was to handle debriefings of overseas travelers and the recruitment of agents, Ober was encountering resistance from contact service officers wary of the increased demands for domestic intelligence gathering. Relations between Ober and the senior contact service officers finally grew so tense that a meeting was convened at Langley. The subject of the meeting, according to a contact service chief, was the "seemingly domestic nature" of Ober's operation. Ober countered that he had backing from the very top of the CIA and, furthermore, that none other than Henry Kissinger and Attorney General John Mitchell were depending upon his reports. Trying to pull rank, Ober instructed the contact service officers to continue feeding him information on the underground press activists and other war dissenters. The meeting broke up, but one contact service chief went back to his office and created a paper trail to protect himself. In a May 20, 1970, memo, he wrote that "at least one field chief expressed doubts about subject case."

During the meeting, at least one significant procedural change was made. In the future, DCS officers who expressed doubts about MHCHAOS would be dealt with individually by Ober himself. "It was agreed by all that a personal explanation would most likely dispel any doubts," as the memo of May 20 put it.[13] However, the DCS director continued to be nervous. He sent a notice to the chiefs of his U.S. field offices on June 29, 1970. "Although this is a statement of the obvious," the director began, referring to MHCHAOS, "we wish to emphasize once again the extreme sensitivity of this case." His message ended with a striking indication of his discomfort. Ober had been soliciting information from the contact service for two years "in verbal pitches," but now Ober would be asked to put his requests in writing. At this change, however, Ober balked. To put anything in writing would be handing his critics ammunition that they could use against him.

———

Yet another recalcitrant CIA officer was giving Ober trouble over MHCHAOS. With a lifetime secrecy contract in hand, Ober approached the man and showed him the paper. The single sheet had three typewritten paragraphs on it:

> I understand that I am not to discuss with or disclose to any person any information designated MHCHAOS unless such a person is also currently authorized to have access to MHCHAOS information. I am aware that it is my responsibility to ascertain that such authorization for another person is valid and current. . . . I am further aware that if a change in status renders it no longer necessary

for me to have access to MHCHAOS information, my name will be removed from the list of those so authorized. I also understand that removal of my name from the list will not relieve me of the responsibility of remaining silent about MHCHAOS information.

The CIA officer read the following paragraphs:

I hereby affirm my understanding that no change in my assignment or employment, including termination, will release me of my obligation as stated above.

A current list of Agency personnel cleared for MHCHAOS information is maintained in the office of the Chief, Special Operations Group, Counter Intelligence Staff, extension [phone number].

Below these paragraphs, there were three blank "signature" lines. The agent signed the form, and dated it "14 Oct 70." [14]

Ferrera was an old *Quicksilver* hand by now. He had stood by Becker from the beginning, defending him against the mutinous volunteers and assisting with the new startup. Thus, even though Ferrera refused to live at the commune, he was able to keep his access to Becker long after other nonresidents had been totally cut off.

On October 23, 1970, Ferrera reported on the current state of affairs: "Budget for each issue, $2,000. Printing costs $600–$700 per issue. The day following each issue going to the printers, a staff meeting of all workers, lasting all day and night, goes into every phase of operations . . . to decide articles for the next issue. There is a discussion of current events which are to occur nationally . . . emphasis on campus activities. Add humor, comics. Underground press from around the nation is clipped and placed in copy books. A vote is taken on each article. Those with the greatest number of votes are included in the next issue."

From another infiltrator, Ober learned about the new level of security at the *Quicksilver* office: "They are convinced there may be an attack on the paper . . . there are two-by-fours fastened across each window, screwed into walls. Three bolts have been installed on front door . . . the building contains no explosives, no sizable amounts of ammo; some members do own rifles and pistols."[15] It was this unrelenting emphasis on security that began to force Ferrera to the periphery. So, at the beginning of December 1970, Ferrera moved his base of operations to Chicago, using his *Quicksilver* staff credentials to gain entry to underground newspapers there. While he returned at intervals to the *Quicksilver* commune, his reports to Ober now covered a variety of other antiwar groups.

In Chicago, Ferrera focused on divisions within the antiwar movement. Cranking film through his 35-mm camera, he photographed the National Peace Action Coalition convention at the Packinghouse Community and Labor Center on Chicago's South Side in December. Nearly one thousand delegates were planning antiwar demonstrations for the coming year, but their ranks were split between the Mobilization Committee, headed by Rennie Davis, and the Young Socialist Alliance. Ferrera spied on each side. In the end, the convention failed to agree upon a single date for a united mass antiwar demonstration. Ferrera's reports of a divided antiwar movement were welcomed at CIA headquarters and at the White House as well.

After spending the Christmas holiday with his family in Chicago, Ferrera returned to Washington, where he reported to Ober on January 26, 1971, that the *Quicksilver* commune had become involved in the planning of a big antiwar demonstration for the first week of May. *Quicksilver* staffers had obtained a house for Rennie Davis, who was looking for demonstration organizers.[16] The goal was to create upheaval in Washington for ten days, stretching from April 28 to May 8. "The demonstration will use stalled cars to block Route 1," Ferrera reported.

Relying on impeccable sources, Ferrera provided important advance warnings to the White House. Furthermore, he developed psychological profiles of Davis and his associates. Always alert to any factionalism, Ferrera kept an eye on Davis's power struggle with the Young Socialist Alliance. He reported that there would be opposition to the May action by Young Socialists who believed demonstrations were of no use to the antiwar effort. Ober wanted reports of infighting among leaders, reports that his other agents could exploit, but Ferrera's accounts were unsatisfactory in that regard: "Haven't heard that Rennie Davis has been the center of political infighting. Talk is about the Mayday rally." It seemed that Davis had the diplomacy and charm to keep most of his rivals at bay. The Students for a Democratic Society, a national campus group, had approved the Mayday action, Ferrera related, and the underground press, especially the hometown *Quicksilver Times,* would give it ample publicity. Ferrera also reported that Davis was to be in charge of logistics, tactics, and strategy in advance of the event but would remain in the background and give little or no tactical direction at the actual demonstrations.

Ferrera infiltrated the Mayday organizing committee and in the crucial weeks before the protests his reports to Ober concentrated on tactics and logistics. The Mayday base camp would be at Potomac Park, central to twenty federal buildings and two bridges across the Potomac River. The park has a large number of exits, which, Ferrera predicted, would make it difficult for authorities to move effectively against the encampments. Ferrera added that *Quicksilver Times* was preparing a map of the park for printing on April 28. In another report, Ferrera mentioned there would be no influx of drugs, no intended assassinations, no foreign funding, and no bombing.

The importance of Ferrera's excellent intelligence work, from the earliest planning stages of the gigantic Mayday protests, cannot be overestimated. It was espionage with a political bent, and it was relayed directly from the CIA. By this point in his administration, Richard Nixon was extremely defensive about protests. With Ferrera's reports, local police and federal officials would be able to find a means of containment. Ferrera explained that this would not be easy because the Mayday plans were so disorganized: "Davis said Mayday is the most disorganized demonstration he's ever seen."

On April 22, Ferrera reported to Ober that there was "going to be a big meeting that night at *Quicksilver Times* to decide the contents of the April 28 issue. This would be the last word on the Mayday plans to be published, including a regional map of the Potomac Park campsite and other housing locations, plus the all-important final schedule of protests." Another report revealed that *Quicksilver* was in a financial bind, and the bookkeeper was negotiating with the real estate agent about overdue rent.[17]

At about this time, Ferrera entered the offices of the College Press Service collective, where he met Chip Berlet, an editor of the news syndicate that sent weekly packets of news and photographs to several hundred subscribing college newspapers. Once an arm of the National Student Association, the news agency had gone independent after the *Ramparts* exposé and was also struggling to survive financially. Berlet later described his meeting with Ferrera: "[He said he] was planning to go to Europe, and he asked if we needed a Paris connection. We checked with *Quicksilver* and found that Sal hung out with the Mayday organization."[18] So when Ferrera offered to make his apartment in Paris the foreign news bureau for College Press Service, Berlet gratefully accepted and, in turn, agreed to give Ferrera credentials and $21 a month for one or two dispatches from Paris. The trip to Paris apparently was a kind of escape valve for Ferrera, once the Mayday action was over. Until then, he continued to monitor the meetings of the protest organizers.

The Mayday action itself came off as advertised. Bridges were blocked. Tear gas burned the eyes of demonstrators. More than seven thousand were arrested. Included among those sent to jail were many of the writers and photographers at the College Press Service, along with almost all the *Quicksilver Times* staffers—except Ferrera. Staffers of Liberation News Service, the New York antiwar syndicate, who were staying at the *Quicksilver* commune, were arrested, too. All were held in large outdoor stockades.

Before Ferrera left for Paris, he also reported to Ober on the *Barb* and *Tribe* (Berkeley), the *Old Mole* (Boston), the *Guardian* (New York), *Harry* (Baltimore), the *East Village Other* (New York), and Dispatch News Service (Washington, D.C.), which had distributed Seymour Hersh's story of the My Lai massacre.

As such reports came in, Richard Ober grew increasingly hard-pressed to keep his operation secret. In August 1971, inspectors from the Office of Management and Budget, who were assigned to review the CIA budget, set off a near panic in Ober's basement vaults. Fearing that the inspectors might stumble onto MHCHAOS, Ober sent out this order: "I have confirmed with [deleted] that the OMB visiting your area between 19 August and 19 September is not aware of the MHCHAOS program and should not be made aware of it during the [deleted] briefings to be held in the near future . . . should any questions concerning MHCHAOS be raised by the OMB team, the team members should be referred back to headquarters."[19] Simultaneously, though, Ober's stature within the intelligence community was growing. Richard Helms had appointed him to the top secret interagency Intelligence Evaluation Committee, where Ober met with officials of the Department of Justice, Secret Service, Department of Defense, and National Security Agency. The committee reported directly to John Dean at the White House. The top item on the committee's agenda was domestic political intelligence, and the top task—communicated directly from Nixon via Dean—was to devise better methods of preventing leaks.

The leak considered the most embarrassing to all in the intelligence community was the publication, in 1971, of the so-called Pentagon Papers. Four years earlier, the Office of the Secretary of Defense had requested Daniel Ellsberg of the Rand Corporation (a government-funded research institute) to join the Vietnam Study Task Force. The result of this group's work was the Pentagon Papers: the forty-seven volume *U.S.-Vietnam Relations, 1945–1968.* This official study, analyzing the U.S. involvement in Vietnam, relying on secret documents and itself classified, was what Ellsberg had turned over to the *New York Times.*[20] As a direct consequence of Nixon's concern about the release of the Pentagon Papers by Ellsberg, the White House ordered the Intelligence Evaluation Committee to write a special report on how to stop this sort of leak. Entitled "The Unauthorized Disclosure of Classified Information," it was edited by Ober; it was so secret that only twenty-five copies were printed.[21] Each page was stamped "SECRET."

Ober's report admitted that leaks are sometimes in the government's interest, which was tantamount to saying the government is willing to give away secrets that make it look good but must fiercely protect any that make it look bad. Because there was no uniform procedure governing news leaks, individuals who leaked information were difficult to prosecute. Any trial might result in more releases of secret information, and, besides, the leakers were often people at the highest levels of government.

Ober's recommendations were to restrict contacts by federal officials with journalists and to record any contacts through a central office under clearly defined procedures. He further recommended that leakers be tracked down and fired and that new laws be enacted to punish unauthorized disclosures. In the years ahead, as the Republican administration of Ronald Reagan came into office, Ober's report would be used as the foundation for the largest peacetime secrecy-and-censorship apparatus the United States has ever known.

THREE

The CIA Tries to Censor Books

IN MARCH 1972, A TYPESCRIPT OF AN ARTICLE and a related book proposal were purloined by a CIA agent from a New York publisher and forwarded to Langley. For Richard Ober, the manuscript was right out of a bad dream. A former senior CIA official, Victor Marchetti, was planning to write a book exposing CIA deceptions. Marchetti had been the executive assistant to the deputy director of Central Intelligence and had attended regular planning and intelligence meetings attended by Richard Helms. He had also been a courier for the Agency group that approves covert operations. The most carefully guarded CIA information was called Sensitive Compartmented Information, or SCI, and was distributed to officials strictly on a need-to-know basis. But his position had allowed Marchetti an overview of the Agency purposely denied to most CIA officers.

Over time, Marchetti had become troubled by the Agency's role in the overthrow of democracies on behalf of dictators and by CIA manipulation of other nations' internal policies. He saw evidence of corruption in overseas operations. Marchetti's intellectual honesty was also offended by intrigue inside CIA headquarters that disrupted the accuracy of intelligence estimates. Furthermore, the Vietnam War had disillusioned Marchetti, whose sons would soon reach draft age. And when Eagle Scouts from a troop he served as scoutmaster began dodging the draft, Marchetti began to feel his CIA job was isolating him.

Upon quitting the Agency at age thirty-nine, after a highly successful fourteen-year career, Marchetti wrote a novel called *The Rope-Dancer.* Prior to its publication by Grosset and Dunlap in 1971, a CIA officer read a version of the manuscript at Marchetti's home, in keeping with the rules set out in the CIA secrecy contract Marchetti had signed. The CIA officer found no security breaches, and publication went forward.

What troubled Ober and Ober's immediate supervisor, Thomas Karamessines, was one particular line in the novel. Marchetti's central character is speaking with jaundiced anger about the fictional CIA: "Somebody should publicize the Agency's mistakes."[1] Suppose Marchetti got it in his head to write about MHCHAOS? Concerned, Helms himself ordered Marchetti placed under surveillance beginning on March 23, 1972.[2]

Within days, an article written by Marchetti appeared in the April 3 *Nation* under the headline "CIA: The President's Loyal Tool." Marchetti wrote that the CIA was using the news media to create myths about the Agency and was fooling such influential publications as the *New York Times* and *Newsweek.* Additionally, he claimed, the CIA had continued to control youth, labor, and cultural organizations in the United States, notwithstanding the scandals triggered by the report in *Ramparts.* Marchetti also castigated Helms for spending too little time engaged with the intricacies of intelligence analysis, satirically calling him a "master spy" who conducted his most important weekly meetings in less than twenty minutes. Marchetti concluded: "Secrecy, like power, tends to corrupt, and it will not be easy to persuade those who rule in the United States to change their ways."[3]

Now Marchetti was circulating a proposal at New York publishing houses to write a book-length version of the article. Who knew what secrets he might divulge?

CIA Executive Director William E. Colby appealed to the Agency's deputy general counsel, John S. Warner, for help. Warner proposed asking a court to require Marchetti to submit the book manuscript to the CIA for prepublication censorship. Warner's reasoning was this: Marchetti had signed a secrecy contract, which might have the same legal weight as a private corporate contract that prohibits employees from revealing trade secrets. The problem was that the validity of the CIA secrecy contract had yet to be upheld by any court.

Karamessines, Colby, and Helms approved Warner's strategy for moving ahead to validate the contract, recommending it to the White House, where Nixon aides John Ehrlichman and David R. Young took charge of the matter. Ehrlichman was chief of a not-yet-famous unit in the White House basement known as the Plumbers. Richard Nixon had become obsessive about stopping leaks like that of the Pentagon Papers, and to that end Young had assembled a team of former CIA agents. It was the Plumbers who had been receiving the MHCHAOS intelligence about the antiwar movement. Young's ace wiretapper was James McCord, who had been a senior CIA officer under Karamessines. McCord's arrest in connection with the wiretap of the Democratic National Committee offices in the Watergate complex was just a few weeks away.

Meanwhile, Warner met with Young in late March 1972 and obtained White House approval for the plan to take Marchetti to court. Wasting no time, Warner and Karamessines then walked into the chambers of U.S. District Court Judge Albert V. Bryan Jr., in Alexandria, Virginia, and showed the judge bits of the purloined Marchetti manuscript. The lawyers explained their legal theory to Judge Bryan. Karamessines had brought an affidavit from Helms, who asserted that CIA censorship relied upon "special authorities" granted in the 1947 National Security Act for "protecting intelligence sources and methods from unauthorized disclosure."

Judge Bryan approved Karamessines's request and issued an injunction on April 18, 1972. Within hours, a process server found Marchetti in his backyard garden and handed him a judicial order requiring him to submit all his writings to the CIA for approval. Marchetti immediately asked the American Civil Liberties Union to help him overturn the injunction. Recognizing the historical importance of Judge Bryan's order—the first injunction to enforce peacetime censorship—the ACLU agreed to take the case. A team of lawyers, headed by

Melvin Wulf of New York, was assembled. Irwin Goldbloom led a Department of Justice legal team that represented the CIA. The two sides brought their arguments to Bryan's court. The CIA was asking that the temporary injunction be made permanent; Marchetti was asking that it be lifted in its entirety. The trial began on May 15, 1972.[4]

Before starting, though, the government lawyers requested that all reporters and spectators be removed from the room, that the doors be sealed, and that the proceedings be conducted with utmost secrecy. The ACLU attorneys objected, though not in principle. They argued that the courtroom should be cleared only for presentation of classified testimony. The government lawyers agreed.

The first witness was Karamessines, who was suffering such lower back pains that he had to appear in a wheelchair pushed by a medic. Karamessines identified himself as the CIA officer responsible for overseas espionage and counterespionage. Goldbloom asked that the record be sealed for Karamessines's testimony. Judge Bryan instructed federal marshals to empty the room of everyone but the court staff and the attorneys.

This landmark censorship case thus got under way in secret, and so it seemed destined to remain. Later, not even Marchetti's ACLU attorneys would speak about the trial's proceedings. "As interesting as it would be to describe the day in detail," Wulf noted, "I am forbidden to, for the public was excluded and the testimony of the government witnesses is classified."[5] The only copy of the sealed transcript of the proceedings was subsequently lost, according to a court clerk who told CIA attorneys, "We can't find it." "And they never have!" CIA counsel Warner later wrote.[6]

In fact, the copy had only been misplaced. The following account of the trial is based on that still-classified transcript.

Karamessines went on the attack, testifying that as he read Marchetti's book proposal he determined that publication would compromise intelligence operations, although he did not mention his two principal concerns—MHCHAOS and the Plumbers unit. Instead he cited other examples, such as Marchetti's revelation that CIA officer Jack O'Connell was the control agent for King Hussein of Jordan. "This information would constitute such an embarrassment to the

Government of Jordan, coming as it would from an authoritative source," Karamessines testified, "[that] it would compel the Government of Jordan to seriously delimit, if not discontinue . . . collaboration with our Service." He also warned against making public the existence of electronic collection devices in India aimed at Chinese and Russian advanced weapons systems, as well as CIA financial assistance to the political machine of Tom Mboya and Jomo Kenyatta in Kenya. Karamessines insisted that Marchetti had to be censored so the other U.S. intelligence agencies' foreign allies would continue to trust the CIA. At stake, he said, was the CIA's reputation among the world's community of spies. It was an argument the CIA would repeat in courtrooms and before Congress for the next twenty years.

Marchetti had also named a CIA agent who was instrumental in the capture and execution of Che Guevara in Bolivia. The danger, Karamessines claimed, was that Cuban intelligence might try to retaliate against the CIA operative. But under subsequent questioning by Wulf, Karamessines admitted that the agent named by Marchetti had been previously identified in the *New York Times* and that no harm had befallen him.

Wulf asserted that the sole ground that some intelligence sources might be adversely affected was insufficient reason to censor Marchetti and limit his First Amendment rights. Such censorship was acceptable only if there was "an immediate, direct, and irreparable effect upon the security of the United States," the standard suggested by several U.S. Supreme Court justices in the earlier case about the Pentagon Papers. Goldbloom countered that this was not a First Amendment case: the United States was seeking neither to stop publication nor to censor. Rather, the United States was seeking "specific performance" of a contract. This rather clever attempt to sidestep the obvious conflict between censorship and the First Amendment was persuasive to the judge. Bryan agreed that censoring Marchetti was a question not of the First Amendment but of contract law.

To prevail, all the government would have to do was produce a signed secrecy agreement and demonstrate that Marchetti was trying to publish information learned at his place of employment. While Wulf was unable to turn Bryan around on this point, he did succeed in raising questions about the arbitrary nature of the CIA's classification process. On cross-examination, Karamessines testified that, in essence, information was classified when he himself read and classified it. A puzzled Bryan said he was having difficulty understanding why a more precise system did not exist. Karamessines was describing a system that seemed to the judge to be far too open-ended. Even information that had been previously published could be reclassified as secret if a top CIA official so decided.

For the government, Goldbloom called another CIA witness, Howard J. Osborn, CIA director of security, who had run the *Ramparts* operation before Karamessines gave it to Ober. Osborn told the judge that Marchetti had given radio and TV interviews around the country in which he had revealed classified information about the National Reconnaissance Organization's spy satellites and about two CIA "fronts," Southern Air Transport (which would later be used in arms shipments to the Nicaraguan Contras) and Rocky Mountain Air. Osborn backtracked somewhat under cross-examination, withdrawing his claim that U.S. spy photography, alluded to by Marchetti, was classified.

As his chief witness, Wulf called to the stand Marchetti, who charged that "most CIA activities are being carried out without the advice and consent of Congress, or even without their knowledge." Looking directly at Karamessines and Osborn, Marchetti said he wanted the CIA to stay out of operations in the United States: "My main purpose is to try and . . . avoid the problems that have sometimes occurred in the past in other countries where secret organizations turn into—eventually—into secret police type–organizations. They become obsessed with counterespionage in their own country and with putting down social unrest, and so forth."[7]

Marchetti later recalled the reaction of Karamessines and Osborn: "When I said that [referring to domestic operations] they shit their pants. Domestic operations were the big sin and I had a whiff of it. They knew I knew something but didn't know how much. But they assumed I knew a lot."[8]

Most likely, this courtroom drama was brought about by the fear at the CIA that someone would leak word about MHCHAOS. The secrets actually cited by Karamessines and Osborn were of little importance; many had already been reported in the press. But Karamessines and Osborn were not about to tell a judge that their true purpose that day was to cover up violations of the 1947 National Security Act. At 4:15 P.M. on the day the trial had started, after less than eight hours of testimony, Bryan granted the permanent injunction that Karamessines had requested, requiring Marchetti to submit all his writings, even novels, to CIA censors prior to sending them to his editors. Bryan ruled that "the [secrecy] contract takes the case out of the scope of the First Amendment[;] . . . to the extent the First Amendment is involved, the contract constitutes a waiver of the defendant's rights thereunder."

The ruling was of immeasurable significance, effectively nullifying the First Amendment rights of any government worker willing to submit to a secrecy contract, although the repercussions were not immediately obvious. Marchetti appealed the ruling on the basis that no contract should negate a constitutional right, but on a 6–3 vote the U.S. Supreme Court subsequently declined to review the case.

———

Even while MHCHAOS was surviving the Marchetti scare, the CIA inspector general, an internal cop, was the focal point of a second emergency. Worried that the inspector general might discover MHCHAOS and expose it, Helms called in Colby, Ober, and Karamessines for a meeting on December 5, 1972. Helms emphasized the importance of running a cleaner, less dubious-looking operation. There was a need to proceed cautiously, he said, to avoid a showdown with "some CIA personnel." Nonetheless, Helms was adamant that MHCHAOS not be abandoned. It will not be "stopped simply because some members of the organization do not like this activity," he insisted.[9]

Helms cautioned Ober against attending meetings of the Justice Department Intelligence Evaluation Committee, because security was lax and its role in domestic politics might lead investigative reporters to MHCHAOS. Helms had come up with a solution to the problem of CIA officers who doubted the legality of MHCHAOS. Henceforth, it would be described within the Agency as an operation against international terrorism. "To a [*sic*] maximum extent possible, Ober should become identified with the subject of terrorism inside the Agency as well as in the Intelligence Community," Helms ordered.[10] Afterward, Colby sent Karamessines a summary of the meeting: "A clear priority is to be given in this general field to the subject of terrorism. This should bring about a reduction in the intensity of attention to political dissidents in the United States not apt to be involved in terrorism." The change in label was evidently intended to improve the Agency's image and cover, on the assumption that "terrorists" were more believable as a genuine threat than "dissidents."[11]

But there was in fact to be little change in targets. MHCHAOS continued to hold radicals in its sights, specifically radical youths, Blacks, women, and antiwar militants. The label "international terrorist" was designed to replace "political dissident" as the ongoing justification for illegal domestic operations. And in the final move to clean up Ober's act, in December Helms put an end to the operation of the five-year-old MHCHAOS by formally transforming it into the International Terrorism Group—with Ober still in charge.

Only seventeen days later, Helms and Karamessines announced their resignations from the CIA. Nixon named James Schlesinger to replace Helms as director, and Schlesinger in turn replaced Karamessines with Colby as deputy director for plans. In a euphemistic change, Schlesinger and Colby renamed the Directorate for Plans as the Directorate for Operations, which was the CIA's way of saying, "Let's call domestic spying a response to terrorism."

Toward the end of August 1973, Marchetti submitted his completed manuscript to the CIA for prepublication review. The CIA officers who read the manuscript were pleased to discover that Marchetti and his coauthor John Marks had not written about MHCHAOS. The CIA censorship process took thirty days, and Marchetti was ultimately told to eliminate about 20 percent of the book—339 separate deletions. Among them were several paragraphs that described how Helms had perjured himself in testimony before the Senate when he denied any CIA involvement in the 1970 elections held in Chile. The exact censored words from Marchetti's text were these:

> The agency's chief of station in Santiago, working with the close cooperation of Ambassador Korry, put the money and his under-cover agents to work in a last-minute propaganda effort to thwart the rise of Allende to the Presidency. But despite the CIA's covert action program, Salvador Allende received a plurality in the September 1970 popular vote.
>
> During the next two months, before Allende was officially endorsed as President by the Chilean congress, the CIA and Ambassador Korry, with White House approval, tried desperately to prevent the Marxist from taking office. Attempts were made to undercut Allende through continued propaganda, by encouraging a military *coup d'état*, and by trying to enlist the support of private U.S. firms, namely ITT, in a scheme to sabotage Chile's economy. None of the secret actions, however, proved successful.[12]

On September 7, Marchetti and his publisher, Alfred A. Knopf, responded to the CIA's deletions by filing suit in the federal district court in New York City. The government countered by seeking a change of venue back to the Virginia courtroom of Judge Bryan. New York City was the center of the publishing industry, and Knopf was one of publishing's most respected names, whereas Bryan's courtroom was just miles away from CIA headquarters in Langley, Virginia. The change of venue would tilt the proceedings in the CIA's favor, as well as burden Knopf with the extra financial costs of an out-of-state trial. The government once more was able to prevail.

Back in Bryan's court, the government lawyers offered a compromise, a reduction in the number of deletions from 339 to 168. This sudden change, though, only reinforced Bryan's impression that CIA classification was done on the basis of "it's secret because we say so."

On March 29, 1974, Bryan ruled that the CIA had failed to show proper cause in 141 of the 168 deletions. The remaining 27 contained satellite intelligence. The CIA decision to classify information as secret, Bryan observed, "seems to have been made on an *ad hoc* basis as he [Karamessines] viewed the manuscript, founded on his belief at that time that a particular item contained classifiable information which ought to be classified."[13] In other words, information Marchetti wrote about was not classified when he worked at the CIA; it was merely classifiable. When the CIA officers read his manuscript, they classified it.

Perhaps even more significantly, Bryan recognized the First Amendment implications of Marchetti's censorship, ruling that judicial oversight of the CIA's censorship was necessary to protect Marchetti's First Amendment rights against "the whim of the reviewing official." Bryan's essential point was that CIA officers seemed to be censoring spontaneously and capriciously as they turned Marchetti's pages, in violation of the First Amendment. It was a significant reversal of Bryan's initial view of the CIA's case against Marchetti fifteen months earlier.

The CIA quickly moved to file an appeal, a process that promised to be lengthy. Rather than delay publication of *The CIA and the Cult of Intelligence* any longer, Marchetti agreed to go ahead with a version that showed 168 blank spaces. It was the first book sold in the United States that contained page after page on which the word "DELETED" appeared in bold type to indicate portions censored by the government.[14] Marchetti said later, "The CIA thought I deliberately did not talk about MHCHAOS when they saw the book . . . I was relieved . . . they asked me to do jobs with them afterwards. They said, you didn't spill your guts."[15]

The government's appeal of Judge Bryan's ruling in the Marchetti case came before Chief Judge Clement F. Haynsworth of the Fourth Judicial Circuit. Haynsworth had gained national notoriety in 1969 when the Senate rejected his nomination for the U.S. Supreme Court for failure to reveal a potential conflict of interest: he had refused to step down from labor cases involving textile mills with which he had once had business ties.

Haynsworth decided to throw out part of Bryan's ruling on the grounds that the courts had no right to entertain the question of whether CIA secrets were bona fide. Information was secret "when the legend was affixed to the document," Haynsworth ruled. He also came to the conclusion that Marchetti "effectively relinquished his First Amendment rights" when he signed his secrecy contract.[16] In Virginia, Bryan unhappily went about complying with Haynsworth's decision. "It does not appear to me that there is a great deal the District Court can now do except sustain the government's position as to all deletions," Bryan wrote in a letter to an assistant U.S. attorney.[17]

CIA officers were relieved. Even longtime CIA censors would later confess that Agency censors had cut Marchetti's book arbitrarily, in a "cavalier" fashion. "The review was amateurish," said the chief CIA censor, Charles Wilson, after he retired. "It was a review the Agency lived to regret."[18]

The outcome of the Marchetti case elevated contract law to a rank above constitutional rights. CIA attorney Warner later observed, "For the first time the CIA had taken the initiative in the courts to prevent the unauthorized disclosure of intelligence sources and methods."[19] The "sources and methods" language of the 1947 National Security Act had become the legislative foundation of censorship.

As the Marchetti suit was proceeding through the courts, so was another CIA censorship case involving an attempt to halt the publication of *The Politics of Heroin in Southeast Asia,* written by a twenty-six-year-old doctoral candidate at Yale University, Alfred W. McCoy. In the book McCoy revealed that the CIA had entered into dealings with heroin traders in Southeast Asia.[20]

McCoy had already embarrassed and angered the CIA by testifying to the Senate Appropriations Committee that the Agency—and thus the federal government—was implicated in the heroin epidemic plaguing the nation. In Indochina, the CIA had provided substantial military support for mercenaries, right-wing rebels, and tribal warlords who were engaged in narcotics traffic. "In northern Laos, Air America aircraft and helicopters chartered by the CIA and USAID have been transporting opium harvested by the Agency's tribal mercenaries on a regular basis." McCoy also testified that in Thailand, the CIA had "worked closely with Nationalist Chinese paramilitary units that controlled 80 to 90 percent of northern Burma's vast opium exports and manufactured high-grade heroin for export to the American market."[21] McCoy told the senators his full findings would be published in his book, due out in a few months.

The CIA assigned Karamessines's colleague, senior CIA official Cord Meyer, to stop McCoy and his publisher, Harper and Row. Meyer traveled to New York to call on Cass Canfield, senior editor and member of the board of directors of Harper and Row, who belonged to the same social circles as Meyer. In their meeting, he asked Canfield to freeze McCoy's contract, in a way that not only would have killed the book at Harper and Row but would have prevented McCoy from going to another publishing house.[22] Canfield refused. On July 5, 1972, CIA general counsel Lawrence R. Houston sent a letter to Harper and Row formally requesting a copy of McCoy's manuscript prior to publication.

Editors and lawyers at Harper and Row debated what to do. Meyer had claimed that publication of the book would put overseas operatives in mortal jeopardy, and a Harper and Row attorney, Brooks Thomas, thought that on this basis the submission of McCoy's manuscript to the CIA was morally correct. "How would you feel if you published and fourteen people were killed because of it?" Thomas asked. He argued that if Harper and Row maintained complete and unilateral control, a CIA review would not amount to censorship. After some weeks of discussion, McCoy's editor, Elisabeth Jakab, asked him to come to New York. McCoy met with the president of Harper and Row, Winthrop Knowlton, who told McCoy the publishing house had decided to submit his manuscript to the CIA. McCoy felt ambushed and refused to give his permission. Knowlton gave him until the next morning to change his mind.[23]

McCoy took the elevator down to the streets of midtown Manhattan and found a phone booth. Calling different editors, he discovered that changing publishers would involve lengthy legal fights and at least a six-month delay in publication. In all likelihood the delay would be fatal to sales. McCoy called his editor and arranged a meeting that night with her and Harper and Row counsel James Fox. They talked through the night about McCoy's concerns. How might they make ground rules for a process that he felt was illegal under the First Amendment? By morning, McCoy had reluctantly agreed to give the CIA censors ten days to offer their objections, and for each point he insisted on full documentation. McCoy took a shower and returned to the Harper and Row offices to write out the agreement. That same morning the *New York Times* reporter Seymour M. Hersh appeared at Harper and Row on the trail of a story that subsequently made the front page of the *New York Times:* the CIA was attempting to censor a book that linked the Agency to the trafficking of heroin.[24]

The manuscript, meanwhile, was forwarded to CIA counsel Lawrence Houston. The CIA returned a twenty-page document listing the Agency's objections, but Harper and Row editors and lawyers found no merit in any of them. Holding firm to the manuscript as McCoy had written it, Harper and Row sped up publication. The irony was that all the publicity regarding the CIA's attempts at censorship was about to make his book a success. "It would have been an obscure book without them," McCoy later said.[25]

The CIA had miscalculated. Unlike Marchetti, McCoy was not a government employee and had signed no secrecy agreement. The CIA had no contractual handle on him and no recourse in the courts; the Agency could only apply pressure in the executive suite of the publisher, and that had resoundingly backfired.

———

Toward the end of 1972, the CIA ran into new fiscal restraints, and Cord Meyer was assigned to look at Richard Ober's Special Operations Group for potential reductions. Ober and Meyer were old acquaintances. Back when Karamessines had ordered Ober to organize MHCHAOS, Meyer had been on the shortlist of other CIA officials capable of setting up the operation. Now, five years later, Ober sat in his basement vault and compiled facts and figures to defend the costs of MHCHAOS to Meyer.

Because the basement was still officially a secret, Ober walked over to Meyer's offices; there he began laying out the tremendous scope of MHCHAOS. He spoke of how he would rush orders to agents in the field, who were required to act quickly on the basis of recently obtained intelligence. Ober and his staff had "unilateral" control over eighty agents like Sal Ferrera. On average Ober was sending and receiving 5,000 "action cables" a year, and another 1,300 "action dispatches." More than 700 intelligence reports were disseminated to the White House and other agencies. FBI informants were supplying an additional 10,000 reports annually.

For such a large operation, the MHCHAOS budget for agents in the field was very small, less than $100,000. But what was most impressive to Meyer was Ober's close relationship to the Nixon administration. Ober confided that MHCHAOS files were going directly to John Dean at the White House, even as Dean was involved in the Watergate cover-up.[26]

When all was said and done, the MHCHAOS budget was left unscathed by the austerity cutbacks that otherwise were mandatory throughout the Agency. Ober could keep his agents inside the underground press.

One of the most productive agents, Sal Ferrera, was at this stage operating overseas, where his targets were Americans. Upon first landing in Europe in the summer of 1971, Ferrera had moved fast. He was in Zurich on July 7 and in Rome on July 15. In September he was in Copenhagen, spying on peace activists who were involved in an underground railroad for U.S. GIs who had deserted because of qualms over Vietnam. Ferrera then based himself in Paris, site of the Vietnamese embassies, where unofficial and official peace-seekers from the United States and Vietnam were trying to negotiate an end to the war. In his nice guy role, Ferrera sought out and befriended Americans sympathetic to the peace effort. He introduced himself to the five-member youth contingent attending the Versailles Peace Assembly, an international conference of antiwar activists.

Ferrera's cover was the same as it had been in the United States, that of a leftist journalist. College Press Service distributed his writings to its U.S. campus subscribers. In one article, Ferrera wrote about German radical political groups and the divisions between them. Another article, syndicated by the Alternative Features Service to underground newspapers in the United States, was headlined "Just Another Day in Derry" and analyzed the ideological conflicts within the Irish Republican Army.

Ferrera had proved adept at penetrating the CIA's political opponents in the United States. He was well established as a MHCHAOS star. But his new assignment was his most sensitive yet. He was to befriend former CIA officer Philip Agee, who was writing a book filled with one CIA secret after another—revealing far more than those divulged by Sheinbaum, Wood, Marchetti, and McCoy put together. Because Agee had served as a CIA case officer on the streets in South America, he had been privy to more intelligence work than the office-bound Marchetti. But, like Marchetti, Agee had grown disenchanted, responding to a general cultural wave of doubts about the U.S. imperial role in Vietnam. Agee had moved to Paris, out of the reach of U.S. courts. In France, the CIA could not enforce the secrecy contract Agee had signed.[27]

Living in the same expatriate community, however, was Ferrera, who began to frequent the Paris cafe Le Yams, where Agee often sipped coffee and socialized. Ferrera introduced himself as a reporter for College Press Service. Once he had become a familiar fixture at the cafe, Ferrera introduced Agee to a young woman he invitingly described as an "heiress." Agee had spent all his savings while at work on his book and was desperately poor. When the woman expressed an interest in financing him while he finished the book, Agee allowed her to read the unfinished manuscript over a weekend. She responded with enthusiastic support, giving Agee enough money to see him through several months of writing.

Of course, Ferrera now had the perfect rationalization to see Agee's manuscript at any point. As Agee grew more and more dependent on Ferrera, he began using Ferrera's address as his own. One of the letters that came to Ferrera's apartment was from Agee's father, and it described CIA Counsel John Greaney's visit to the Agee family home in the United States. Greaney had given Agee's father a copy of his son's secrecy contract, along with a copy of the recent Marchetti court decision.[28]

Ferrera also apparently arranged a typewriter swap, allowing him to introduce into Agee's apartment a portable Royal typewriter and a case crammed with microphones and transmitters. Agee soon discovered the surveillance device and had it photographed; eventually the photo of the bugged typewriter would appear on the cover of his book. In the meantime, though, Ferrera had learned that Agee was about to identify CIA operatives in South America. This advance notice enabled the Agency to move the operatives, as well as to take preventive measures to reduce the embarrassment from a host of other stories in Agee's book.

The book itself, *Inside the Company: CIA Diary,* was published in 1975 without prior censorship. In a twenty-two-page appendix, Agee named scores of individuals and organizations controlled, supported, or used by the CIA. Agee had by this time realized that Ferrera was an undercover operative, and Ferrera's name was included in the appendix, linked to the impressively wired typewriter case pictured on the cover. The book jacket excerpted a *Washington Post* reference to Marchetti's blank-filled book and boasted, "There are no blanks in Philip Agee's." Seizing on the Agee case, CIA officials in Washington began to agitate for a law to imprison anyone who publicly identified intelligence agents.

Ferrera returned to Chicago. After legally changing his name to Allen Vincent Carter, he fled to the Southern California suburb of Costa Mesa. In 1980, I discovered his hideout and knocked on the door of 2410 Harbor Boulevard, apartment C104. Visibly discomfited, Ferrera denied he had worked for the CIA. He said he was working for the Wonderful World of Travel, a company that "did not exist yet." When I showed him copies of the informant reports he had sent to CIA headquarters, his face registered shock. He flipped up his middle finger and slammed the door.

FOUR

Bush Perfects the Cover-up

SPEAKING BEFORE FIVE HUNDRED GUESTS at the Four Seasons restaurant in New York in February 1973, at his fiftieth birthday party, Norman Mailer was drunk. He opened his speech with a dirty joke that made the crowd groan and catcall. Then Mailer announced that he was beginning a foundation called the Fifth Estate, intended to be a "people's FBI, and a people's CIA." The foundation would investigate those two government agencies. "If we have a secret police to keep tabs on Washington's secret police," Mailer said, "we will see how far paranoia is justified. Let's look into the idea that the entire government of the United States is conceivably being managed secretly."[1]

John Leonard, commenting in the *New York Times Book Review* a couple of Sundays later, dismissed the Fifth Estate as an ill-advised vigilante group. But in the weeks after Mailer's party, the Watergate scandal developed and its antidemocratic implications began to sink in. As more information about secret political spying became known, Mailer seemed less foolish. In July 1973, the *Village Voice,* a New York City paper friendly to Mailer, ran an article headlined "Who's Paranoid Now?" In it many of the city's literary elite now said Mailer was right. "Not only was Mailer right, he was prophetic," the article concluded.[2]

Village Voice columnist Nat Hentoff noted that three former intelligence men were already publishing a magazine in Washington, D.C., called *CounterSpy*, which, as Mailer had proposed, was regularly exposing a side of the government that operated in secret. "Norman," Hentoff wrote to Mailer, "these three ex-intelligence agents are legitimate[;] . . . any source of financial support is eagerly welcomed."[3] In response, Mailer telephoned *CounterSpy* editors Tim Butz and Winslow Peck and invited them to join him for a drink at the Watergate complex bar.

Butz had served in the air force during the Vietnam War. At the main airbase outside Saigon, Tan Son Nhut, Butz was chief of a ground crew assigned to an unarmed RF4C Phantom 2 photo-reconnaissance aircraft that was flying spy missions over North Vietnam, Laos, and Cambodia. Home from the war, he enrolled at Ohio's Kent State University. There in 1970 National Guard troops shot to death his friend Allison Krause, prompting him to organize a Kent State chapter of the Vietnam Veterans Against the War. In 1971 he helped with the Mayday antiwar demonstrations that Ferrera had spied on.[4]

In March 1973, Butz and his partners had launched *CounterSpy*, a monthly with a cover price of 75 cents. The first issue accused the FBI of using a right-wing group, the Secret Army Organization, to attack antiwar activists in San Diego, California. "We all know that Big Brother is watching," stated the magazine's editorial. "No one in our government has taken the time to explain who is being spied upon, and why we are being watched. . . . The secrecy with which the government surrounds itself must stop."[5]

The meeting with Butz and Peck convinced Mailer to host a fundraising party for *CounterSpy*. With this infusion of money from Mailer's activities, *CounterSpy* was moved out of Butz's apartment into an office on Dupont Circle. The next issues were larger. *CounterSpy* revealed that the intelligence community was attempting to use fears of terrorism as an excuse to engage in domestic political spying. An editorial accused espionage agencies of promoting terrorists as the new bogeymen.

Another *CounterSpy* article uncovered the police record of the Symbionese Liberation Army leader Donald David DeFreeze, whose group had assassinated a California school superintendent and kidnapped newspaper heiress Patricia Campbell Hearst. *CounterSpy* accused DeFreeze of having been a police informant in the late 1960s, a period when he was arrested repeatedly for armed and violent crimes but released repeatedly from jail. The question was whether DeFreeze was a terrorist or a government provocateur.[6]

While on a national campus speaking tour, Mailer continued to send donated funds back to *CounterSpy.* Mailer and *CounterSpy* were the embodiment of growing anti-CIA resentment. By the middle of 1974, the CIA was in the position of having to deny involvement in the Watergate scandal.

Amid the numerous scandals of the Nixon administration and under particular pressure from partisans of Ralph Nader, Congress was moving toward a new openness. Amendments to strengthen the 1966 Freedom of Information Act were drafted. The FOIA had been reduced to near uselessness by bureaucratic intransigence and judicial refusals to restrain executive secrecy. The U.S. Supreme Court, in deciding the 1973 FOIA case *Environmental Protection Agency v. Mink,* had said the courts should not be allowed to inspect classified national security records unless Congress directed otherwise.[7] By rejecting judicial review, the Supreme Court had in the *Mink* case adopted basically the same line of reasoning as had Chief Judge Haynsworth in the Marchetti case.

In the fall of 1974, however, Congress amended the FOIA to reverse the *Mink* decision. The main proponents of the amendment were Edward Kennedy in the Senate and John E. Moss in the House. The amendment explicitly authorized federal judges to inspect classified records in chambers in order to determine whether the government was warranted in withholding them from public release. In addition, Congress added teeth to the FOIA in several other ways. In the future, the government would have to prove why secrecy was necessary for each specific case. Government agencies would have to publish indexes identifying information that had been made public, as a means of assisting citizens in locating government documents. And the fees charged to citizens for copies of government records, which sometimes were prohibitively high, could be waived under a new range of circumstances, thus ensuring that fees could not be used as barriers to disclosures.[8] Bureaucratic delays in the release of data also were sharply curtailed. A new deadline of ten working days was imposed on the government for all FOIA requests. In a case in which the government denied a request, a twenty-day appeal period was established, after which the case could be taken to court.[9]

The CIA would spend the next two decades fighting the release of documents to citizens who requested them under the FOIA. For CIA officials, whose lives were dedicated to secrecy, the logic behind the checks and balances of the three-branch system of government may have been incomprehensible. The idea that federal judges not trained in espionage could inspect CIA files and even order their release was enough to curdle the blood of secret operatives like Richard Ober. CIA officers felt that neither Congress nor the courts could comprehend the perils that faced secret agents. Their instinctive reaction, therefore, was to find any avenue by which they could avoid judicial or journalistic scrutiny.

A month after Congress enacted the new FOIA amendments, someone at the CIA leaked the news of MHCHAOS to Seymour Hersh at the *New York Times*. Hersh's article appeared on the front page of the December 22, 1974, issue under the headline "Huge C.I.A. Operation Reported in U.S. against Antiwar Forces, Other Dissidents in Nixon Years." Although sparse in detail, the article revealed that the CIA had spied on U.S. citizens in a massive domestic operation, keeping 10,000 dossiers on individuals and groups and violating the 1947 National Security Act. Hersh reported that intelligence officials were claiming the domestic operations began as legitimate spying to investigate overseas connections to dissenters.

Gerald Ford, who only four and a half months earlier had assumed the presidency in the wake of Nixon's resignation, took the public position that the CIA would be ordered to cease and desist. William Colby, who had replaced James Schlesinger as CIA director, was told to issue a report on MHCHAOS to Henry Kissinger. Apparently

Ford was not informed that Kissinger was well aware of the operation. A few days later, after Helms categorically denied that the CIA had conducted "illegal" spying,[10] Ford named Vice President Nelson Rockefeller to head a commission that would be charged with making a more comprehensive report. Ford's choice of Rockefeller to head the probe was most fortunate for Ober. Rockefeller was closely allied with Kissinger, who had been a central figure in the former New York governor's 1968 presidential primary campaign. Although Rockefeller was well regarded in media and political circles for his streak of independence, it was all but certain from the beginning that his report would amount to a cover-up.[11]

In fact, Colby ran into trouble because he was willing to be more forthcoming about MHCHAOS than Rockefeller and Kissinger desired. After Colby's second or third appearance before the commission investigators, Rockefeller drew Colby aside and said, "Bill, do you really have to present all this material to us? We realize there are secrets that you fellows need to keep, and so nobody here is going to take it amiss if you feel there are some questions you can't answer quite as fully as you seem to feel you have to."[12]

Because of MHCHAOS and Watergate, Congress began to investigate the CIA. On September 16, 1975, Senators Frank Church and John Tower called Colby to testify at a hearing about CIA assassinations. Colby showed up carrying a CIA poison-dart gun, and Church waved the gun before the television cameras. It looked like an automatic pistol with a telescopic sight mounted on the barrel. Producers of the evening newscasts recognized this as sensational footage, and just as surely Colby recognized that his days as director were numbered. He had not guarded the CIA secrets well enough.

Colby was fired on November 2, 1975. His successor was George Herbert Walker Bush, who had been serving as chief of the U.S. Liaison Office in Beijing. Bush's job would be delicate, perhaps impossible, and probably thankless; but as the former chairman of the Republican Party, he had already been in a similar position, guiding the party through the worst days of the Watergate scandal. He had supported Nixon as long as it was politically feasible, then finally had joined those who insisted on Nixon's departure.

While preparing for his confirmation hearings, Bush received a letter from Nixon, who asked that the CIA's domestic political operations be kept hidden. "You will be greatly tempted," Nixon wrote, "to 'give away the store' in assuring members of the Senate committee that everything the CIA does in the future will be an open book. This, of course, is the surest way for you to be confirmed and to reduce the number who will vote against you. It will also be the surest way to destroy an agency that has already been terribly weakened by the irresponsible attacks that have been made upon it by both the Senate and House investigating committees." In his autobiography, where he published this letter, Bush explained how he had understood Nixon: "Nixon's mention of giving away the store was an oblique reference to the policy of the man I'd replaced at the CIA, Bill Colby. As CIA director, Colby had been criticized by Agency professionals and others in government for what they perceived as his 'open book' candor whenever he testified before a Congressional committee."[13]

In contrast, Bush hewed more closely to the strategy advocated by Nixon. At his confirmation hearings before the Senate Armed Services Committee, he remarked, "Some people today are driven to wantonly disclose sensitive information—not talking here about the Congress—to friend and foe alike around the world. In many instances this type of disclosure can wipe out effective operations, can endanger the lives of patriotic Americans, and can cause enormous damage to our security." In the daylong hearings, Bush alluded to Operation MHCHAOS, which had been made public in the newspapers, and in doing so seemed to confirm an allegation denied by the CIA. "This Agency," he said, "must stay in the foreign intelligence business and not harass American citizens, like in Operation CHAOS."[14] CIA officers were still maintaining that no such harassment had occurred and that MHCHAOS was instead merely a program that investigated intelligence connections between domestic dissent and foreign powers—an alibi that Bush would later come to adopt himself.

Bush told the Senate that he wholeheartedly endorsed secrecy contracts. At this date, of course, no one knew that Bush would become vice president and president and would sit on the National Security

Council for twelve years; no one knew that his support of secrecy contracts would have far-reaching effects.

On January 27, 1976, Bush was confirmed by the Senate, and a few days later he was sworn in as CIA director inside the gray CIA "bubble," a domed auditorium that squats in front of the seven-story CIA headquarters in Langley, Virginia. The bubble was packed with CIA officers. President Ford arrived on the speaker's platform with his entourage. His speech made it clear that Bush was expected to carry on in the tradition of previous directors. Keep the Agency out of public scandals. Keep the secrets. Improve the Agency's image.

"George Bush," Ford said, "assumes the leadership of the intelligence community at a very critical point in its history—critical because national and international attention is focused on your work now as never before. Because much of your work depends on secrecy and because secrecy adds a new aura of mystery and intrigue." Abuses of the past have "more than adequately been described. . . . The irresponsible release of classified information by people who should know better must cease." Ford continued, "George Bush shares my commitment to these principles. As a former member of Congress and as the son of a very great man, a distinguished statesman, the late Senator Prescott Bush of Connecticut, George has known all his life that the people are sovereign."[15]

Supreme Court Justice Potter Stewart administered the oath of office. A Republican from Ohio, Stewart had written in the Pentagon Papers case that he believed in the "sovereign prerogative" of the president to keep secrets from the people—a throwback to British common law. Such kingly prerogatives had, two hundred years earlier, produced the Revolutionary War.

A continuing series of scandals had eroded the CIA's public credibility. In November 1975, Frank Church's Senate committee reported that the CIA had tried to assassinate Cuban leader Fidel Castro and had engineered the murder of Patrice Lumumba, ex–prime minister of the new Republic of the Congo. The Church Committee also contradicted the sworn testimony of Richard Helms by revealing that the CIA had helped engineer the 1973 coup in Chile. Morever, several former CIA operatives—Victor Marchetti, Philip Agee, and Stanley

Sheinbaum—had joined the *CounterSpy* advisory board to help consolidate the outside pressure against the CIA.[16]

The CIA was not without resources, of course. In 1975, former CIA officers, including David Atlee Phillips, organized the Association of Retired Intelligence Officers to undertake a public relations campaign to enhance the Agency's image. Phillips also operated behind the scenes. He told Marchetti, whose name was on the *CounterSpy* masthead, "Get your name off. We're going to land on them." Marchetti respected the CIA's power and took the warning to heart. He withdrew from the magazine and talked others into leaving with him.[17]

Just before Christmas 1975, a tragedy had provided an opportunity to shift the scrutiny away from the CIA scandals. In Athens, Greece, the CIA chief of station Richard Skeffington Welch was assassinated on December 23, gunned down as he returned to his house from a party at the U.S. ambassador's residence. His death focused attention on the danger inherent in publishing the names of CIA agents. Welch had been identified as a CIA officer in a letter to the editor published by the *Athens News* a month earlier on November 25. The letter, signed by the "Committee of Greeks and Greek Americans to Prevent Their Country, Their Fatherland, from Being Perverted to the Uses of the CIA," denounced the CIA for its role in the installation of a reactionary Greek government.[18] While Welch's assassins most likely learned about his CIA affiliation from this letter (or from his decision to live in an Athens house well known as a CIA residence), most of the blame for his death was aimed at *CounterSpy,* which also had printed Welch's name.

In the midst of the Senate vote to confirm George Bush in January 1976, intelligence officials were making no secret of their outrage over Welch's death and their fury at *CounterSpy.* A well-known reporter told editor Tim Butz that his own life had been threatened by angry former intelligence officers, and Butz began to carry a gun.[19] Members of the New York intelligentsia, who had been drawn to *CounterSpy* by Norman Mailer, began to keep their distance. It was unseemly to be contributing money to a magazine accused of having blood on its hands.

Even though CIA critics were put on the defensive by the Welch assassination, it did not take Bush long to appreciate that he had his work cut out for him when it came to casting the Agency in a positive light. Less than a month after taking over, he had to answer questions about a report by the House Select Committee on Intelligence. Although the House had voted to suppress the report at President Ford's request, someone leaked it. The whole report, known as the Pike Report after U.S. Representative Otis Pike, Democrat of New York, was reprinted in the *Village Voice* issues of February 16 and 23, 1976.

The Pike Report was shocking because it provided the first official overview of CIA excesses: the Agency ran large propaganda operations, bankrolled armies of its own, and incurred billions in unsupervised expenses. The report revealed that top CIA officials had tolerated cost overruns nearly 400 percent beyond the Agency budget for foreign operations and 500 percent beyond the budget for domestic operations, for years concealing their profligacy from Congress. The CIA also was said to have secretly built up a military capacity larger than most foreign armies; the CIA and FBI between them had spent $10 billion with little independent supervision. Further, the CIA's single biggest category of overseas covert projects involved the news media: it supported friendly news publications, planted articles in newspapers, and distributed CIA-sponsored books and leaflets. The phony CIA dispatches had often found their way into domestic news stories, thus polluting with inaccuracies the news received by Americans.

George Bush's workday began at 7:30 A.M., when his CIA driver in a gray Chevrolet picked him up at his Washington home. Bush read the morning's packet of secret reports on the fifteen-minute drive to headquarters. The curved road toward the guardhouse of the CIA compound took Bush past a chain-link fence, topped with strands of barbed wire held in place by triangular frames. The compound was made doubly secure by black pressure sensors that would alert security officers if anyone emerged from the woods to try to break through the fence. Inside headquarters, a special elevator sped Bush up to his narrow office on the seventh floor. On the flat roof above him, smoke-stacks vented the document incinerator in the basement.

Bush came to understand that the CIA was protected by a system less visible but as effective as a fence with sensors—the secrecy contracts all CIA officers signed on their arrival at the Agency. As a result, few of Bush's activities as director would ever become public. Biographers would be given little material about his CIA tenure. John Ranelagh, the author of *The Agency: The Rise and Decline of the CIA,* an encyclopedic history, would relegate Bush's year at the CIA to a footnote: "Bush's success . . . is demonstrated by the paucity of information about his year as DCI."[20]

Bush hoped to persuade congressional leaders that the investigations of the Agency should be curtailed. He made numerous visits to Capitol Hill, where his low-key personal charm was welcomed. On March 31, 1976, in a hearing before the Senate Committee on Rules and Administration, he issued a formal call for reducing congressional oversight. He complained that Congress was leaking secrets with abandon. With eight congressional committees involved in oversight, and eleven other committees or subcommittees that could make claims on the CIA, Bush proposed that all congressional powers over the CIA be invested in a single person: the chairman of one joint committee who would be the sole recipient of information about CIA secret operations. This flew in the face of a long-standing Senate rule that allowed all members access to information possessed by other members, but Bush would not be denied. "I can see no justification for unlimited dissemination of this Agency's sources and methods," he testified, relying on the language of the 1947 National Security Act.

Bush's lobbying was successful. In large measure, his proposal was adopted: Congress consolidated the oversight process, drastically restricting its own access to CIA secrets. From now on, only two committees, the Senate Intelligence Committee and the House Intelligence Committee, would oversee the CIA.[21] As an extension of the same strategy, Ford gave Bush authority to spread secrecy contracts throughout the executive branch and increased his control over all intelligence budgets. In his capacity as CIA director, Bush was to manage the entire U.S. intelligence community, including a separate staff that administered the National Security Agency (which intercepts radio signals) and the National Reconnaissance Organization (which operated eye-in-the-sky satellites)—thirteen separate agencies in all.

These changes were accomplished with executive orders issued by Ford, but for the next phase of the strategy—enacting more restrictive secrecy laws—Bush had to resort again to his charm and lobbying abilities. He moved, first of all, to mollify CIA critics within the major media. In a speech to the American Society of Newspaper Editors on April 15, 1976, Bush stated, "One of the things that troubles this group, and I want to get it out in the open, is the whole question of secrecy." Protecting sources and methods, little noticed at the CIA's inception in 1947, was becoming the Agency's refrain, he said, and what was needed was for Congress to pass a new set of secrecy laws. "Most of you are concerned, as I am, about the Official Secrets Act connotation," he went on, referring to the 1911 British censorship law that makes it a criminal offense for any unauthorized person to release or receive official government information. Bush tried to reassure the assembled editors that he wanted only to penalize the person leaking the information, not the journalist receiving it. Bush also mentioned that secrecy contracts would be used more widely throughout the federal government.[22]

Almost none of the editors reacted negatively to Bush's speech, a response that had to embolden him. The tacit cooperation of the journalists was critical as Bush prepared to return to Congress to lobby for the new legislation. It appeared that journalists would not seriously oppose the legislation so long as they themselves remained unaffected—a historic quid pro quo that was to become a hallmark of the CIA's relationship with the media.

Later in 1976, Bush was called to testify before the House Subcommittee on Government Information and Individual Rights.[23] The panel was chaired by New York Congresswoman Bella S. Abzug, who was distinguished by a relentless and penetrating oratorical style. She had been a forceful opponent of Joseph McCarthy's witch-hunts and of the Vietnam War. Recently, she had obtained a portion of her CIA dossier, and she was appalled to find that the Agency for the past twenty-three years had been spying on her, opening letters between her and her legal clients, and recording her antiwar speeches.

At the high hearing bench with Abzug were other members of Congress who likewise had a personal interest in the CIA. Michael Harrington, a Massachusetts Democrat, had been pilloried after he passed on information to other members of Congress from secret testimony given a year earlier by William Colby. (The testimony concerned Colby's confession of CIA involvement in the Chilean coup and the death of President Salvador Allende.) Harrington's correspondence with his colleagues had leaked to the press, and for these leaks he had been called to account by CIA loyalists in Congress.[24] Also present were John Conyers Jr., the Michigan antiwar Democrat whose friends had been spied upon by the CIA, and John E. Moss, father of the FOIA.

Abzug went immediately to the heart of the matter. "The subcommittee," she said, "today begins consideration of an extremely timely and important subject—the rights of individuals who were subject to surveillance and harassment by programs such as the FBI's COINTELPRO and the CIA's CHAOS." (COINTELPRO was the FBI acronym for its counterintelligence program against antiwar activists and newspapers, run in collaboration with MHCHAOS.) "Another subject," Abzug said, "is the impending resumption by the intelligence agencies of their programs of destruction of documents. We are frankly concerned that before Congress can act . . . the agencies may dispose of the evidence of past wrongdoing."[25]

Abzug told George Bush she intended to see to it that the CIA notified the thousands of citizens who had been the subject of "intercepts" and surveillances. Any or all of them should have a chance to review their dossiers, she said. Bush's consternation was plain. Such a wholesale opening of CIA files would be a nightmare for Ober and Karamessines. Even during publicity about MHCHAOS, the CIA had managed to keep under wraps the larger political operations conducted by Sal Ferrera and others like him.

Before Bush could reply, Abzug had him sworn in under penalty of perjury. Bush then proceeded to defend Operation MHCHAOS as "a proper foreign intelligence activity within the charter of the Agency." "However," Bush acknowledged, "the operation in practice resulted in some improper accumulation of material on legitimate domestic activities. . . . Only a very small fraction of reporting on the activities of American citizens in the United States was done by the CIA." Typical of CIA denials, Bush's statement was true, up to a point, but it was also misleading. The FBI, military intelligence, and local police had more voluminous collections than the CIA—but much of their undercover work had been done in collaboration with and coordinated by the CIA, where their reports had been forwarded. "CHAOS . . . did not involve any type of positive action against [domestic] subjects," Bush asserted, contradicting his earlier statement at his confirmation hearings, when he had used the word "harass" to describe the actions of CIA operatives.

As for Abzug's notification program, Bush waved his arms and sputtered that it was unworkable. "The CHAOS program was not designed to identify individuals, but rather to examine the possibility of foreign connections with certain kinds of activity. Most of the information collected or maintained under the program is not complete enough to sufficiently identify or locate the individuals concerned," he claimed.[26]

A CIA file without names and addresses is exceedingly rare, and there is no doubt Bush was being less than candid. When released years later, the MHCHAOS files on College Press Service, *Quicksilver Times, Ramparts,* and other journals, for instance, would prove to have a full complement of names and addresses and even the identities of sexual partners. At that time and under those circumstances, Bush's statement was difficult to refute, however, for Abzug could not inspect MHCHAOS files in the Langley basement.

Bush had a different solution in mind: to allow the CIA to "destroy such material, including all the information which was improperly collected under the so-called CHAOS program." Abzug responded, "You suggest that the orderly notification of an individual, where it is possible, is not proper. In view of the enormous harm that was done these individuals, in view of what has been the admitted invasion of both criminal law and the Constitution in the maintenance of these files, are we not going to be more effective in seeing to it that this does not happen again by showing the confidence to show citizens who were wrongly acted against that we can deal with it and we can notify them and make amends?"[27]

Bush's aide, CIA Legislative Counsel George Cary, leaned into his microphone and offered another ingenious argument. He said that a number of people who had been spied upon "have written to us [and] have asked that the information be destroyed." (Cary later was forced to admit that the CIA had received only five such requests.)[28]

Later in the hearings, Representative Harrington directly confronted Cary and asked him if any of the information collected by the CIA on U.S. citizens, "improper or not, and its origins questionable or not, [has] been exchanged with local law enforcement officials?"

"Not by us," Cary answered.

"Not by the CIA?" Harrington said, attempting to pin Cary down.

"No," Cary said pointedly.[29] But the CIA had trained local police department intelligence units, and in an exchange of information that was usually one way, to the CIA, MHCHAOS did accumulate information from local police.

The outcome of the hearings was that Bush agreed to have Americans ask for their CIA files under the FOIA or the Privacy Act, a law that gave citizens the right to inspect files on themselves. However, those who later tried to obtain their MHCHAOS dossiers discovered the CIA would fight them every inch of the way.

After the hearings and scandals abated, Bush pridefully reported on June 6, 1976, that "eighteen months of investigations have come to an end."[30] Bush had been on the job five months. He had quieted the storm. He spoke before Cleveland's City Club and expressed his delight that Congress had begun to consolidate CIA oversight with its creation of the Permanent Select Committee on Intelligence, which he called "a step in the right direction."[31] The only drawback, he said, trying to elicit laughs, would be if the committee were chaired by Abzug.

Also in June 1976, at Bush's direction, the CIA organized the Publications Review Board—the first U.S. government prepublication censorship body established during peacetime. The formalization of a censorship process was consistent with Bush's pledges to enforce secrecy contracts. While it gave the appearance of an orderly, even-handed approach, its purpose was to increase the CIA's ability to censor the writings and speeches of CIA officers.

The new board was necessary to compensate for the CIA's tenuous legal position in the courts, the result of the Agency's appearing to be arbitrary. In the Marchetti case, 85 percent of the CIA deletions had been rejected by the presiding judge. Bush's CIA General Counsel Anthony A. Lapham, who worked on censorship cases, later explained that the Agency was getting "bumped around in court. The process wasn't working well. It was sloppy and haphazard." He said there was "a recognized need to create a more formal, more orderly footing, . . . a process of reviewing and sending manuscripts to the various CIA reviewing elements in a regular, well-understood way."[32]

The duties of the board's members and the means by which they would clear manuscripts were outlined in a single headquarters bulletin.[33] Under the new Publications Review Board, there would be for the first time a standardized procedure for circulating manuscripts to relevant experts within CIA divisions for their recommended changes and deletions. CIA Associate General Counsel John Greaney, who described himself as a "gofer" in the Marchetti case, sat on the Publications Review Board. He later called it "a bureaucratic cover-your-ass" procedure designed to deflect charges that the CIA censors deleted only negative characterizations but left in positive ones.

In actuality, Greaney said, the board's censorship process did not markedly differ from the traditional CIA procedure. Officers with operational knowledge of a manuscript's subject would decide what should be deleted, and the board would usually rubber-stamp these recommendations.[34] But the board did allow the CIA to claim in court that its censorship process was now disciplined and impartial.

Although Bush never took credit for it when he later ran for higher office, the Publications Review Board was a monumental achievement. It was a key to preventing embarrassing disclosures, halting congressional inquests, quieting public controversy, and keeping the lid on further disclosures about MHCHAOS.

FIVE

Censor Others as You Would Have Them Censor You

WHEN DEMOCRAT JIMMY CARTER WON the 1976 presidential election, George Bush made him an intriguing offer. Bush would forgo political activity for six months if Carter would retain him as CIA director for that period. Carter politely declined.[1] As Bush prepared to quit his offices at Langley, he had to try to rein in one more dissident CIA officer who was writing a book that promised to be another embarrassing critique of the Agency. The resulting censorship case would be the most significant yet, going all the way to the U.S. Supreme Court.

CIA General Counsel Anthony Lapham informed Bush in January 1977 that the new threat was coming from former CIA officer Frank W. Snepp III, who had resigned after a tour of duty at the Saigon CIA station. Bush was told that Snepp's book was likely to criticize the Agency's handling of the American withdrawal from Vietnam. But if Snepp did not submit his book to the CIA censors, as also seemed likely, he could be taken to court for violating his secrecy contract.[2] Lapham proposed that Bush ask the U.S. attorney general to seek a federal court injunction against Snepp similar to the one granted against Marchetti.

Snepp's credentials included a degree in international affairs from Columbia University and work as a researcher for CBS. A Columbia professor had recruited him into the CIA, which at the time gave him a draft exemption. Ironically, the CIA ran short of volunteers for Vietnam, and in 1969 Snepp was ordered to the Saigon station. The station chief, William A. Christison, rated his performance "very high."[3] Snepp wrote reports on North Vietnamese and Vietcong activities, intentions, and capabilities and interrogated high-ranking Vietnamese prisoners. He also grew accustomed to making public statements on behalf of the CIA. Snepp recalled that he became the embassy's principal briefer of journalists and visiting members of Congress. It was left to him to determine what to say at the briefings. "I was given . . . the discretion to determine what was classified and what wasn't, as every Agency officer is," Snepp testified.[4]

On April 29, 1975, as Communist troops entered Saigon, Snepp escaped Vietnam on one of the last CIA helicopters off the roof of the U.S. Embassy. As he prepared to leave the embassy, he heard the cries of Vietnamese CIA agents left behind. This memory remained with him. Saigon fell the next day. Snepp grew bitter over what he saw as a clumsy and irresponsible retreat by the CIA, which left agents and intelligence files behind. For him, it was another example not only of the Agency's lack of professionalism but of its disregard for human life. Earlier, when he was interrogating Vietnamese prisoners, he had been shocked to learn that a prisoner had been killed by being pushed from a helicopter.

Snepp returned to CIA headquarters at Langley with a reputation as "one of our outstanding analysts," according to his superior, Paul V. Walsh.[5] But when Snepp complained about the Saigon withdrawal and instigated an official investigation, he felt he was not taken seriously and that the final outcome was a whitewash. He began thinking he would have to write a book for the truth to become known. Snepp discussed his book idea with an old CIA associate, William K. Parmenter, who told him it was highly unlikely the Agency would approve the sort of writing he had in mind.[6] But Snepp would not be warned off. He decided to go ahead with the book.

Word of Snepp's project soon reached John Greaney in the CIA general counsel's office, and on January 26, 1976, Greaney ordered Snepp to go downstairs immediately to take a lie detector test. The two pivotal questions were, did he have a manuscript, and was he in touch with a publisher? It was the last straw for Snepp. He stormed out and submitted his resignation that night.[7]

A year later Lapham, who was Greaney's boss, ascertained that Snepp was indeed at work on a book. Lapham told George Bush that Snepp was refusing to submit the completed portions of his manuscript for censorship, in violation of his secrecy agreement. As one of his last decisions as CIA director, Bush followed Lapham's recommendation and sent a letter to the attorney general. But nothing was done immediately. The Justice Department lawyers failed to see how Snepp's manuscript could rise to the required level of an imminent threat necessary to support legal action. If censorship was to be approved again, the case had to be perfect. Snepp was not in the same category as Marchetti, who had already published classified information in periodicals before he was taken to court. Besides, the courts had never specifically addressed exactly what constituted a violation of a secrecy contract.

By this stage, Bush was no longer at Langley. Admiral Stansfield Turner had been appointed as his replacement. In a conversation with Snepp, Turner got the impression that Snepp would submit his book for CIA review. When Snepp's book, *Decent Interval,* was published by Random House in November 1977 without prior review by the CIA, Turner felt personally betrayed. He initiated a lawsuit, which the Justice Department filed in the U.S. District Court for the Eastern District of Virginia, the same court that had supported the CIA suit against Marchetti. The suit asked for an injunction that would force Snepp to submit any future manuscripts for censorship, plus monetary damages for his failure to submit *Decent Interval.* The government argued that censorship authority was vested in the director of Central Intelligence under the 1947 National Security Act, because he was required to protect secrets from unauthorized disclosures. The government complained that Snepp had caused irreparable damage to the national security and asked the court to order Snepp to hand over all earnings from sales of his book.

Snepp, for his part, argued that he was adhering to his secrecy contract, because his book contained no classified information. The CIA agreed that the book had no classified information but countered that

Snepp's secrecy contract compelled him to submit any and all writings related to intelligence. As in the Marchetti case, the government said its reputation in the intelligence community had been severely injured by uncensored publications.

The subject of intelligence secrets and censorship was new to the presiding judge, Oren R. Lewis. He disagreed with Snepp's view that a CIA officer could discern (as Snepp had during his Vietnam briefings) the subtle differences between classified information and unclassified information.

Snepp had turned to the traditional defenders of the First Amendment, the American Civil Liberties Union. The lawyer assigned to Snepp's case was Mark H. Lynch, a tall, thin attorney in the ACLU's Washington office, known for his academic, understated style. Lynch, while working for consumer advocate Ralph Nader, had helped draft the 1974 FOIA amendments.

Lynch felt Snepp was in no position to ignore or fight the precedent of Marchetti. Rather, Lynch focused on the fact that Snepp had put no secrets in his book. It seemed reasonable to Lynch that, with no secrets, no violation of the secrecy contract could exist. However, Lynch's strategy came undone in the courtroom. The question became, "How can the CIA be assured a manuscript contains no secrets unless prior censorship is permitted?" Lynch's mistake was that he acquiesced in the Marchetti precedent.

At one of the key hearings before the trial, Lynch told Judge Lewis, "We accept the ruling of the Fourth Circuit that a CIA agent cannot divulge any classified information or information which has not been made public by the CIA."

Judge Lewis asked, "Do you accept the ruling that he is not the judge [of what is secret]?"

Lynch said, "No, we do not."

Judge Lewis, fuming, replied, "So, therefore, he is the sole judge of whether giving away—if he thinks it's not classified because somebody else already knows about it—an atomic energy secret, that he can give it away?"

"Our position is that he need not seek Agency prior review if he is confident—" Lynch said. He was going to add that Snepp need not seek CIA prior review if Snepp were confident no secrets were contained in his book, but the judge interrupted: "I understand. You take the position that the writer has a right to be the sole judge of whether it would injure the United States or not; and therefore, under the First Amendment he has the right to expose anything he wants to expose, as long as in his own mind, according to you, in his own mind it is neither classified nor injurious to the security of the United States? If that is your position, I respectfully disagree."

Judge Lewis subsequently stated that Snepp "willfully, deliberately, and surreptitiously breached" his secrecy contract and wrote his book not to save the United States from "some great crime" nor "to let the American public know all of these things[:] . . . he did it for money." Lewis characterized Snepp's profits as "ill-gotten" and a breach of "the highest public trust that you can have."[8] On August 2, 1978, the judge ordered Snepp to account to the court for revenues from the book and pay the profits to the U.S. government. In addition, Lewis ordered Snepp to submit all future writings about intelligence to the CIA for censorship, whether or not his writings contained secrets.

Ultimately, the Snepp decision was allowed to stand by the U.S. Supreme Court. The Supreme Court approved contracts of the kind that Richard Ober had used as leverage to quiet dissident CIA officers who questioned MHCHAOS. The mere existence of the contract required that manuscripts be submitted to censors. This decision gave the CIA the authority to institutionalize its censorship program. It would provide the precedent for censorship to be extended to more than fifty other federal agencies.

———————

After leaving the Agency in 1980, ex-Director Stansfield Turner four years later finished writing a book on the CIA. Having signed a secrecy contract, he too was obligated to submit to the censorship apparatus. But when he himself was censored, Turner saw the experience differently from when he had sued Snepp. Recalling what happened to his book, *Secrecy and Democracy: The CIA in Transition,*[9] Turner's voice rose to an angry pitch. The censorship by Publications Review

Board Chairman Charles Wilson was totally unreasonable, he said. Wilson censored information that was already public, and he classified speeches that were unclassified when Turner gave them. Admiral Turner saw the censorship board's decision to release certain data as political. "It was that stupid Casey line that we can classify whatever we want," Turner said, referring to his successor, William Casey. The line of censorship, he observed, gets drawn in a crazy way.[10]

For his part, Charles Wilson was surprised that Turner was criticizing the very CIA review process Turner had himself used against Snepp. "What changed?" Wilson wondered. "I used to lie awake nights asking that question," he added. "I can't answer it."[11] Turner said that as director he did not understand the ramifications of CIA censorship. But as an author on the receiving end of the process, "I have seen the abuse to come from it." Victor Marchetti felt satisfaction at Turner's predicament. "The former directors of the CIA have been burned by the very precedents that they helped to establish."[12]

It seemed to escape Stansfield Turner that he had described the very nature of censorship, which necessarily involves the drawing of lines between permissible and forbidden. Where to draw that line is seldom anything but a subjective judgment made by the censor. In practice, the CIA's Publications Review Board found that while inevitably its members' judgments about a manuscript varied, the author saw no hint of disagreement—only a unified opinion.[13] Turner blamed his negative experience with CIA censorship on "the personality of one man . . . and his tyrannical manner";[14] but tyranny is the essential element of censorship.

As for George Bush, when he subsequently wrote a book about intelligence matters, he simply avoided the Publications Review Board. CIA documents reveal that between 1977 and 1983, Bush submitted only one piece of his writing to the censorship board: a ninety-eight-page chapter of his autobiography, *Looking Forward*.[15] "One chapter—that's the only thing I remember," said Charles Wilson. The CIA requested no changes, according to Victor Gold, Bush's coauthor. Bush also failed to submit his statements on intelligence matters during his presidential and vice presidential campaigns of 1980, 1984, and 1988, according to Wilson. Bush's apparent violation of the secrecy contracts he favored was dryly pointed out by a member of the House Permanent Select Intelligence Committee, Romano Louis Mazzoli of Kentucky: "Ambassador Bush has been saying a great many things about the CIA as part of his presidential campaign."

Bush, like Turner, approved of censorship—except in his own case.

One important member of the CIA's Publications Review Board was Ernest Mayerfeld, who was born in Frankfurt, Germany. Short, wide-shouldered, and jut-jawed, he is a classic CIA hush man. He became a U.S. citizen in 1944 and served in the U.S. Army Counterintelligence Corps until 1946, then earned a law degree before being hired by the CIA. During the 1950s he was posted to Zurich and Helsinki. Upon returning to the United States, he rose steadily in the Agency, helped by an iron will and a smooth gentility that would later charm even some civil liberties lawyers.

By 1979 Mayerfeld was convinced that demands under the FOIA for access to CIA files constituted a crisis for the Agency. Mayerfeld was up against such celebrities as actress Jane Fonda and her husband, Tom Hayden. Hayden, a former antiwar activist, had filed FOIA lawsuits seeking the dossiers the CIA had maintained on them. Fonda and Hayden were joined by other wealthy Americans who were not put off by the expense and complexity of suing the CIA in federal court. One of Mayerfeld's jobs was to work with the Justice Department to defend the CIA against those lawsuits. At the beginning of 1979, Mayerfeld expressed his apprehension about the lawsuits in a memorandum to the CIA deputy director for operations: "So far we have been successful in defending the deputy director of [sic] Operation's secrets from the onslaught via the courts. . . . But I must state that it is getting tougher."[16]

Mayerfeld's solution was to try to reverse the 1974 FOIA amendments that allowed greater public access and more sweeping judicial review. On April 5, 1979, Mayerfeld and Deputy Director of the CIA Frank C. Carlucci appeared before the House Select Committee on Intelligence, Subcommittee on Legislation, in Room H 405 under the

Capitol dome, in an electronically shielded room for the conduct of intelligence business, its door carefully guarded.[17] Although Mayerfeld was concerned about the possibility of the court-ordered release of MHCHAOS documents, he and Carlucci did not mention the pending lawsuits. Instead they claimed that the intelligence agencies of foreign allies were afraid to trust the CIA because of their perception that U.S. control over secrets was not tight enough.

Relying on this pretext, Mayerfeld and Carlucci presented the committee with a proposal that appeared to empower the CIA director to exempt from FOIA release any documents he wanted kept secret. The exempted documents would include counterintelligence and operational records such as MHCHAOS files, although Mayerfeld and Carlucci neglected to make this clear to the committee.[18] While Mayerfeld left an impression with the committee that the CIA's biggest problem with the FOIA had to do with paranoia in foreign capitals, the MHCHAOS counterintelligence files were among the documents sought by Fonda, Hayden, and other American targets of the spying operation.[19]

A year later, Mayerfeld had to return to Congress to renew his plea for a revision of the FOIA. Congress had not moved forward, because of opposition from the Washington office of the ACLU. Morton Halperin, director of the ACLU-sponsored Center for National Security Studies, had raised the alarm that Mayerfeld's proposal would put MHCHAOS files on domestic political organizations out of reach.[20] Halperin's group had claimed in print that the counterintelligence programs were breaking the law, were corrupting political institutions, and had been used to spy on Martin Luther King Jr. In one congressional hearing, Halperin warned, "The CIA understates the adverse impact of the exemption on the public's right to know." Halperin saw Mayerfeld's proposal as a cover-up.[21]

Halperin had a professional understanding of secrecy. As a former official of the Defense Department, he had helped write the Pentagon Papers and later served Henry Kissinger on President Nixon's National Security Council. But Halperin fell out of favor when Kissinger suspected him of leaking the news that the United States was bombing Cambodia. Kissinger had the FBI tap Halperin's home and office telephones. When Halperin discovered he was the target of eaves-dropping, it changed his perspective: he was suddenly an outsider. In 1980 he was promoted to be the director of the ACLU's Washington office while maintaining his position at the Center for National Security Studies. Now the CIA had to deal with him to get what it wanted on Capitol Hill.

SIX

Did Congress Outlaw This Book?

BECAUSE OF THE FIRST AMENDMENT, the incarceration of a journalist is a rare event in the United States. Even while the CIA was mounting various campaigns to stop leaks, the prevailing stance toward the media protected journalists from being penalized. Nonetheless, as the CIA grew more and more frantic in trying to prevent the publication of its secrets, the threat of prison became a weapon used against writers, editors, and publishers.

During his term at the Agency, George Bush had lobbied Congress on behalf of a law that would imprison journalists and government employees who identified CIA agents. Such legislation was introduced on January 24, 1980, by the acting Senate Intelligence Committee chairman, Daniel Patrick Moynihan, a Democrat from New York who was then an avid CIA supporter. Moynihan believed that such criminal penalties, though unprecedented, were necessary to protect operatives of the CIA, FBI, and military intelligence. Moynihan's counterpart in the House, Chairman Edward P. Boland of the House Permanent Select Committee on Intelligence, sponsored a similar bill.[1]

Although the House and Senate proposals varied somewhat, both provided that "whoever, having or having had authorized access to classified information that identifies a covert agent, intentionally discloses any information identifying such covert agent to any individual not authorized to receive classified information . . . shall be fined not more than $50,000 or imprisoned ten years, or both." This provision was aimed at intelligence officers and meant to silence the likes of Victor Marchetti and Philip Agee. The proposals also targeted journalists, stating that "whoever intended to expose covert agents shall be imprisoned three years and fined not more than $15,000, or both."[2] This provision was aimed at magazines such as *CounterSpy.* In addition, the drafted bill prohibited writing about domestic CIA operatives who, like Sal Ferrera, also worked abroad. (His infiltration of underground newspapers for MHCHAOS was still secret.) Ferrera's name and activities would have been protected from disclosure because he was someone who "within the last five years served outside the United States." So long as CIA domestic agents were rotated abroad, as Ferrera had been, they would be covered by the new law.

Moynihan's proposed legislation ran into opposition from Senator Edward Kennedy, then chairman of the Senate Judiciary Committee. Kennedy rewrote the bill so that it would protect rather than punish whistle-blowing. Kennedy's bill would have strengthened First Amendment safeguards for those who reveal governmental abuses and failures. But that was hardly a popular view in Congress. As a result, the bill died when Congress went home for the 1980 presidential election.

Ronald Reagan won that election convincingly over Jimmy Carter. Then, in a move that made seasoned spies raise their eyebrows, Reagan rewarded his campaign manager, William Casey, by appointing him the new director of the CIA. Casey had made a fortune investing in Capital Cities Broadcasting Corporation and had gained influence with Reagan by pulling in New York City campaign contributions.[3] Never before had such a dyed-in-the-wool political operator been placed in charge of the CIA, an agency that ideally should have been above politics.

Casey soon was pushing Congress to enact a reconstituted Intelligence Identities Protection Act, telling the House Intelligence Committee on April 7, 1981, that for his agency "secrecy is the life blood."

He cited tragic reminders of the cost of unauthorized disclosures: Richard Welch, now five years dead from an assassin's bullets; an innocent young girl wounded by a fusillade of bullets fired into a CIA residence in Jamaica, whose address had been given at a news conference in that country by an editor of *Covert Action Information Bulletin,* an offshoot of *CounterSpy.* Casey also testified that the CIA's access to foreign intelligence was being impaired. U.S. allies, he said, could not comprehend why the U.S. government allowed disclosures, and they were increasingly reluctant to cooperate with the CIA.[4]

Accompanying Casey to the hearing was a young conservative from the Justice Department, Richard K. Willard, who had been assigned by Casey to raise the government's preoccupation with secrecy to a new level. Willard had learned about the operational side of intelligence from 1970 to 1972 in Vietnam, where he was an officer of the Army Security Agency (the army counterpart of the National Security Agency). His military unit directed eavesdropping on North Vietnamese radio transmissions. Willard was the unit's historian. After his service, he had graduated from Harvard Law School in 1975 and had clerked for Supreme Court Associate Justice Harry A. Blackmun. After the huge Reagan victory in 1980, Willard was one of many young ideologues caught up in the enthusiasm for a new conservative era in Washington. He signed on to the Reagan transition team and then took a temporary job with the White House counsel. Meanwhile, a friend of his, Kenneth Starr, had landed a better position at the Justice Department, and Willard agreed to come to work with Starr without a definite position in mind. When the personnel managers at the Justice Department searched for an appropriate job for Willard, his stint of duty in Vietnam came up. "They saw I had an intelligence background," he explains, "so they proposed to me that I take over the Office of Intelligence Policy."[5] There, with a staff of ten lawyers and four secretaries, he was adopted by Bill Casey as a sort of protégé.

At the House hearing, Willard testified, "The First Amendment is not absolute." Specific harm to the government necessitates curbs, he said; more important than the sanctity of the First Amendment was the necessity to shield the government from exposure of its intelligence operations.[6]

The biggest obstacle to Casey and Willard's proposal was the influence that the ACLU and allied journalism trade groups had with liberal members of Congress. But on July 13, one of the ACLU's leading experts on secrecy laws, Morton Halperin, and ACLU attorney Jerry Berman paid an unusual visit to CIA headquarters for private discussions of the Intelligence Identities Protection Act. Halperin and Berman were convinced that liberal opposition to the bill was weak and that the Reagan administration would be able to steamroller it through Congress. As they saw it, their best hope was to salvage the situation. Offering a compromise, they tried to convince CIA lawyers to insert language that would retain a partial protection for journalists. Under the compromise, in order to obtain a conviction prosecutors would have to prove that journalists had "intent to harm" intelligence operations. Theoretically, this would have barred prosecution of reporters who were just doing their job. In exchange, Halperin and Berman agreed to switch their position: the ACLU would refrain from opposing the Intelligence Identities Protection Act. Further, Berman and Halperin promised the CIA that their supporters in Congress would not try to delay the bill.[7] It was a historic agreement between the ACLU and the CIA, two old political enemies.

Halperin, who prided himself on his skill at bureaucratic maneuvering, was infatuated with the deal. Although his compromise contained an unprecedented capitulation, giving the government carte blanche to prosecute its own employees, Halperin felt certain he had saved the day for journalists. Essentially, the compromise would keep in place the quid pro quo as George Bush had outlined it: journalists would be left alone at the expense of those government employees with the courage to blow the whistle. The one difference from Bush's proposal was that, in some circumstances, prison terms for journalists would be tolerated by the ACLU.

More significantly, Halperin's compromise was a signal that the ACLU would not mobilize its quarter million members to lobby Capitol Hill in defense of the First Amendment rights of government employees or reporters. As the ACLU position became clear in the ensuing months, the traditional liberal coalition against secrecy began to disintegrate both inside and outside Congress. Over the next twelve years, the Reagan and Bush administrations were emboldened to invent new means to control information. The ACLU acquiescence also helped lull the press. The *New York Times* editorialized that the bill should be restricted "to the punishment of people like Philip Agee, the former spy who first specialized in agent exposure," thus accepting the old bargain.[8] The *Times* was claiming First Amendment protection for itself, but not for government workers.

From the other side of the aisle, conservatives in Congress denounced the ACLU-CIA deal because it would weaken the Intelligence Identities Protection Act. Representative John M. Ashbrook, an Ohio conservative, renounced the compromise and reinserted language more to the liking of Casey and Willard. Ashbrook proposed to make sufficient grounds for conviction a journalist's having "reason to believe" that disclosure would impair or impede an intelligence activity.[9] Other conservatives quoted Cord Meyer, the CIA officer who had been involved with MHCHAOS and had tried to suppress McCoy's *Politics of Heroin in Southeast Asia*. In a newspaper column, Meyer had written, "The assassination of [Welch] shows how tragic can be the consequences of the fingering of CIA officials abroad. . . . Let us hope that we don't have to wait for a replay of the Welch assassination to shock the Congress."[10] As Halperin watched, his compromise steadily lost support. The divisions in the liberal camp made it impossible to rally a united front against Ashbrook. The final House vote was 226 to 181 in favor of Ashbrook's tougher standards.[11]

Representative Lee H. Hamilton, an Indiana moderate who stood on the House floor in favor of the bill but later voted against it, contended that "legitimate journalists" would be safe from prosecution. This was an interesting phrase, marking a departure from tradition. U.S. journalists had seldom been licensed, sanctioned, or otherwise made legitimate by their government. Now it appeared that Congress was taking the first step in that direction. A senior congressman from California, Don Edwards, a liberal Democrat and former FBI and naval intelligence agent, objected, "For the first time in American history, the publication of information obtained lawfully from publicly available sources would be made criminal." Edwards, chairman of the

House Judiciary Subcommittee on Civil and Constitutional Rights, cautioned, "It is clear that the name need not actually be revealed to constitute 'identifying information.' In some circumstances, simply noting the agent's title and location may be sufficient to reveal his identity."[12] Edwards further warned that prosecution would be directed by political appointees.

When the House bill reached the floor of the Senate in 1982, Senator Joseph Biden asked whether a 1977 *New York Times* series on CIA propaganda operations and its ties with the media was of the type to warrant prosecution under the proposed law. In the series, *New York Times* reporter John Crewdson had identified more than twenty-five CIA officials, agents, and sources of assistance.[13] Biden also wanted to know if the investigative reports of Carl Bernstein and Bob Woodward in the *Washington Post* might land their authors in prison, and whether *New York Times* writer Robert Pear could have been prosecuted for disclosing the names of CIA agents when describing CIA knowledge of South Korean influence peddling in Washington.[14]

The questions were, in part, prompted by Richard Willard, who had pleaded with Congress to enact broad language to let him prosecute people who should reasonably have foreseen that their disclosures would harm either the covert agents or the intelligence operations in which they were involved. Democratic Senator Henry "Scoop" Jackson of Washington State said he understood the bill to be targeted against reporters who established a pattern of exposing covert agents. But investigative reporting is inherently a pattern of activity that often includes naming names, another senator observed. In that case, Jackson replied, a jury should determine guilt or innocence.[15]

This extraordinary debate went virtually unnoticed; even *New York Times* reporter Robert Pear, one of the journalists whose hypothetical prosecution had been discussed by the Senate, told me he was completely unaware his name had come up. As the debate continued intermittently for days, Senator Moynihan, an early sponsor of the proposal, began to have doubts. He worried that the *New York Times* would have to defend its intelligence stories in court. Desiring to make prosecutions more difficult, Moynihan told Willard, "We are not enacting this bill to ease the burdens of the U.S. attorneys." "After all," he said, "even the *New York Times* can only afford to defend so many reporters in a year. It costs money. The U.S. Government can destroy a newspaper by suing it."[16]

As Moynihan spoke, Vice President George Bush slipped into the Senate chamber to take up the gavel as president of the Senate. Moynihan interrupted himself to point out Bush's unusual presence, then resumed the debate, noting that when he had served as the ambassador to India it was well known that U.S. spies worked in his embassy. The CIA had provided only nominal cover for American intelligence operatives. Spies who work in American embassies "might as well all be Alabamians or Georgians with a deep accent, or Texans with high-heeled boots," he said, "so conspicuous in evidence and well known are they. And it is almost beyond the capacities of an American journalist in a foreign capital not to know the names of the intelligence community operatives." "I make this point," Moynihan continued, "only to make it clear that we are on the edge of making a crime out of the publication of information which is commonly available."[17]

When the vote was finally tallied, Moynihan and five other senators voted against it. Ninety senators voted for it.[18] For a bill to become law, each chamber has to enact identical language, and the slightly different versions of this legislation had to be reconciled at a special conference. This accomplished, both chambers approved the bill in June 1982. Typically, a report is also issued to specify the exact intentions of Congress; it can be used later by judges who need to interpret a law. Although the report in this instance stated that the law "does not affect the First Amendment rights of those who disclose the identities of agents as an integral part of another enterprise such as news reporting of intelligence failures or abuses," the plain language of the legislation made journalists liable to prosecution for what they wrote. It would be up to the Justice Department to resolve this conflict on a case-by-case basis. The government now had powerful new weapons to wield against any whistle-blower who talked to a reporter and against the reporters themselves. Subsequently, the FBI would investigate the nation's best reporters—including *Washington Post* reporter Bob Woodward—for violating the new law.

After President Reagan signed the bill into law, John Kelly, who had become editor of *CounterSpy,* feared a car might swoop to the curb and federal agents jump out and snatch him. In the next several issues of the magazine, Kelly refrained from listing the names of CIA operatives. But the law was most effective at intimidating government employees who might have wished to disclose secrets. Richard Willard, keenly aware of this fact at his desk in the Justice Department, incorporated notice of the new law's penalties into an updated version of the CIA secrecy contracts.

The CIA had been secretly investigating exactly how Richard Welch's assassins had identified him. Immediately after the assassination, Bush had let the blame fall on *CounterSpy.* But the results of the CIA investigation, finally released under the Freedom of Information Act, made clear that about a month before the assassination, the *Athens News* had printed a letter to the editor that identified seven people, including Welch, as CIA officers. The CIA determined that Welch's identity as a CIA officer had also been previously published in East Germany in a 1968 book titled *Who's Who in the CIA,* written by Julius Mader (presumably with help from the East German intelligence services). In addition, a publication in Lima, Peru, had identified Welch as a CIA officer when he had been chief of station there, prior to his transfer to Greece. The CIA investigation also debunked as "untrue" a *Washington Post* story that claimed the *Athens News* had verified Welch's identity with *CounterSpy* before publishing the letter to the editor.

The CIA investigation strongly implied that publication of Welch's name in *CounterSpy,* which had placed him in Lima, did not necessarily lead to his exposure in Athens. Former editor John Kelly, who was not working at *CounterSpy* when it published Welch's name, traced the source that revealed Welch's CIA affiliation to members of Maryknoll, a Catholic order, who had collected Peruvian newspaper clippings about Welch. Kelly said that the editors of *CounterSpy* did not know Welch had left Lima for Athens until after his assassination.

CounterSpy editors instead laid the blame for Welch's death to the CIA's defective spy policies. "After the *Athens News* publicly identified him, there was no excuse for the CIA to keep him there," the *CounterSpy* official statement pointedly observed. "For many Greeks the name of the CIA brings back horrid memories of U.S.-supported tortures, imprisonment, and death, as well as intervention in the country of Cyprus."

SEVEN

Trying to Hush the Fuss

IN 1981, THE DEMAND FOR MORE SECRECY, as it had before, originated in the White House. While Congress debated methods of controlling reporters, Reagan was troubled by an outbreak of back stab-
bing among top officials of his administration. They were leaking
nasty tips about each other to the media—and in the process, they
were sullying Reagan's image and weakening his leadership.

In the roiling controversy, Reagan, too, went public, complaining
about loose talk. It took a while for him to rally his forces. The urgent
job of stopping leaks went to his close friend, Judge William P. Clark,
his chief of staff when he was California governor. It then took more
than a year to establish a strongly led interagency secrecy group whose
work eventually resulted in a great expansion in the use of secrecy.

Clark was a wealthy fourth-generation California rancher who had
only a high school education, but who passed the bar exam and then
left law for politics. After his election to the White House, Reagan
nominated Clark as deputy secretary of state. It was an unhappy
choice. Clark knew little of foreign affairs; at his confirmation hearings, he repeatedly had to plead ignorance. Although Clark was confirmed, his role within the administration soon turned away from foreign intrigues and toward conflicts much closer to home.

As it turned out, Clark's boss, Secretary of State Alexander Haig, was one of the Reagan officials given to public feuding. A snappy dresser who liked his Jack Daniels whiskey, Haig once settled a dispute with Jeane J. Kirkpatrick, the U.S. representative to the United Nations, by showing *New York Times* and *Wall Street Journal* reporters the notes from a secret National Security Council meeting. Haig also had characterized Britain's foreign secretary as "a duplicitous bastard." When news of Haig's feuds with National Security Adviser Richard V. Allen hit the press, Reagan was jolted again. This was not the image Reagan wanted for his presidency. At a news conference he complained, "There seems to be too much just loose talk going around."[1]

It got worse. Budget Director David A. Stockman became the biggest talker of all, speaking straight into the tape recorder of journalist William Greider at a series of breakfast meetings held over the course of a year. Greider published an article based on these interviews in the December 1981 issue of the *Atlantic Monthly.* Stockman's indiscreet comments provided front-page stories for several days. Stockman criticized defense spending, tax cuts, and the budget deficit—the essential elements of the Reagan program. The Department of Defense "got a blank check," Stockman said, and Americans were "goddamn greedy" and "out of control" as they clamored for tax cuts. "Do you realize the greed that came to the forefront? The hogs were really feeding."[2] Although Reagan had promised to eliminate the deficit, Stockman estimated that tax breaks would increase the federal deficit $200 billion per year by 1985.

Partly as a result of Stockman's disclosures, public support for Reagan's policies began to ebb. In mid-November 1981, Reagan retreated from Washington to hunt turkeys in Texas with his chief of staff, James A. Baker III. Baker told a crowd that before he and Reagan left the White House, "We turned off the lights, we turned down the thermostat and we bound and gagged David Stockman."[3] For Reagan, though, it was no laughing matter. Many of his advisers were growing distrustful of one another, concerned that any mistake they made would be leaked to the media.

In January 1982, Reagan elevated Judge Clark to be his National Security Adviser. Clark's mission was clear: stop the leaks. Almost immediately, Clark fired off a set of instructions for dealing with leakers. But his order had been hastily written and issued without consultation with the Justice Department, which would be charged with implementing it. Further, Clark was advised that his order would not stand up to a legal challenge and that the controversial constraints it would place on reporters would be bound to rile the news media. So Clark turned for help to U.S. Attorney General William French Smith. Smith proposed that Clark put his order on hold and convene an interagency group to come up with a better one. In due course, with Clark's approval, Smith handed the assignment to Richard Willard. The interdepartmental group, as Willard described it to me later, was to be a policy-formulating body asked to come up with recommendations for action, with a short deadline. The proposal met with Willard's approval because, in his words, "it promised this would not be studied to death, something would be done quickly."[4] Proud to have been selected, Willard drew together lawyers from the Departments of State, Treasury, Defense, Energy, and the CIA, presumably consulting with the National Security Agency and the relatively unknown Information Security Oversight Office (ISOO).

On June 28, 1978, President Carter had created ISOO with Executive Order 12065, "in order to balance the public's interest in access to Government information with the need to protect national security information from disclosure," known as the "balancing test." ISOO's mandate from Carter had been to eliminate excess secrecy, not at all what Willard had in mind for his group. The executive order that set up ISOO also defined the various categories for classifying government information, according to how serious the damage to the national security caused by unauthorized disclosure would reasonably be expected to be: *top secret,* for exceptionally grave damage; *secret,* for serious damage; and *confidential,* for identifiable damage.[5] The ISOO director had the power to declassify information, though it was rarely used. Further, under Carter's executive order, the ISOO chief was to establish an Interagency Information Security Committee; this became in essence Willard's interdepartmental group.

After little more than a year as a government lawyer, Willard found himself at the center of the White House obsession with stopping news leaks. He also found himself at the head of a working group, some of whose members had considerably more experience with controlling information than he did and who represented departments with varying levels of enthusiasm for secrecy. The interdepartmental group met in Willard's Justice Department offices. Attending one of the first sessions was the representative from the Department of Defense, L. Britt Snider, the civilian director of Counterintelligence and Security Policy. Snider was disturbed by Willard, who seemed to have the zeal of a new convert. The two men had similar backgrounds—Southern upbringing and service in Vietnam—but Snider had a considerable edge in political experience. Working for U.S. Senator Samuel James Ervin Jr., a Watergate folk hero, Snider had investigated Pentagon spying on American antiwar activists. Then, transferring to the Church Committee to work on its broad study of CIA and Pentagon abuses of power, he had investigated Nixon's counterintelligence campaign against domestic dissidents. The Church Committee's final and lengthy report, highly critical of the U.S. intelligence agencies, contained several sections written by Snider. For a brief time, he had quit politics and started a small-town law practice in his home state of North Carolina, but, bored with real estate transactions and divorces, he had returned to Washington in 1978 to take the counterintelligence and security position at the Pentagon.

"Richard [Willard] was new to this kind of problem," Snider said later, referring to leaks. "Others in the group had been dealing with it a long time. At the start, people were letting Richard be Richard. He was fairly naive, I thought. He thought things were far . . . [more] clear-cut and black and white than they . . . were in practice. He sort of came in as a man with a mission. He thought he was doing what the administration wanted." It seemed to Snider that Willard acted as if secrecy had been part of Reagan's election mandate. "He felt that this is why they got elected. They wanted to tighten security and stop leaks." Snider had a more complex view of leaks: "In the Carter years and early Reagan years the political people were upset about leaks, and they wanted to stop the problem," Snider said. In certain cases, the concern about unauthorized disclosures seemed appropriate to Snider, but as he pointed out, "in time you get—what's the word—convinced it's a waste of time to worry about leaks." Snider understood that little can be done to keep government officials, up and down the ranks, from talking.[6]

Moreover, the Pentagon, which was accustomed to running a sophisticated public relations and lobbying effort, was far less paranoid about leaks than the CIA. While the CIA's appropriations were secret, the Pentagon had to wage public struggles for its budgets. This essential difference in how the Pentagon and the CIA received funding made for different cultures within these two federal enclaves. Secretary of Defense Caspar Weinberger had ordered his subordinates to counter bad publicity with an official Pentagon version. The CIA, in contrast, was seldom willing to issue comments. For both agencies, espionage was occasionally a problem—but espionage and leaks are two different things. The Defense Department's security relied more on patriotism and common sense than did the CIA's, although the Pentagon for many years also had requested some employees to sign various kinds of promises not to disclose secrets. On occasion Pentagon engineers and auditors who revealed waste to the public or to Congress were discharged or transferred to remote outposts. But compared to the CIA, the Pentagon ran an open shop.

Both the Treasury and Energy Departments, on the other hand, were little concerned about leaks. Jordan Luke, speaking for the Treasury, made it clear to Willard's group that he was interested in law enforcement rather than secrecy, and Energy's Assistant Secretary for Security Affairs James W. Culpepper showed he did not share Willard's intense interest in relations with the news media. Congress had prohibited Energy Department contractors and employees from passing to unauthorized persons "restricted data" concerning atomic weapons and nuclear material, particularly if there was reason to believe it would be used to injure the United States or give advantage to a foreign power. However, there had been few occasions to prosecute under those laws. The State Department's representative, Deputy Legal Adviser Daniel W. McGovern, had a more sophisticated and positive view of leaks since the department had a tradition of using leaks for strategic purposes. Diplomats often drop bits of information to reporters, all the while being discreet enough not to offend foreign dignitaries. The State Department, however, was certainly not casual about unauthorized disclosures. It used secrecy contracts with selected employees to forestall such disclosures. The CIA, by this time, tried to tie down all employees by insisting on such contracts.

The director of the ISOO, Steven Garfinkel, was among the most influential members of Willard's group. He had been an attorney at the National Archives, the official repository of old papers, which is frequently raided by journalists and historians trying to make sense of the federal government. As general counsel, Garfinkel had the job of preventing the release of classified information from the archives; he did it so well that he was appointed director of ISOO in May 1980. There he instituted inspections to determine if agencies were properly protecting classified information. Garfinkel and Willard saw eye to eye on a key point: Garfinkel thought too great a volume of information was routinely classified. The quantity was so great that the classification system was threatened with overload. If fewer documents were classified, he thought, they could better be protected.[7]

The CIA's representative to the Willard group was Ernest Mayerfeld, an elder statesman of secrecy campaigns. Mayerfeld had participated in CIA attempts to censor Marchetti and Snepp. And while Bush was director, Mayerfeld had organized the Agency's pioneering Publications Review Board to censor CIA employees. Casey's assignment of Mayerfeld to the Willard interagency group was indicative of a long-term shift in the role of the CIA. In 1972, Richard Ober had represented the CIA on the Justice Department's interdepartmental Intelligence Evaluation Committee, which, like Willard's group, studied the unauthorized disclosures of classified information. But at that time the CIA clearly considered the committee to be outside its jurisdiction under the 1947 National Security Act, and Ober was subsequently removed from the interagency group in order to avert a scandal. A decade later, any concerns about the impropriety of CIA participation had disappeared. Indeed, Mayerfeld would become the most influential member of Willard's group.

Willard and the other members of the group worked furiously in early 1982 to meet a March 31 deadline for issuing their report. While they worked, political leaking continued from within the Reagan administration, and so did urgent demands to stop it. Willard felt pressured from officials at the White House and from Casey at the CIA. Mayerfeld also felt badgered by Casey, who had his own obsession with leaks and who sent letters to other agencies bemoaning the sievelike nature of government. Casey had many secrets to keep. One example: as Reagan's campaign manager, he had set up a secret intelligence operation run by former CIA Office of Security Director Robert W. Gambino, who, in the days before the 1980 election, tracked Carter administration attempts to rescue or negotiate the release of the Iranian hostages.

President Reagan himself added to the pressure, complaining bitterly about unauthorized stories in the media. In an interview with *TV Guide* in March 1982, Reagan said, "[As president] you might be in the midst of some pretty delicate negotiations and suddenly a leak or a story has endangered—threatened—what you're trying to do. If you push another country in a corner openly on the front pages and on the air—in many cases you make it impossible for that country to accede to what you're trying to get it to do." Reagan cited damaging stories about U.S. sales of fighter planes to Taiwan, complaining, "We didn't want Taiwan or China to hear our decision . . . in the papers . . . until we'd had a chance to say, 'Look, this is what we're going to do,' to each one of them. But then it was leaked." Reagan asked news reporters to "trust us" and to exercise "a kind of editorial self-censorship."[8]

Under these pressures the Willard group quickly narrowed its agenda to concentrate on leaks to the media and decided to focus on consolidating existing laws and practices rather than to break new ground. "The whole idea [was] to use what was in place and build on it," Willard told me. Further, in the interest of speed, the group also agreed to seek a consensus on recommendations, leaving formal department-by-department approval until after the report deadline had been met. Limiting proposals to the use of existing techniques, however, was sometimes not a solution.

One problem the group encountered, for instance, was that under existing laws the Justice Department could not prosecute most leakers. Those who leaked information to reporters to influence policy could theoretically be charged with espionage, but the Justice Department reserved this for the most extreme cases. Furthermore, Richard Willard discovered no single statute that made it a crime, as such, for an employee to disclose classified information—though his advocacy of the Intelligence Identities Protection Act, which was then being debated, attempted to rectify that omission.

Congress had never passed laws to prohibit government officials from talking to reporters. Indeed, a relatively free exchange between the two groups was a tradition dating from the earliest days of the republic: disclosures were routine. Willard would have liked to prosecute bureaucrats under the espionage statutes for talking to reporters, but in all likelihood that goal was out of reach. Talking to the media was simply no crime. But if it were possible to convince federal judges that the government owns information, then the Justice Department could prosecute leakers for theft. However, Willard's group doubted that the Supreme Court would uphold such criminal proceedings.

Making their mission more difficult, the group found that the FBI was reluctant to investigate leaks. "The FBI would opt out of leak investigations because they would not lead to criminal prosecution," Britt Snider said, adding, "If the FBI chased all the leaks in this town they'd never have time to do anything else."[9] Also, because of the ongoing turf war between the CIA and FBI, dating from 1947, the FBI was reluctant to extend itself to protect CIA information. The members of the interdepartmental group did agree to ask the FBI to increase the vigor of its investigations so that leakers could at least be identified and fired. With Mayerfeld exercising considerable influence, they urged the FBI to assign squads to trace the sources of reports in the news media. Despite the varying opinions on secrecy of the agencies represented in the group, its recommendations were to substantially tighten control of information.

The group considered whether it was possible to control the contacts between federal employees and journalists. Reporters regularly used departmental phone books to dial government experts. Nowhere did formal procedures stand in the way of reporters talking directly to bureaucrats, except at the CIA. There, it was standard practice to refer all phone calls from journalists to public affairs officers, who were efficient at deflecting prying questions. The system was also designed to prevent CIA officers from becoming acquainted with reporters and letting down their guard. The system was not perfect and was on occasion ignored, but in general it worked. After some discussion, the Willard group decided this was a model that could be institutionalized throughout the government.[10] A method of chaperoning journalists was one way, it was thought, to change the tenor of reporting in the capital.

A far more dramatic change, however, could be wrought by Bill Casey's call for a new statute to imprison leakers of classified information for up to three years. Generally, the group supported Casey's plan, but Willard and several others were dissuaded by the consideration that the Democrats who controlled the House would never vote for the law. "We were concerned that the search for criminal penalties was counterproductive," Willard told me later. Willard was chairman of the group, and Mayerfeld was smart enough to act as if he was just another one of the fellows around the table. In the end, however, Willard adopted Casey's proposed statute.

The Willard group also decided to adapt another CIA method, the one relied on so consistently by Richard Ober—lifelong secrecy contracts—which had so recently been approved by the courts in the *Marchetti* and *Snepp* cases. This, too, followed Casey's lead. In the wake of the *Snepp* decision, Casey had directed that the secrecy contracts be rewritten for consistent application throughout the intelligence community. Willard and Mayerfeld had done the rewriting; once the Willard group was organized, it was logical for it to consider requiring more government employees to sign. In essence, an employee's signature means, "I'll never talk about what I learn at work without first asking my boss, and if I do write about it without asking first, you can sue me in federal court." The CIA's blanket use of secrecy contracts differed from anti-leak tactics at the State Department and the Pentagon, where nondisclosure oaths were used only on occasion. At the CIA, secrecy contracts were the first line of defense against unauthorized leaks.

On the March 31, 1982, deadline, after threading through the legal difficulties, the Willard group delivered its final set of recommendations to Attorney General Smith, who forwarded the report to the White House.

The Willard report recommended that, even if no criminal laws were violated, the FBI should more vigorously pursue leakers for the purpose of weeding them out of government. To that end, the group urged the use of polygraph tests. The report also recommended new regulations that would prevent unchaperoned conversations between bureaucrats and journalists: "Agencies should adopt appropriate policies to govern contacts between media representatives and government officials, so as to reduce the opportunity for negligent or deliberate disclosures of classified information."

A suggestion with far-reaching consequences was that information be considered government property, thus making prosecution far easier. This was a throwback to the British system, which lacks constitutional protections for speech: since government information belongs to the Crown, a leak is considered theft. In the United States, copyright law is the primary statute controlling the ownership and use of words and images. It expressly prohibits the government from owning works created by officials in the performance of their duties: "Copyright protection under this title is not available for any work of the United States Government."[11] Yet the Willard group wanted leakers prosecuted for theft of the very information that, according to the copyright law, the government cannot own. "Such prosecutions [of leakers] have not been undertaken because of a variety of legal and practical problems," the group disingenuously reported. While the United States Code provided criminal penalties for converting any government record or thing of value to personal use or gain, convictions under that statute had not been obtained when information had been leaked.[12] Nonetheless, the Willard group recommended that the Justice Department should attempt to use the statute for prosecutions. It was, prima facie, a stretch of the legal imagination. Theft implies the owner is deprived of the stolen item; one cannot effectively accuse a person of stealing a chair that the owner is sitting in. But because information exists in the mind, the theft of it usually deprives no one of its use. In any event, the information involved in leaks was gathered at taxpayers' expense. Thus, the theft of government information was difficult to prove in U.S. courts.

The Willard group stopped short of saying all leaks were bad. To the contrary, it said that "many of these disclosures occurred in the context of revealing improper government activities." However, as the Willard report also stated, leaks were a "routine daily occurrence," providing "valuable intelligence for our adversaries concerning the capabilities and plans of the United States for national defense and foreign relations." Concurring with a Reagan complaint, the group declared that a "single bureaucrat" can "thwart our democratic system" if he is freely allowed to disseminate information.[13]

The Willard group's report echoed the report with the identical title, "The Unauthorized Disclosure of Classified Information," edited by Richard Ober ten years earlier. Ober had recommended restricting contacts between federal employees and journalists, as well as investigating leakers even when no crime occurs. Significantly, though, Ober had not stressed the secrecy contracts that he himself had used so effectively at the CIA. An important change had occurred in the intervening decade: federal courts had approved the secrecy contracts.

The Willard group attached to its report a proposed National Security Decision Directive (NSDD) for the president's signature. Presidents use NSDDs to give orders to the bureaucracy, and in many cases they become a kind of secret law. NSDDs have the authority to direct the actions of employees of the executive branch even when they are never made public.

The Willard report, together with the proposed NSDD, amounted to a proposal for an unprecedented governmentwide secrecy program. It called for two kinds of secrecy contracts to be signed by government workers. The first was for employees with access to lesser secrets. This mandatory contract did not specifically require submission of speeches and manuscripts for censorship. However, submitting to censors would be recommended to employees as a way of ensuring compliance. Most employees of the government had never signed anything of this nature.

The second kind of secrecy contract covered higher echelons—secret departments walled off from one another—under the control of the director of Central Intelligence. "For persons with access to the most sensitive kinds of classified information, these agreements should also include provisions for prepublication review," the report stated. This type of contract had previously been used only at the CIA and the National Security Agency. Other agencies had no regulations concerning prepublication review.[14]

In the use of secrecy contracts, Willard's group was advocating that the United States reject a tradition of openness born with the 1776 revolution and embrace the British model of secrecy in government. Specifically, officials of the British government must sign declarations saying that they recognize the Official Secrets Act, that all the information acquired in their jobs forever belongs to the Crown, and that any disclosure is a crime. Further, the British lifelong secrecy contract requires that before publication two copies of any manuscript be submitted for censorship.

Willard assumed that in a matter of weeks President Reagan would affix his signature to the NSDD. For nearly one year, however, the NSDD languished because aides expected its signing to cause a political backlash. Soon, then, it fell to the secrecy team—particularly the core members, Willard, Garfinkel, and Mayerfeld—to turn their efforts elsewhere.

EIGHT

Overcoming the Opposition

TWO HOLES IN THE SECURITY SYSTEM that worried secrecy group leaders were the relatively open FOIA corridor between government files and the public and the Carter executive order "balancing test" for declassifying secrets. By playing up each potential perforation in the government's shield of secrecy, they hoped to outflank and weaken the congressional opposition to these new and drastic measures for the control of information.

The increasing numbers of American citizens filing FOIA requests for information about Operation MHCHAOS heightened anxieties. When the CIA refused to release documents, some citizens—including Jane Fonda and Joan Baez—sued the CIA in federal courts. The suits came to Ernest Mayerfeld at the CIA Office of General Counsel and to Richard Willard at the Justice Department Civil Division. They did their best to seal the MHCHAOS files and other CIA secrets from judicial review and public inspection, citing the national security exemption of the FOIA. But because Congress had said in 1974 that FOIA exemptions were not to be used to hide illegalities, Mayerfeld and Willard were on thin ice. At any time, a federal judge could rule that MHCHAOS was illegal under the 1947 National Security Act, denying them any basis for withholding the files. The prospect of such a ruling caused great concern. The credibility of the CIA's secrecy program might be seriously compromised, and the Agency's reputation might never recover.

The national security exemption under the FOIA, known as the "B-1 exemption," shields information that is properly classified under the authority of an *executive order* in the interest of national defense or foreign policy. The tighter the executive order, the less the information that will flow through the FOIA to the public. The easiest way, then, for Willard and Mayerfeld (and Steven Garfinkel at the Information Security Oversight Office) to protect CIA secrecy was to have President Reagan revoke President Carter's Executive Order 12065 on the classification of information and its release and then sign a new order.

As far as Willard, Mayerfeld, and Garfinkel were concerned, Carter's executive order contained a dangerous opening. The criteria for declassifying secrets included a "balancing test" between the public interest and national security, which invited judicial review to decide whether it was being properly applied. But it was in the CIA's interest to keep judges away from the MHCHAOS files. The new executive order would eliminate that balancing test. The tactics of strengthening the executive order involved legal complexities so arcane that few journalists tried to analyze them for the public. However, Willard and Garfinkel soon landed in trouble on Capitol Hill.

After Reagan signed the new Executive Order 12356 on April 2, 1982, Willard and Garfinkel were dispatched to conduct a briefing of a House government operations information subcommittee. Willard told Congressman Glenn English, the subcommittee chairman, that the protection of national security is a "fundamental constitutional responsibility" of the president and that both the courts and Congress have recognized that responsibility. Willard intended the executive order to shield the CIA from inspection by federal judges, an examination that, he said, threatened to damage national security. He believed judges had no need to know CIA secrets.[1] Willard was only being faithful to the Reagan policy, but his arrogant announcements were not well received by English.

The chairman denounced the new executive order, telling Willard he would not be a party to an action that kept the American people in the dark about their own government.[2] However, English failed to build a consensus among his colleagues. He had trouble explaining away a simple fact: Congress had itself legitimized the executive order by enacting the B-1 exemption for national security in the first place. Nevertheless, CIA Director William Casey continued to be wary of congressional opposition. Casey worried that if challenged too directly, Congress might be stirred into a fighting mood. To head off such a confrontation, Casey wanted the secrecy measures themselves to remain secret, and he frowned on Willard's appearance before English's subcommittee. "Casey took a more cynical view of the process," Willard recalled. "He certainly supported the measures to deal with leaks. He wanted reporters to be called in front of grand juries to find leaks, to reveal sources, and to threaten prosecution for disclosing classified information. He believed in doing the most that you could, but not explaining it in the press"—or to Congress. On the other hand, Willard, younger and brash, felt sure the public would embrace the wisdom of secrecy, in whose importance he so fervently believed, if he just explained it properly.[3]

Another reason Casey wanted Willard to keep a low profile on Capitol Hill was that he believed it was now possible to get a congressional majority to add a new exemption to the FOIA. The exemption originally proposed in 1979 would have permitted the CIA director to designate counterintelligence files, such as Ober's MHCHAOS records, exempt from the FOIA. To date, the ACLU had been able to block this exemption, making the credible contention that the CIA would use it to cover up domestic spying. Casey was therefore counting on being able to neutralize the powerful ACLU, a job he entrusted to the able Mayerfeld.

On June 28, 1982, Ernest Mayerfeld visited Mark Lynch at Lynch's ACLU Washington office. Lynch agreed that the ACLU would no longer oppose the exemption, if, in return, the CIA would not seek to be totally exempt from the FOIA. After the meeting, Mayerfeld set down the agreement in a letter dated July 2, 1982, written on CIA letterhead, and sent it to Lynch.[4]

Behind Lynch's deal with Mayerfeld was Morton Halperin, Lynch's boss and the man within the ACLU responsible for national security issues, who was influenced by several factors. The ability of the Reagan conservatives to storm through liberal opposition had left Halperin—like most liberals—feeling overwhelmed and ineffective. Given Reagan's tremendous sway over Congress, Halperin thought the CIA might win both the B-1 exemption and total immunity from the FOIA. In this atmosphere, he believed it sensible to settle for a more limited B-1 exemption. Like any lobbyist who talks only about gains and never about losses, Halperin would argue vociferously that his compromise would result in no meaningful loss of information to the public. Halperin felt he was saving the FOIA.[5]

In truth, however, much had been given away in the secret compromise between the ACLU and the CIA. The deal was part of a much larger scenario. It meant that the comprehensive secrecy plan contained in the Willard group's National Security Decision Directive, which had been delayed at the White House for fear of political obstructions from liberals, would now move ahead. The new FOIA exemption ended CIA worries about its MHCHAOS domestic spying files. In addition, all pending FOIA requests seeking files on CIA operations would be dismissed.[6] In my case, pending in court, the CIA had reluctantly agreed to an incremental release of Richard Ober's files on CIA investigations into twenty-seven U.S. underground publications. But if Mayerfeld could keep the ACLU deal intact and get Congress to act quickly, the new law might make this lawsuit moot and allow the CIA to retain sole possession of Ober's files.

Lynch, negotiating as Halperin's representative, continued to meet with Mayerfeld over the next several months to work out details of the proposed legislation. The most important remaining dispute, according to Lynch, was whether files of illegal CIA activities would be shielded. This above all else should have given Halperin and Lynch some notion of the CIA's true intent. If they failed to grasp it, then they somehow missed the obvious: the CIA intended to use the proposed law to cover up domestic operations of questionable legality. Halperin seemed to be engaged in wishful thinking. In the final analysis, however, what Halperin thought would be the use and effect of the law mattered little; its interpretation would be left to Mayerfeld's office at the CIA and Willard's office at the Justice Department Civil Division. Another critical point was whether the judiciary, under the new exemption, would have the authority to review CIA files designated as operational. Halperin denied to inquiring reporters that the CIA proposal would hide CIA files on U.S. publications from judicial review, despite every indication to the contrary.[7]

On March 11, 1983, Lynch and Mayerfeld met in the offices of Congressman Romano L. Mazzoli of Kentucky, a House Intelligence Committee member, who was present primarily to witness this historic ACLU-CIA agreement. Mazzoli said that congressional passage was likely and that Mayerfeld and Lynch should work out the final language and send the draft to him. He would introduce it in the House. After the meeting, Lynch and Mayerfeld exchanged a flurry of phone calls and memos to narrow their differences. Mayerfeld had won over the gracious and personable Lynch. Of their negotiations, Lynch later said, "Mayerfeld was a guy who had been involved in FOIA litigation since the effective date of the 1974 amendments and he was extremely knowledgeable. In my dealings with him, he was always very trustworthy. In court and in legislative discussions, he never tried to pull any fast ones. He was the kind of guy I thought you could negotiate with in good faith."[8] CIA officer training includes courses in befriending the opposition; Mayerfeld could have been the dean of instruction.

———————

The importance of the ACLU's concession to the CIA can be discerned from another event, whose timing seems more than coincidental. A few hours after Lynch and Mayerfeld sealed their deal in Mazzoli's office, President Reagan authorized Richard Willard's secrecy program, embodied in National Security Decision Directive 84 (usually referred to as NSDD 84). It had been on hold for nearly one year, yet that same afternoon, Willard released NSDD 84 to reporters in the Justice Department conference room. Mayerfeld's extensive defusing of the ACLU was a necessary condition for White House officials to overcome their political fears of executing NSDD 84.

Willard was pleased to make the secrecy directive available. Only a few reporters were in the conference room, but it got their attention. Section one made four demands:

1. "All persons with authorized access to classified information shall be required to sign a nondisclosure agreement as a condition of access." The secrecy contracts were to be signed by newly hired employees at the Departments of Defense and State. At other agencies all employees with access to secrets would sign them.

2. People with access to the restricted category of Sensitive Compartmented Information (SCI) had to abide explicitly by contract to prepublication censorship. "All such agreements," NSDD 84 read, "must include a provision for prepublication review to assure deletion of SCI and other classified information." This meant that high-level officials, current employees, and new hires would be compelled to submit to lifetime censorship.

3. "All agreements . . . must be in a form determined by the Department of Justice to be enforceable in a civil action by the United States." These contracts were to provide the basis for Marchetti-type court orders to silence potential leakers.

4. "Appropriate policies shall be adopted to govern contacts between media representatives and agency personnel." This provision would, in short order, mean a new era in government-journalist relations, as the agencies tried to regulate reporters' conversations with bureaucrats.

Section two contained five provisions to detect, discipline, or fire employees who might talk to journalists without authorization.

1. News leaks must be evaluated to determine what was disclosed, who had access, and who was therefore suspect.

2. Each agency must investigate its own leaks, seeking FBI help as needed: "The agency shall conduct a preliminary internal investigation prior to or concurrently with seeking investigative assistance from other agencies." (This condoned the CIA's investiga-

tion of published reports about its operations, much as it had done in the *Ramparts* affair.)

3. For the purposes of oversight, records of each leak investigation must be kept on file.

4. In the search for leaks, each federal agency must cooperate with all other agencies.

5. Leakers shall be disciplined or fired: "Persons determined by the [employer] agency to have knowingly made such disclosures or to have refused cooperation with investigations of such unauthorized disclosures will be denied further access to classified information and subjected to other administrative sanctions as appropriate." Thus those who refused to be interrogated or polygraphed would be demoted, stripped of security clearances necessary to their jobs, or dismissed. (This policy, incidentally, provided bureaucratic infighters a new tool, the leak investigation, with which to dispatch their opponents.)

In addition, the NSDD called for the Justice Department to review reports of unauthorized disclosures to determine whether FBI investigations are warranted. Such investigations would be encouraged, even where no criminal prosecutions were warranted, so that offending employees could be identified and sanctioned.[9] The FBI had not previously been very concerned with leak investigations because violations were rarely uncovered.

Willard announced that all agencies of the federal government that handle secret information were covered by the NSDD, and secrecy contracts would be spread throughout. Expecting criticism of these contracts, he was surprised when reporters focused instead on the use of lie detectors. A Justice Department tape of the March 11 afternoon conference preserved an unidentified reporter's challenge to Willard on this point: the reporter cited the refusal of some high-level FBI officials themselves to take lie detector tests when they were under suspicion for leaking an FBI report, because they thought the tests unreliable. Would those senior FBI officers be fired pursuant to the directive? Willard sidestepped, replying that it would depend on whether the government believed their claim that test reliability was the real motivation for their refusal to take the test. The reporter sarcastically asked if a lie detector would be used to determine the real motivation of those who refuse a lie detector test.

Another reporter asked Willard to give some concrete examples of damage to national security caused by a leak. Willard refused. To do so would compound the damage, he said. This refusal became a refrain: We can't tell you what leaks would constitute a criminal violation because that's secret. Yet another journalist began a monologue, taunting Willard with the accusation that he was trying to keep people's mouths shut with NSDD 84 because the government couldn't go to court and convict anyone for talking: so "rather than going back to Capitol Hill and getting a law that maybe you could enforce, you're going to, in effect, make your own law administratively." Willard did not respond.

Much about Willard's secrecy order was unclear, even to him. Commanding federal employees to act is one thing, but no one could expect universal compliance from a bureaucracy so large and multifaceted. How many people would NSDD 84 really censor and silence? Would leaks really be fixed? Even years later, Willard was not sure.[10]

The next step was for Willard, Mayerfeld, and Garfinkel to revise the existing secrecy contracts to give the Justice Department firmer legal ground for Marchetti-type injunctions in favor of prepublication censorship. The revisions were intended to "prevent a book from being published," Garfinkel later conceded. "The most obvious action is injunctive relief, to prevent publication and to deprive the person of profits from that publication, even in the case of the agreements that do not call for prepublication review."[11] To enforce the secrecy contracts, Garfinkel predicted the creation of Publications Review Boards at many agencies—modeled on the CIA example.

About the same time in 1983 that President Reagan signed NSDD 84, former CIA officer Ralph McGehee, who had joined the CIA in 1952, was touring the United States to sell his book on his days at the Agency, *Deadly Deceits*.[12] With help from the ACLU's Washington office,

McGehee had fought Mayerfeld's censoring of 397 items from the book and had partially succeeded. Much of the material Mayerfeld wanted cut had appeared already in the Pentagon Papers,[13] so ACLU lawyers were able to persuade a judge to restore many of the deletions. McGehee had written his book because he discovered the CIA had tampered with facts that undermined U.S. policy in Southeast Asia. In his interrogations of Vietnamese and Thai villagers in the mid-1960s, he had learned that Communists were organizing the countryside to a much greater extent than had been previously reported to CIA headquarters. His reports suggested the United States would have a tougher time in Vietnam than had been anticipated. But when he returned to CIA headquarters, he found his intelligence estimates had been doctored. Both his respect for truth and his sense of patriotism were offended.

On his book tour, McGehee stopped in Berkeley, California, and in a friend's living room, he had his first chance to review NSDD 84. His first reaction: "That directive is scary. People in government who become disillusioned and quit at an earlier age than me will virtually lose their freedom of expression. The people most able to give informed views will be unable to comment."[14] McGehee shook his head as he looked at the two types of secrecy contracts called for under the new NSDD. The first type, for government employees with access to highly classified "compartmented" information, required prepublication review of their writings and speeches. The other type—the nondisclosure agreement, Standard Form 189—for bureaucrats with access to less-restricted information, did not specifically demand prepublication review. But McGehee felt there were no important differences between the two forms. "I've got a real problem distinguishing between a nondisclosure contract and a prepublication review form," he said. "They are the same thing. You have to review to make sure you aren't disclosing classified information." And indeed there would prove to be much confusion between the two forms.

The effort to silence independent or dissident bureaucrats began finally to raise the ire of civil libertarians in Congress. Congressman

Don Edwards, a former FBI agent and the senior member of the powerful California Democratic delegation, oversaw a panel on civil and constitutional rights. In late April 1984 he requested Garfinkel, Willard, and the ACLU lobbyists to testify not only about NSDD 84 but also about the rest of the Reagan administration's secrecy program.

An elderly man with parchmentlike skin and white hair, Edwards sat next to Congresswoman Patricia Schroeder, a Denver liberal, who chaired the Subcommittee on Civil Service. Edwards, also a liberal, began with a harsh criticism of the Willard group's proposed law to imprison public servants three years for talking to reporters about secrets. He noted that President Nixon had classified even White House menus as secret—and "I presume they still are," Edwards said sarcastically, "so you can go to jail for three years for telling someone what you had for breakfast at the White House." Schroeder weighed in with her own criticism. "If this section works, it will ensure that pro-administration policy leakers get to the press while critics and whistle-blowers are cut off." She denounced NSDD 84 as a Republican effort to silence critics of the administration.[15]

Edwards then invited New York attorney Floyd Abrams to speak as an expert on the First Amendment. Abrams asserted that NSDD 84 strikes at the heart of the right of the public to be informed about the government. Since Congress had given secrecy power to the CIA in 1947, he said, Congress could take the power away. Next came Mark Lynch of the ACLU, who had in 1979 denounced prepublication censorship as unconstitutional. Now he condemned NSDD 84, but he also tempered his condemnation with praise for the CIA, referring to but not naming his friend Ernest Mayerfeld, the Publications Review Board's lawyer. "I would like," Lynch said, "to express my very firm conviction that, to the extent the Agency has performed well with respect to prepublication review, it is because people in key positions out there are at the moment acutely sensitive to the power that they have been given to exercise by the *Snepp* Supreme Court decision."[16] Not only was this a compliment for Mayerfeld, the legal and legislative adversary of the ACLU, but Lynch's guarded approval of CIA censorship also revealed that he had grown to accept censorship as a fact of public life.

Lynch's testimony was a significant signal from a leading civil libertarian to the allies of the ACLU who made up the traditional opposition to censorship. At a time when censorship boards were about to be instituted at fifty federal agencies, it seemed odd for an ACLU spokesman to praise, even slightly, an architect of the censorship scheme. Yet the ACLU's attitude toward the intelligence community over the years had always been a little equivocal. Although the ACLU had won many victories for civil rights, the organization also had a long, if little-known, history of cooperating with powerful violators of civil rights. During the 1950s, for example, many ACLU officials and important members—including its president—were informants for FBI Director J. Edgar Hoover.[17]

So it was not entirely a break with ACLU style for Lynch to accommodate his friendship with Mayerfeld. For eight years, while fighting against Mayerfeld in court over the FOIA, Lynch had grown to respect his opponent, despite the fact that the men seemed in every respect such opposites—Mayerfeld, a shrewd, tough fireplug of a man; Lynch, tall and fragile-looking with an unfortunately naive demeanor. Lynch's idealism compelled him to follow his vision of what ought to be, while Mayerfeld was a crafter of opportunity, carefully exploiting each opening. Mayerfeld was expert at creating the impression that he might accommodate his opponent's desires—without ever doing so. But Mayerfeld was also careful never to lie to Lynch, at least where Lynch could catch him, or to display indecisiveness. Instead, Mayerfeld painstakingly built and preserved trust between the two in a brilliant demonstration of spycraft.

Also central to the relationship of the two was a simple political reality: the ACLU in this heyday of Reagan conservatism was politically weaker than the CIA. If Lynch and Halperin had been inclined to activate their beehive of 250,000 ACLU members, they might have been a credible force on Capitol Hill. Instead they pursued a strategy of working by themselves in the back rooms at Langley and on Capitol Hill, even though their opposition far surpassed them in strategic ability.

———

Although NSDD 84 was a great victory for the Willard group, it had more on its agenda. The CIA was pressing for passage of its new

FOIA exemption. To amend the FOIA would require an act of Congress, a much more difficult task than obtaining the president's signature, but now there existed a working relationship between the CIA and ACLU. Mark Lynch and Ernest Mayerfeld were working together on the FOIA amendment. On April 8, 1983, Mayerfeld reported to his superiors at the CIA that Lynch "has said that he is in total agreement with the bill provided that some provisions . . . are deleted."[18]

On June 14, 1983, CIA lawyers compiled a list of FOIA lawsuits against the Agency that could be dismissed under the new exemption—an unmistakable indication of CIA intentions to use the exemption to hide information. This list went through several revisions. The first estimate comprised twenty-three pending lawsuits, including dismissal of twelve actions that sought CIA files on the assassination of President John F. Kennedy. Also on the "may be affected" list was my lawsuit requesting CIA documents from Richard Ober's operations inside the U.S. dissident press, including those involving *Quicksilver Times.*

In addition, CIA lawyers hoped the new exemption would partially or entirely frustrate lawsuits that sought information on other topics: churchwomen in El Salvador; the Unification Church; and Commander Nicholas Shadrin, the Soviet naval defector to the United States who disappeared in Vienna, Austria, and was never found by the CIA. Editors at *Reader's Digest* had filed the Shadrin lawsuit, expecting that the CIA documents "would show the CIA was inept in its handling of the case," writer Henry Hurt explained. "Why else would they want it secret? Protecting intelligence sources and methods? From my experience they are protecting their butts. The material would make them look like a patch of monkeys."[19]

The CIA list also showed how badly the ACLU negotiators had misjudged their counterparts. While Lynch and Halperin were repeatedly assuring reporters that the FOIA exemption to which they had agreed would not affect the release of documents on CIA domestic operations, CIA lawyers clearly thought otherwise. The *Nation,* America's longest-published weekly, first exposed the CIA-ACLU deal in its issue of June 18, 1983. "Unfortunately, the Agency has convinced the American Civil Liberties Union to agree to exempt 'operational files' from the Freedom of Information Act. It is a dangerous exemption," the *Nation* concluded. However, the ACLU protested to *Nation* editor Victor Navasky that it had not agreed to anything, and the magazine, taking the ACLU at its word, ran a "clarification" two weeks later.[20]

Meanwhile, at Langley, CIA lawyers in Mayerfeld's office predicted that the new exemption would also lead to a dismissal of a lawsuit that was seeking the Agency files on its connection to the National Student Association. Up to that point, the student organization's lawyer, David Sobel, had obtained from the CIA an index that described documents that were being withheld. According to the index, the CIA had some kind of involvement with the student group as late as 1979, in apparent disregard for the 1967 "divorce" agreement with the association. The CIA had accumulated more than 372 pages on the student group after February 1969, including 28 pages in 1978. The index was the basis of a story that ran in the *Washington Post* on July 16, 1983, in which I reported that the student association was trying to convince U.S. District Court Judge June L. Green to order the release of a total of 1,500 CIA documents. All CIA-originated material regarding the organization from 1978 onward was withheld by the Agency on the grounds that the documents would reveal "intelligence methods" as well as CIA employee names, "intelligence sources," and "cryptonyms and pseudonyms." The index noted that one document, dated August 4, 1978, "consists of brief statements which would identify a method used to support intelligence activities." Another, dated July 27, 1978, "states in precise detail, step-by-step, a method used to support intelligence activities."[21]

This was the kind of exposure through the FOIA that Mayerfeld was trying to stop. But Mayerfeld's office had overlooked one element of the student association case. Attorney Sobel had insisted upon a clause in a partial settlement of the case stipulating that the lawsuit could not be dismissed by any future legislation. Sobel had outflanked Mayerfeld.

On September 24, 1983, another story by me appeared in the *Nation,* based in part on interviews with Lynch and Mayerfeld.[22] Contrary to the earlier "clarification" in the *Nation,* this article asserted that there indeed was a deal between the CIA and the ACLU. Lynch was quoted on his relationship with Mayerfeld: "We're two guys who've spent a lot of time in court together shooting the shit, and I've always told him if they get off the total exemption thing we might be able to work something out." In the same issue, Morton Halperin cowrote a response headlined "There Is No Deal." Halperin addressed only the Senate bill, although his "deal" was with Congressman Mazzoli in the House. In the clever manner of a Capitol Hill insider, Halperin's denial was literally truthful, while being wholly misleading.

In the lawsuit I filed for CIA files on dissident U.S. publications, the CIA had decided to disregard its previous agreement to keep to a schedule of release, obstinately refusing to produce documents on its operations against *Ramparts, Quicksilver Times,* the *Guardian,* and Liberation News Service. The Senate had passed the exemption in November 1983. As soon as the House followed suit, the lawsuit regarding CIA operations against U.S. publications could be dismissed, and the schedule of release could be permanently abandoned. The documents might then remain secret forever, as Richard Ober had intended. But in January 1984 the FOIA exemption became stalled in the House.

Consequently, on January 19, 1984, the Justice Department and the CIA asked the judge in the *Quicksilver* and *Ramparts* case for an unlimited extension of time in which to produce documents.[23] The CIA had fought the release of Ober's records administratively, in federal court, and on Capitol Hill; now the battle was again joined in federal court.

This latest maneuver was foiled within a few weeks when questions about the constitutional prohibition of ex post facto laws were raised. On February 8, 1984, Congressman Mazzoli called Lynch and Mayerfeld to an Intelligence Committee hearing in Room H 405 of the Capitol to discuss the ACLU-CIA agreement in public. The hearing was sparsely attended and little reported. Mazzoli praised the unusual agreement between the CIA and ACLU, insisting, "It is neither immoral nor a sellout to talk with the other guy and try to compromise differences."[24]

As the hearing continued, Mazzoli kidded Lynch for spending so much time on Capitol Hill, where he was a frequent visitor to the offices of the Intelligence Committee. "Does the sergeant-at-arms think you may be earning a congressional pension up here?" he asked. "When he sees you around long enough, he may think you are one of the members." Lynch was an insider. During his testimony, Lynch outlined where the ACLU stood: "Now, our position on this bill is that if, in fact, it will not result in the loss of any meaningful information to the public, and if it will result in expedited processing, it will be a plus for the public, and it is something that we would support." In Lynch's interpretation of the FOIA exemption, the MHCHAOS documents would still be subject to search and review. But some of those documents were already included in Mayerfeld's "may be affected" list of lawsuits the CIA wanted to have dismissed.

When Mazzoli said it might make things simpler if the House cut out of the bill the section to dismiss pending litigation, Lynch took the CIA position, saying he was agreeable to the dismissal of some lawsuits to help the CIA reduce the backlog of requests in its FOIA office. However, Mazzoli was concerned about the legal difficulties with ex post facto laws—a type of law generally prohibited by the Constitution. To this prohibition Mazzoli now alluded: "If I understand correctly, around here, typically we have made laws prospective." Mazzoli struck from the bill the troublesome section, leaving a version that would permit pending lawsuits to continue. Thus changed, Mazzoli introduced his bill to Congress on March 15.

Only after Mazzoli eliminated the ex post facto provision did the CIA, on May 15, 1984, release the information on its investigations of U.S. publications used in this book.

Mazzoli's bill was titled the CIA Information Act and came up for consideration by the House on September 19, 1984. Representative Ted Weiss of New York handed leaflets to his colleagues as members walked onto the floor to vote, asking them to keep the CIA honest by voting no. The House members slipped their plastic voting cards into the slots on the back of each bench, and the tally rolled up on the screen over the floor. Despite Weiss's last-minute lobbying, Mazzoli's bill passed 369–36.[25]

Upstairs, outside the observation galleries of the House, Mayerfeld stood surrounded by younger CIA officers and intelligence committee staffers, grinning and shaking hands. He had pulled off a coup. Forthwith, court challenges to the CIA would be curtailed, as would be the authority of judges to conduct in camera inspections of files.[26] After this victory, Mayerfeld had every reason to believe he and Willard would see their secrecy program succeed beyond their initial expectations.

———

One odd and unexplained aspect of this whole affair was how Morton Halperin arrived at his conclusions. Halperin and Lynch's rationalization for their deal with Mayerfeld was the need to limit a CIA proposal that would pass despite their opposition. But their claim that they were powerless to stop the legislation was flatly contradicted by ACLU Executive Director Ira Glasser, who told a colleague, "We could have killed the bill at any time, as you know, if we had wanted to and thus avoided *any* legislation."[27] Halperin's judgments had been clouded.

At one point Halperin sent a memorandum to Glasser stating that the legislation was drafted to ensure access to all files relating to CIA domestic spying. This simply was false, as indicated by the CIA "may be affected" list. Compounding this error, Halperin in the same memo told Glasser that CIA domestic counterintelligence activities "are conducted by the Office of Security which does not have authority to designate those files as 'operational' files" to shield them from release."[28] But CIA documents that Halperin's own office had obtained under the FOIA proved the contrary. Richard Ober had run Operation MHCHAOS not out of the Office of Security, as Halperin had claimed, but out of the Directorate of Plans, which later had its name changed to the Directorate of Operations. The CIA "may be affected" list proved that MHCHAOS files on the underground press were being shielded by the legislation Halperin supported. Such mistakes of fact were astonishing for someone who served as a national security expert.

––––––––––

The importance of placing CIA operational files beyond public reach soon became apparent. In 1984, CIA Director Casey, Vice President Bush, and other top officials of the Reagan administration were involved in a series of secret maneuvers that would become, when publicized in 1986, the Iran-Contra scandal. At stake was nothing less than possible criminal indictments of White House officials and the impeachment of President Reagan. The administration's secret arms shipments to Nicaraguan counterrevolutionaries in violation of the congressional ban on such activity involved the CIA, whose operational files were being put out of reach by the new FOIA exemption.

President Reagan convened a meeting of his top advisers, the National Security Council Planning Group, to discuss his Central American policies. Despite Reagan's popularity, polls showed opposition to his policy of arming the Contras and to U.S. involvement in the El Salvadoran civil war.

Casey and Bush were at the meeting, along with U.S. representative to the United Nations Jeane Kirkpatrick, Chairman of the Joint Chiefs of Staff John W. Vessey Jr., Secretary of State George P. Shultz, Attorney General Edwin Meese III, National Security Adviser Robert C. McFarlane, and Admiral John M. Poindexter. McFarlane opened the meeting by noting that Congress had banned military aid to the Contras. How would the administration buy weapons for them? Casey wanted to seek support from "third" countries, such as Saudi Arabia. Kirkpatrick agreed.

Shultz cautioned that the Constitution prohibits the spending of funds not appropriated by Congress. "If we go out and try to get money from third countries, it is an impeachable offense," he said. Casey replied that he already had permission from senior members of the congressional intelligence committees to arm the Contras with funds solicited from other nations.

Meese said his lawyers could "find the proper and legal basis which will permit the United States to assist in obtaining third-party resources for the anti-Sandinistas." One of the laws that would be called into play was the 1961 Foreign Assistance Act. This act contained a 1974 amendment, referred to as the "Hughes-Ryan Amendment," that prevented the CIA from spending any funds appropriated by Congress for foreign operations unless and until the president "finds" that each operation is important to the national security. Thus before the CIA could conduct a secret operation, such as arranging funding for the Contras, the president would have to sign a "finding" that such activity was critical to national security and then report the finding to senior members of the congressional intelligence committees.[29]

Powerful players in group discussions often sit back to evaluate everyone else's positions, then at the last moment propose a "consensus" view. At the end of the two-hour meeting, Bush said to Reagan, "How can anyone object to the United States encouraging third parties to provide help to the anti-Sandinistas under the finding? The only problem that might come up is if the United States were to promise to give these third parties something in return so that some people could interpret this as some kind of an exchange." Although Bush would later claim to be "out of the loop," he clearly was supporting third-nation funding of the Contras to avoid the congressional ban on U.S. arms shipments. Bush's role at this meeting would become an important secret to keep when he himself tried to gain the presidency in 1988.

Reagan said, "If such a story gets out, we'll all be hanging by our thumbs in front of the White House until we find out who did it."[30] The meeting adjourned.

Two years later, in 1986, the Iran-Contra scandal broke. By 1987, with Bush the heir apparent to Reagan, the question was: Where was Bush while the scandal was unfolding? Trying to put the question to rest, Bush appeared on CBS-TV and said, "What I do is advise the president. I don't speak up in these meetings. I haven't done it for six and a half years. I'm not going to start now."[31]

The White House transcript of June 25, 1984, would later reveal that Bush's claim of silence was false, but the electorate did not know this fact until after the 1988 election. Keeping secrets was the priority. The Willard group's secrecy program, designed to silence officials who might blow the whistle, helped secure the Reagan administration's Iran-Contra dealings from public knowledge. The staff and secretaries of the National Security Council had signed secrecy contracts, as had members of the interdepartmental working groups that implemented the policies. Everyone was bound by the rules promulgated under NSDD 84.

During the same period, White House officials continued an intense lobbying campaign with Congress, trying to persuade Congress to support the Contras. However, for this to happen, liberal supporters of the Sandinistas had to be politically neutralized, and that was to be done by implementing NSDD's nondisclosure agreements.

1. Congressman John E. Moss of California wrote the Freedom of Information Act in 1954 after being denied information by the Civil Service Commission; the act was eventually passed in 1966.

2. CIA agent Salvatore John Ferrera as he appeared in 1969 when he was infiltrating the Washington, D.C.–based *Quicksilver Times* and other news organizations in Illinois and California. (Photo courtesy *Quicksilver Times* and Terry Becker.)

3. American Civil Liberties Union legislative counsel Mark H. Lynch announcing his support for the CIA Information Act in 1984.

4. Morton Halperin, when he was director of the American Civil Liberties Union office in Washington, D.C., cut controversial deals with the CIA and FBI, dropping ACLU opposition to secrecy legislation.

5. Richard K. Willard in his law offices at Steptoe and Johnson, after leaving the Justice Department. His Interdepartmental Group to Study the Unauthorized Disclosures of Classified Information authored the 1983 secrecy program.

6. Steven Garfinkel, director of the Information Security Oversight Office, in 1984.

7. Michael Pillsbury, a former aide to Senator Orrin Hatch, was fired from his Pentagon post for talking to reporters during a policy dispute with the White House. His security clearances were later restored.

8. Central Intelligence Agency assistant general counsel Ernest Mayerfeld at the hearing in 1984 at which the American Civil Liberties Union announced its support of a new Freedom of Information Act exemption for the CIA.

9. L. Britt Snider represented the Pentagon in the Interdepartmental Group to Study the Unauthorized Disclosure of Classified Information.

10. Judge William H. Webster, former FBI director and director of Central Intelligence, who lobbied Congress for secrecy laws.

11. Ernest Fitzgerald, a Pentagon whistle-blower and author of *The High Priests of Waste.*

All photos by the author unless otherwise noted.

NINE

Censorship Confusion

WITH NSDD 84 VIRTUALLY A DONE DEAL, the chairman of the House Subcommittee on Legislation and National Security, Texas Democrat Jack Brooks, instructed the General Accounting Office to determine how many federal employees would be required to sign secrecy contracts. GAO Director Frank C. Conahan responded that, of 5,137,280 civilian and military personnel, 4,048,636 held some kind of security clearance and would, therefore, fall under the purview of NSDD 84. A total of forty-seven federal agencies would be affected. Further, the GAO reported, only two leaks of the most highly classified secrets had occurred in the past five years through writings or speeches by current or former government employees.[1] In other words, almost no leaks involving national security information had ever taken place. Brooks, who knew that leaks were merely a political problem, not one that threatened the national security, was not surprised.

The day after Brooks received the GAO report, he called Richard Willard before his committee. Attempting to mollify Brooks, Willard declared that Brooks himself would not have to sign a secrecy contract: "Secrecy agreements do not extend to any elected officials."[2] Willard was trying to ease suspicion that NSDD 84 amounted to a coup by the executive branch to take away from Congress the control of information.

But in fact, the new NSDD did require that Brooks and others in Congress sign the contracts, and it did amount to a coup. In the Republican Senate, two members of Reagan's own party, Charles Mathias Jr. of Maryland and Barry Goldwater of Arizona, were upset enough to challenge the White House. Mathias, who had written about secrecy and foreign policy in a political text published by Oxford University Press in 1974, sent an angry letter to the White House and received a high-handed response: "Your letter has been brought to the President's direct attention and is now being shared with the appropriate advisers for a thorough study and review."[3] When Mathias learned that even Goldwater, the elder statesman of the conservative movement, had received a similar affront, he took the Senate floor to complain.

Mathias proposed an amendment to put a six-month hold on the expenditure of funds for any additional secrecy contracts. Goldwater supported him, saying, "The most used rubber stamp in this town is that red one that says 'TOP SECRET.' " Goldwater knew that few secrets damaging to national security had ever been revealed. Furthermore, contrary to senatorial prerogatives, Congress had been given no opportunity to consider NSDD 84. As the floor debate warmed up, Senator Moynihan pointed out that presidential political advisers are more likely to leak information than are career government professionals. Senator Carl Levin of Michigan added, "Never before has our government attempted to so severely restrict the flow of information between government employees and the people they serve."[4]

Mathias's amendment, riding on a State Department spending bill, passed by a 56–34 vote on October 20, 1983. To great fanfare in the press, the amendment appeared to halt censorship for the time being. However, the actual words of Mathias's amendment need to be scrutinized closely: "The head of a department or agency of the Government may not, before April 15, 1984, enforce, issue, or implement any rule, regulation, directive, policy, decision, or order which (1) would require any officer or employee to submit, after termination of employment with the Government, his or her writings for prepublication review by an officer or employee of the Government and (2) is different from the rules, regulations, directives, policies, decisions, or orders (relating to prepublication review of such writings) in effect on March 1, 1983." Although the new secrecy contract authored by Willard and Mayerfeld in 1983 was ruled out by the amendment, an older and nearly identical version could still be used.

Journalists across the nation overlooked this loophole in their reports of the Mathias amendment. "Senate Shelves Plan to Censor Federal Workers," read the *San Francisco Chronicle* headline. "Senate Would Bar Strict Censorship Urged by Reagan," announced the *New York Times*. These accounts of the amendment were repeated in subsequent commentaries. Columnist William Safire, in an opinion piece appearing January 19, 1984, wrote that "Congress, at the instigation of Senator Charles Mathias, put a hold on directive 84." Similarly, columnist Anthony Lewis, in a piece headlined "Meese and Secrecy," reported, "Last October the Republican-controlled Senate voted, 56 to 34, to suspend enforcement of the order until April 15 for further study. The House agreed and the suspension is now in effect."[5]

Once this misinformation was printed, it was preserved in newspapers' clip files, which ensured the perpetuation of the mistakes. Thus, it seemed impossible for the correct story to appear. *New York Times* reporter Hedrick Smith, in an article headlined "A Public Call for Secrecy," wrote that the presidential order that required lifetime censorship was eventually "blocked by Congress."[6] Those most opposed to the spread of censorship, believing that the order had been rescinded, were lulled into complacency.

Richard Willard himself was fooled by the misreporting. Believing that his superiors in the administration had not backed him up, he felt he had been stuck with a losing cause. "It was not possible for someone at my level to be the only person defending the program," a crestfallen Willard said. "I was not going to be successful with Mathias, as a mid-level bureaucrat."[7]

However, security officers were engaged in the unnoticed but widespread distribution of the 1981 secrecy contract. Though not as legally sophisticated as the outlawed 1983 contract, the old one still required lifetime prepublication review and was quite effective, under the circumstances. In practical terms, for the public servant, the old and new contracts were equivalent. Any government employee writing about the government faced the threat of censorship, and the Mathias amendment did little to slow the practice.

The other nondisclosure agreements were totally unaffected. A few days after the Senate vote on the Mathias amendment, I phoned Steven Garfinkel at the Information Security Oversight Office and asked about the Standard Form 189 nondisclosure agreement. "The Senate action on prepublication review agreements did not touch what we're doing in this office," was Garfinkel's reply. He admitted that the newspaper headlines were confusing even to his own people. "Security officials are calling, asking, 'Do we have to stop signing people up?' 'No, certainly not,' " Garfinkel answered.[8]

Yet many information-security officers did believe the media reports that the secrecy program had been abandoned, while other security officers, who were less than enthusiastic about the secrecy contracts, chose on their own to ignore the program. As a result, it was temporarily unenforced. In response, the National Security Council sent out letters to the heads of more than fifty federal departments and agencies just before Christmas 1983, ordering them to implement the eleven sections of the program left untouched by the Mathias amendment. "You should proceed expeditiously with the promulgation of these regulations, with a target date no later than one month from your receipt of this letter," the order read. Congressman Brooks, like so many others, initially did not notice that an older secrecy contract was replacing the new contract that Mathias had banned. When I informed Brooks about what was taking place, he shook his head and said, "Subtleties are overlooked in Washington all the time." He was not pleased and planned further action.

William Casey and the other National Security Council principals could see that congressional and bureaucratic resistance to censorship would not go away in 1984, a presidential election year that additionally bore special connotations because of George Orwell's classic novel about totalitarianism and censorship. On January 30, Brooks introduced a comprehensive bill designed to halt the spread of prepublication censorship beyond the territory of the CIA and the National Security Agency, no matter which contract was used.

Because the bill made exceptions for the CIA and National Security Agency, though, his staff worried about the "me too" problem. Other agencies, like the FBI, might convince a legislator to amend the bill to permit additional exceptions in their case. A runaway number of "me too" amendments might actually authorize the spread of censorship. The problem was delicate and classic: Once any censorship was permitted, where would it stop?

———

Appearing before another hostile congressional panel on February 7, 1984, behind closed doors, Richard Willard was accompanied by the CIA's deputy director for operations, John Stein, and by a representative of the National Security Agency, which intercepts communications. Their job was to prove to the congressional panel the necessity of the secrecy contracts. They proceeded to give impressive examples of intercepted communications, to demonstrate that leaks were a real threat to national security.

But even as Willard was playing his strongest hand in a secret session braced by CIA and NSA officers, he was beginning to crack. He admitted to Congresswoman Schroeder, "I seriously regret this has become such a controversial and political issue over the last year." He continued: "We would like to find a way to solve the problem that is not controversial, that doesn't cause us to have to come up and have hearings every couple of months, to be denounced as people who want to squelch the First Amendment and terrorize government employees. I don't like being called the John Dean of the Reagan administration. . . . If there is a better solution to the problem, we would like to hear it."[9]

In the face of congressional opposition, Willard seemed to be trying to find an acceptable middle ground. Whether he was making a genuine offer to compromise is difficult to judge, because what followed was another political sleight of hand that, like the Mathias amendment, fooled the opposition into thinking censorship was being stopped.

On February 17, National Security Adviser Robert C. McFarlane issued a memo that began, "In order to permit sufficient opportunity to resolve concerns raised in the Congress concerning certain provisions of NSDD 84, the President has directed that implementation of two provisions of that directive be held in abeyance." Those concerned polygraphs and the use of secrecy contracts that called for lifetime censorship for high-level officials with access to top secrets. "All other provisions of NSDD 84 remain in effect and implementation should proceed expeditiously," McFarlane stated. This was the Reagan administration's second fallback position—to hold off on the controversial polygraphs and a few contracts—and it was designed to knock the wind out of Brooks's initiative.

Willard told Congresswoman Schroeder that in light of McFarlane's memo there was no necessity for further involvement by Congress. "We believe that a further discussion . . . would serve no useful purpose," Willard testified. McFarlane later reassured Schroeder that he did not intend to reinstate polygraphs or the high-level contracts for the remainder of the current session of Congress, which had about a year to run. Of course, this meant the suspension was merely temporary.[10]

Again, at a critical moment, the ACLU's national security experts in Washington retreated from a fight over censorship. This time the issue was Standard Form 189, one of the two secrecy contracts. The ACLU had lobbied hard for the Mathias amendment but took a softer line on the wide use of Form 189, treating it as a fact of life. This acquiescence had been signaled by the ACLU's national president, Norman Dorsen, who in a letter to Deputy Secretary of State Kenneth W. Dam on April 13, 1983, deplored Willard's program but nevertheless urged Dam to "focus on how best to implement it."[11] The ACLU president felt that it might be possible to ameliorate the effects of censorship, noting that "the potential adverse impact of the prepublication order will clearly depend on the precise details of the regulations." This was yet more evidence that the ACLU in the Reagan era would accept censorship as long as it was properly regulated.

Dorsen's letter was a far cry from the ACLU position of 1979, taken by attorney Mark Lynch, that "secrecy agreements . . . impose an unwarranted and impermissible burden on the First Amendment rights of CIA employees." Now, only four years later, the civil liberties group—dominated by attorneys—seemed to be accepting the *Snepp* decision and forgoing any recourse to public opinion, as if, having lost in court, they no longer had the political will to mobilize their large nationwide membership. Moreover, Dorsen was mirroring the attitude of Halperin and Lynch in the Washington office. As Steven Garfinkel described it later, "Essentially [the ACLU] position was if they had written Form 189 they might have written a few things differently, but that they could live with the form."[12]

Federal employees who complained to the ACLU about the new restrictions were told of the *Snepp* decision and advised there was little alternative but to go along. When an employee of the U.S. Department of Agriculture appealed to the ACLU, he was told the situation was hopeless in the face of *Snepp*. No court fight against Standard Form 189 could be won, and therefore it was pointless to try.[13] Willard was well aware of the ACLU's conciliatory attitude on Standard Form 189. "Yes, the ACLU reviewed it . . . the ACLU didn't scream about that one," he said afterward.[14]

Although NSDD 84 had never been terminated and, at best, only two of its thirteen provisions had been suspended, even the Washington office of the ACLU mistakenly reported the opposite. In one ACLU publication, *From Official Files,* Willard's NSDD 84 was listed as having been "withdrawn in 1983 in the face of congressional and other oppositions."[15] While the ACLU was operating under a false assumption, the National Security Council, the CIA, and the ISOO were pushing behind the scenes to have nearly four million federal employees sign prepublication review contracts as well as Form 189.[16]

Patricia Schroeder's chief counsel, Andrew A. Feinstein, summed up the situation the following year: "The [false] abandonment was publicly announced, [but] the administration is using the previous prepublication review form, and it is virtually as bad. The administration hasn't drawn attention to itself, but accomplished what it wanted to do anyway."[17]

Broad censorship was so new that it was difficult to grasp the exact implications of the wider use of secrecy contracts under NSDD 84. By looking back at the experiences of CIA officers, however, one could perceive a hint of the future. In 1980, for example, Mayerfeld and his subordinates had tackled the case of CIA agent Wilbur Crane Eveland, who was writing a book critical of the CIA when the *Snepp* decision came down.[18]

Eveland, born in 1918, had enlisted in the army during the Depression and was assigned to the Corps of Intelligence Police. After World War II he was assigned to study Arabic and was posted to Baghdad. Later, the CIA obtained his services and gave Eveland a new name, Perry M. Chapworth; he was dispatched to curry favor with the rulers of Lebanon and Egypt. After Eveland retired, he spent time in Beirut working as an independent consultant for the petroleum industry. He knew the CIA had successfully censored Victor Marchetti's book in 1974 on the basis of a prepublication review contract, but Eveland could not remember signing any such document.

In 1975, when civil war erupted in Lebanon, he left Beirut to finish his book in California. Early in 1980, while the U.S. Supreme Court was deliberating the *Snepp* case, Eveland circulated galley proofs of his book. However, the Supreme Court's subsequent ruling that CIA officers had to submit their writings to the Agency for censorship, even if the manuscripts contained no secrets, disheartened Eveland. To protect himself, he informed CIA Director Stansfield Turner by mailgram on February 29, 1980, that he had already circulated galleys of his book.

Eveland received a call twenty days later from John Payton, the CIA assistant general counsel in Mayerfeld's office, who asked to record the conversation. "We do have a reason to prevent your publication," he said. "We have secrecy agreements which you've signed that prevent you from publishing a book or otherwise writing on the subject of intelligence [without CIA approval]." This warning scared Eveland. Payton recommended to Eveland that he retain ACLU attorney

Mark Lynch to negotiate with the CIA's Publications Review Board. Later Payton's recommendation was reinforced by word from Washington that CIA's general counsel would not meet with Eveland without Lynch. In his fear, Eveland accepted Lynch as his representative.

In a series of complicated exchanges, Lynch advised Eveland to hand over four chapters of his book to Payton and Mayerfeld, and Eveland agreed. "But I would not subject myself to censorship," he said later. "I was willing to discuss it, but not willing in advance to accept their changes. I authorized my publisher, Norton, to send them four chapters." Eveland's fear began to turn into resolve: he did not want to consider any changes requested by the censors, and he did not accept CIA assertions that he had signed any prepublication review contract. However, Lynch continued to negotiate with Mayerfeld, who obdurately took the position that Eveland was in violation of his secrecy agreement because Eveland had sent his manuscript to his publisher before submitting it to the CIA for censorship. At this late stage, Mayerfeld felt that any official censorship of the book would only serve to confirm its sensitivity and accuracy. Mayerfeld refused to review the book and threatened to stop publication with a lawsuit.

Eveland again grew worried, feeling he could never prevail over the CIA in court. In an effort to find a way out of his predicament, he traveled to CIA headquarters to meet with Mayerfeld. "The room was bugged," Eveland recalled. "Their attitude was: You are guilty." There, the CIA officers made their proposition to Eveland. "They would let me off the hook if I'd agree to let them review the book, deleting portions without my having the right to disagree. If I agreed, I'd go to Norton, tell Norton I'd changed my mind, but not why, and take those things out." Eveland declined the offer. He told Mayerfeld that he had no control over his publisher, who planned to print the material regardless of the CIA's objections. The meeting ended with no agreement.

Eveland then gave Norton the go-ahead to print his book, titled *Ropes of Sand: America's Failure in the Middle East.*[19] In an author's note, he acknowledged submitting portions to the CIA for approval but stressed that the book was printed as written. "I still believe that the First Amendment protects a citizen's right to criticize our government," he wrote. "I've accordingly accepted the CIA's refusal to review this book and instructed my publisher to proceed."

Mayerfeld's office sent the Eveland file to Willard at the Justice Department for criminal action. From a legal point of view Willard had a problem because Department of Justice guidelines called for the execution of a precisely worded secrecy contract that specifically obligated the signer to prepublication review.[20] Willard had no such contract in hand. In the meantime, Eveland had filed a FOIA request for a copy of any secrecy contract he might have signed. When the CIA could not produce one, his recollection that he had never signed any such contract was confirmed. (He had joined the CIA through an interagency loan from the army at the request of CIA Director John Foster Dulles, thus bypassing the normal hiring procedure.) The CIA in 1983 finally provided Eveland with a copy of his employment contract, which, the Agency implied, obligated Eveland to the censorship process, but on it appeared no signature of Eveland's in his own name or that of any of his aliases. Even more important, the employment contract contained no explicit assertion of a prepublication review agreement.[21]

Mayerfield made Eveland a final offer to avoid court: a standard secrecy contract that would require Eveland to submit to CIA censorship all future writings and speeches relating to the Agency. Moreover, Eveland would have to pay to the treasurer of the United States any profits from *Ropes of Sand*. If he submitted and cleared any future editions with the CIA, he could keep the money from those cleared editions. Lynch advised Eveland to sign the agreement. Faced with the *Snepp* decision, plus pressure from the CIA and the ACLU, Eveland felt cornered. To be sued by the U.S. government was a terrifying prospect. "I have inoperable cancer of the prostate," he said. "I've got a time limit and don't want to get into litigation." So, on December 17, 1982, he signed the CIA prepublication review agreement, binding him contractually to censorship.

The affair left a foul taste in Eveland's mouth, and for a time he felt he had cheated himself out of his First Amendment rights by signing the contract. Eveland thought Lynch was too cooperative with Mayerfeld. "Mark [Lynch] worked it out with Ernie [Mayerfeld],"

Eveland said later. "They wanted me to shut up, that's all. I can't help but feel there has been an informal cooperative arrangement. On real gut issues . . . the ACLU goes along with the Agency. Mark and Ernie—it's a nice tame arrangement."[22] Nonetheless, Eveland obeyed the agreement he signed and submitted his articles for censorship. The resulting deletions from his work only sharpened his regret. For example, after Eveland wrote that "the CIA and the U.S. Embassy depended on the Phalangists (a right-wing Lebanese party descended from fascists) for intelligence in Beirut," CIA censors scratched "CIA" from the passage.[23] Eveland protested to the CIA censor, "I quoted the *New York Times* on that." But the CIA censor, Paul Schilling, replied, "You may not do it."

When U.S. Marines sailed for Beirut in August 1982 to evacuate elements of the Palestine Liberation Organization, Eveland thought the policy wrong; he had written to National Security Adviser William Clark on July 14 to warn against letting the marines get sucked into the Lebanese civil war.[24] Eveland reminded Clark of the U.S. Marine landing in Beirut during the crisis of 1958 that accomplished nothing. Eveland also wrote to several other Reagan administration officials to urge caution. The deployment went forward, however. Learning that the marines were setting up camp at the Beirut International Airport, which had been a battlefield for seven years, Eveland grew more alarmed. He had conducted espionage in the area and had helped arm three of the factions now at war. Eveland foresaw tragedy. "I knew it from history," he said. Eveland warned anyone who would listen that the airport was a shooting gallery, the worst place for U.S. troops to be.

By this time, Eveland's home was a small apartment in a friend's house in Massachusetts. He was nearly penniless, with no pension because he had not been a salaried employee, and he was dying of cancer. Paul Schilling, a CIA censor and a subordinate of Mayerfeld, wrote a letter to Eveland on September 20, 1983, to quiet him. Schilling cautioned Eveland to quit making speeches regarding "the current political/military situation in Lebanon and the Middle East. . . . [Y]ou have certain obligations under your Settlement Agreement with the United States Government[;] . . . any such statements made in violation of those agreements are made at your peril."

Eveland understood the warning, but now fear was subordinate to other emotions. His illness made him disdain anything the CIA might do to him. He felt he was trying his best to save his country from a disaster in Beirut, and he would not let the CIA shut him up. A month later, on October 21, 1983, during a well-attended lecture at Harvard University's Center for Middle Eastern Studies, Eveland waved his chalk in the air and said emphatically that the marines in Beirut were in mortal danger. He explained that his judgment was based upon information learned while he was a CIA officer. "I drew a map of the Beirut airport on the chalk board," Eveland remembered, "and I said that in my opinion it would take one hundred body bags for Ronald Reagan to understand the marines were in a shooting gallery."

Thirty-six hours later, a suicide bomber sped past marine sentries at the Beirut airport. Loaded with explosives, his truck blew a huge eight-foot-deep crater into which the four-story concrete marine headquarters collapsed, leaving a pile of rubble one story high. Two hundred and forty-one marines died, and seventy were injured.[25]

———

Eveland's anger at the CIA subsided as his cancer progressed. He grew to accept his prepublication contract as a badge of honor for having served the CIA, a service that was the pride of his life. When he was feeling its heat, however, censorship had been difficult for Eveland to accept. It had gone against his beliefs about American liberties.

TEN

The Pentagon Resists Censorship

Now that NSDD 84 was a presidential order, it had to be put into effect. From the beginning Britt Snider, the Pentagon representative to the Willard group, had argued that signing 3.7 million Pentagon and Pentagon contractor employees to secrecy contracts presented "an extraordinary administrative burden," too big to undertake. According to Snider, NSDD 84 was written to meet this objection, requiring only newly hired employees at the Defense Department to sign secrecy contracts.

Even so, the Pentagon continued to drag its feet. Six months after NSDD 84 was signed, Pentagon officials had yet to issue any implementing orders. Leaks were not nearly as bothersome to the Pentagon as they were to the CIA. "We had scads of leaks of defense information," Snider said, "but once they're leaked, they're harmless." Besides, Snider did not believe NSDD 84 put a meaningful crimp on the number of leaks.[1]

At the Information Security Oversight Office, Steven Garfinkel grew frustrated as he tried to get the Pentagon to adhere to NSDD 84. "Their reluctance was that they didn't want to do anything," Garfinkel told me. "It was a pain in the butt for them. They said it would cost a couple of million dollars, and we said, come on, that's bullshit.

There are people signing forms all the time. The big services, the navy and the air force kept hesitating, they did not want to get into this."[2]

The Pentagon had another reason for its reluctance to comply. When the National Security Act was passed in 1947, the CIA had gained espionage power that once belonged to the Department of Defense, setting up a turf war between the two agencies. In addition, Secretary of Defense Caspar Weinberger did not always see eye to eye with CIA Director William Casey over U.S. policy in the Middle East and Central America, and he resented Casey's privileged standing with the president. It was no surprise that Weinberger took a contrary attitude regarding NSDD 84.

The Department of Defense depended upon public debate for its large appropriations and thus ran one of the largest and most sophisticated public relations operations in Washington. Weinberger had even ordered his public affairs officers to release information in response to FOIA requests as quickly as possible, telling them not to fear the disclosure of embarrassing data. His theory was that the more quickly facts got out and into the newspapers, the more quickly mistakes would be forgotten—whereas the hint of a cover-up would prolong a scandal. Conversely, the CIA received its funds in secret appropriations and so did not need, and indeed feared, public debate.

In 1984 Casey gained new political leverage over Weinberger because of the case of Samuel Loring Morison, an eccentric employee of the Pentagon stationed at the Naval Intelligence Support Center in Suitland, Maryland. Morison was the grandson of the historian Samuel Eliot Morison, who had immortalized the revolutionary naval commander John Paul Jones for his cry, "I have not yet begun to fight," during battle with HMS *Sarapis.* As a part-time editor for the encyclopedic *Jane's Fighting Ships,* the authoritative British-based guide, Samuel Morison wrote about the U.S. and Soviet navies. When the publisher of *Jane's* started a spin-off magazine, *Jane's Defence Weekly,* Morison pursued a position on it. Ranking Pentagon officers gave Morison permission to write for *Jane's* in his government office, after hours. But, as everyone in his unit knew, Morison worked for *Jane's* during working hours also.

One day in 1984, Morison picked up some photographs lying on a nearby desk. They showed a Black Sea shipyard where a Soviet aircraft carrier more than one thousand feet long was being built. Morison could see giant cranes raising sections of steel into place and could also discern the ship's silos for launching surface-to-air missiles. A sophisticated spy satellite, the KH-11, had taken the pictures. Morison scissored off the "SECRET" stamps from the top and bottom of the photographs and mailed the images to his editor at *Jane's Defence Weekly*—leaving on the glossy photographic paper one telltale fingerprint.

Derek Wood, his contact at *Jane's Defence Weekly*, received the photos and reproduced them on August 11, 1984. One appeared on the magazine's cover, and three more—two as a two-page spread—were published on inside pages. Subsequently many American newspapers, including the *New York Times* and the *Washington Post*, reprinted the photos. U.S. Navy Captain T. Fritz, one of Morison's bosses, read the *Post* at breakfast and recognized the photo as one of those missing from his unit. At work, he confronted Morison, who disclaimed any involvement. The sixteen people in the unit, including Morison, spent a day or more turning the place upside down in a vain search for the original photographs.

Consistent with NSDD 84, the FBI was summoned to find out how *Jane's* obtained the secret pictures. *Jane's* editors, following standard British procedure, handed over the originals received from Morison, and the FBI identified his fingerprint on one photo. Morison was arrested as he was about to board a plane on his way to vacation in England. He was charged with theft and espionage.

The fingerprint evidence meant that Morison was one leaker the Justice Department could criminally prosecute. The Willard group, after trying to imagine such an ideal case, had concluded that it was too unlikely to anticipate. Now, however, exactly such a case had materialized. The Justice Department brought Morison before a federal judge on a multicount indictment. One count charged that he willfully caused the photographs of the aircraft carrier to be transmitted to a person not entitled to receive them. Another charged him with theft or conversion of the same three photographs. He was also accused of stealing information characterized as "government property," and he was charged with two counts of unauthorized possession of classified material stemming from documents found in the search of his home.

The indictment of Morison was firmly anchored in fact. The unanswered question was whether his acts—leaking classified information to a publication—were illegal. In the past, supplying information to the U.S. press had not been successfully prosecuted. But in this case, the Justice Department was able to prosecute a man who worked as both a government employee and a reporter.

Morison turned for help to the ACLU's Washington office. Morton Halperin and Mark Lynch accepted Morison's defense, which placed them in an interesting position. At a congressional hearing in 1980, Halperin had agreed with former CIA Director William Colby that individuals with access to intelligence secrets should be subject to criminal penalties if they knowingly revealed secrets.[3] In essence, Halperin had given the ACLU seal of approval to prosecution of leakers who were government employees—part of the quid pro quo protecting reporters that was, in effect, also approved by the journalism establishment. Now that Halperin's office was in charge of defending Morison, Lynch denied to a reporter there was any conflict between the ACLU's political support of prosecuting leakers and an ACLU legal defense of them.

Appearing in court, Lynch asked U.S. District Court Judge Joseph H. Young in Baltimore to dismiss the indictment of Morison. He argued that the Espionage Act, under which Morison had been charged, was intended to punish only espionage in the classic sense of divulging secrets to agents of a hostile foreign government. Congress did not intend the espionage law to punish leakers of classified information to the press, Lynch argued, and information is not property subject to indictment under theft statutes. Judge Young denied Lynch's motion, and, in the key ruling of the case, he set a relatively easy burden of proof for the Justice Department. The government did not need to prove evil purpose. The issue of Morison's guilt or innocence would ride on the physical passing of information rather than on the purpose to which the information was put.

Organizations representing reporters and editors backed away from supporting Morison on the grounds that his was not a First Amendment case. "He was a government employee and he was subject to the rules of his employer," commented the Reporters Committee for Freedom of the Press.[4] However, the government considered him to be a reporter.

Morison's trial began in October 1985. The judge had set the tone of the trial in pretrial hearings by ruling that it need only be shown that Morison's disclosure "would be *potentially* damaging to the United States" for the government to win a conviction. The trial was, in a sense, concluded before it started. Potential damage is vastly easier to establish than actual damage. "Potentially, you can get run over by a car every time you cross the street," Lynch said.[5]

The jurors were selected, and in his opening remarks Lynch informed them that William Kampiles had been found guilty of selling to the Russians the operating manuals for the KH-11 photo reconnaissance orbiter—his point being that Morison had revealed nothing new to the Soviets about KH-11 satellite capabilities. The U.S. satellite that took the picture of the aircraft carrier had not changed since the Soviets had obtained the satellite's operational manual. The prosecutor agreed that Morison had some reason to believe that the publication of the photos in *Jane's* told the Soviets nothing new. But the prosecution also produced witnesses who testified that publication of the Morison photos confirmed to the Soviets that the KH-11 satellite had *not* changed since the Soviets had bought the manual to it. Information confirming an absence of change, the experts said, was *potentially* harmful to the United States.

Lynch had a devil of a time getting experts to testify in defense of Morison. One problem was that the government required Morison's witnesses to sign a lifetime secrecy contract before the experts could inspect the classified documents being used against Morison. Lynch called American University Professor Jeffrey T. Richelson, author of several books, including *The U.S. Intelligence Community*, who had worked as a consultant to the Defense Department in the field of satellite reconnaissance.[6] Richelson had also written for the Defense Department a three-volume study about U.S. government means for verifying strategic arms limitations treaties. "It involved no classified information," Richelson told Morison's jury. "It involved purely taking what was in the open press and writing a report on that."[7] The resulting report was classified top secret, however, and because Richelson refused to sign a secrecy contract before testifying for Morison, the judge admonished him against revealing classified information.

While Richelson was on the stand, a further dispute broke out. After the government had tried to prove that satellite data were closely held, Richelson began explaining how, relying on public information, a person could not only deduce the spy satellite's flight path but also identify a satellite as a KH-11. At this point, the prosecutor interrupted and, in a bench conference, protested that Richelson was revealing classified information. A discussion about government classification ensued. Lynch quipped that "as long as the government doesn't identify it's classified [information], no one's going to know it's classified."[8] This off-handed, almost wisecracking approach gained no favor with the judge. The judge ruled that Richelson could only present information he had obtained from "open source material" as testimony, and Richelson completed his statements.

Lynch also tried to find CIA officers to testify on Morison's behalf. One was Roland S. Inlow of McLean, Virginia, who had been coordinator of the KH-11 satellite systems. He told the jury, "In my opinion disclosure of these three photographs would cause no damage or injury to the United States." Also, CIA Deputy Director for Science and Technology Richard Evans Hineman testified that other publications had printed a KH-11 satellite photograph of an airfield near Moscow in 1981. Further, Iranian students had published KH-11 spy pictures left behind when Delta Force helicopters crashed trying to rescue hostages in 1980. But Hineman also damaged Morison's case by saying that photos printed by *Jane's* would confirm to the Soviets that the satellite was still working, a valuable thing to know.

Lynch, for his part, tried to show that Morison's action was neither criminal espionage nor theft; but given the legal parameters set by the judge, Lynch's task was difficult. It was made more difficult by the personality of his client. Lynch decided to keep Morison off the stand, and when asked for an explanation, a member of the defense team replied, "Have you ever met Morison?" The defendant was a bitter eccentric who was unlikely to create a good impression with the jury.

In the end, the jury found potential damage and convicted Morison. The judge sentenced him to two years in prison. His appeals were denied, although two appellate justices did raise First Amendment concerns. Altogether, he spent eight months incarcerated.

With this conviction of Morison, the highest expectations of Willard and Mayerfeld had been exceeded. "Morison was in a sense an ideal case under Willard . . . a leak to a foreign journal for money," observed Britt Snider, the secrecy expert at the Pentagon. "It was not a leak to the U.S. press for ideological reasons, the 'good leak.' "[9]

Morison's arrest and conviction charged the atmosphere inside the Reagan administration. A Pentagon employee had been convicted on serious charges. The Pentagon's security had been breached. This made it easier for the National Security Council to overcome Pentagon resistance and expand NSDD 84 and the rest of the secrecy program to all Pentagon employees, not just the newly hired. It was the first time the Pentagon's millions of workers had ever been asked to sign secrecy agreements, a fact that surprised Steven Garfinkel at the ISOO. "We were working under the assumption that people within the military . . . [in the] Department of Defense had already executed some form of nondisclosure agreement, and we were rather surprised to see that they had not," Garfinkel said. "For the most part they are not signing anything."[10]

After some months of give-and-take, the Department of Defense accepted a five-year timetable for complying with NSDD 84. On February 28, 1985, retired General Richard G. Stilwell, acting as deputy under secretary of policy for the Department of Defense, ordered military secretaries to get the signatures of some 3.7 million employees on nondisclosure contracts. In the two years following the Willard group's report on leaks, opposition to the secrecy program had nearly disappeared, allowing the program to be extended far beyond what the group thought were its practical boundaries.

———————

In contrast to the Morison case, there was little publicity for Lucille Manko, a forty-nine-year-old working mother who drew ocean charts that were sold over the counter to mariners. Occasionally her employer, the Defense Mapping Agency, ordered her to chart for the navy what she identified only as "foreign waters." For those charts, she was cleared to see top secret information. On April 24, 1985, Manko was working at her light table, drawing a map with a Rapidograph pen, when a security officer dropped a package on her desk. He told her to sign the enclosed Standard Form 189.

By habit and by her nature as a bit of a perfectionist, Manko read the fine print of the form. She had dreamed of becoming a writer upon her retirement. It was clear from her reading of Form 189, however, that any kind of book—history or fantasy—would have to be turned over for censorship before she could send it to a publisher. In order to avoid a civil suit for breach of contract and confiscation of all fees and royalties, she would have to submit to government review all books, articles, and speeches, no matter how tangentially related to security concerns they might be—if she signed the contract.

"Form 189 is binding for life. It says you can't disclose any information that is classif*able.* My first thought was everything is classif*able,*" Manko said. "This form would make me liable for life for things that could be classified after I cease working for the federal government." She called the security officer and told him she thought the contract was an abridgment of her First Amendment rights.

At work the next morning, she was ordered to report to the chief security officer at the Defense Mapping Agency. He sat her down and told her the secrecy form was not mandatory, but, if she refused to sign, the agency would begin revocation of her security clearance, which was necessary for her employment. "I considered this blackmail. But I have mortgage payments. I have children I support. So, I signed the form," she said. "Everyone around here agrees with me.

You sign it but you're not thrilled with it. I signed it. I had to, or lose my clearance, and out the door."[11]

Manko had company. Others, much higher up in the government, were also offended by the contracts, including Jeane Kirkpatrick, Reagan's ambassador to the United Nations. A Georgetown University professor, Kirkpatrick had first impressed the Reagan inner circle with an article for *Commentary*, "Dictatorships and Double Standards," which tried to define differences between authoritarian and totalitarian regimes. Kirkpatrick now was at the center of power, the only woman regularly seated in the White House Situation Room. She told a women's forum in New York City on December 19, 1984, "This is where the very biggest decisions get made, the decisions that shape the destiny of the world."[12]

But she would not stay at that center forever. Kirkpatrick obtained a book contract from the New York–based publisher Simon and Schuster to write about life at the White House and terminated her ambassadorship effective April 1, 1985. In September she was also to begin writing a newspaper column for the Los Angeles Times Syndicate.

As Kirkpatrick was shutting down her office, State Department security officers, as a normal part of the separation process, presented her with a batch of standard forms to sign. One caught her eye, and she stopped to give it a particularly careful examination. It was a secrecy contract. "It binds you to not write, not even from unclassified material that may have come to you in the course of your work in the State Department," she later told me, biting off every syllable with clarity. "This is an extraordinary document. You could never write after signing it."

She recoiled at the prospect. "If you write on any subject you dealt with while you were in government, it will be reviewed by State," she said. "I declined [to sign the censorship form]. . . . I'm a writer. I couldn't sign, nor have I signed, anything which binds me to review. I'm interested in writing about foreign affairs. [The form] went way beyond revealing classified information. I'd be happy to sign something saying I won't reveal classified information. It went way beyond that. It means you can't write anything about government." Kirkpatrick researched the legal status of the secrecy contract. "If I'd been required by law, I would have signed it. I obey laws. But it was an internal bureaucratic regulation. I declined it. I did not do it," she said.[13]

After the Society of Professional Journalists' magazine, *The Quill,* reported her action, the *Washington Post* praised her in an editorial, "Saying No to the Censors."[14] At the ISOO, Garfinkel read the news reports and decided to investigate her. He discovered that the form she declined to sign was not Standard Form 189, for which he was responsible, but a State Department form, a leftover from the days before NSDD 84 when many agencies had their own secrecy procedures.

Garfinkel had spent considerable time trying to establish the new, improved Standard Form 189 as a replacement for poorly written contracts used on an agency-by-agency basis. To those who questioned him about the Kirkpatrick incident, Garfinkel pointed out that the State Department forms were inferior to Form 189. "Kirkpatrick didn't decline to sign one of *our* forms," Garfinkel said.[15]

Ultimately, Kirkpatrick suffered no penalty for rejecting the secrecy contract. She was leaving government service and little could be done to force her compliance.

———————————

There remained one recommendation of the Willard group's report that had yet to be followed: instilling "self-discipline" in the news media—asking reporters and editors to censor themselves. Casey now tried that approach.

Washington Post reporter Bob Woodward had learned of a communications intercept code named Ivy Bells, an underwater cable-tapping operation in Soviet territory in the Sea of Okhotsk, southwest of Alaska. A U.S. submarine had been sneaking into Soviet waters every few months to service a listening pod clipped over a Soviet military communications cable. Woodward, believing that the trespassing by a U.S. nuclear-armed submarine in Soviet waters was newsworthy and dangerous, had pursued the story. It was not clear to

Woodward or to his editor at the *Post,* Ben Bradlee, how much the Soviets already knew about Ivy Bells. Bradlee went to see National Security Agency Director Lieutenant General William Odom on December 5, 1985, and told him Woodward's story. Odom replied that the story would contribute to Soviet knowledge, though he would not explain how. While checking through old newspaper articles, however, Woodward discovered that the *New York Times* had already reported that U.S. submarines were plugged into Soviet communications cables.

Bradlee called Odom and told him about the *Times* story. "I hoped you wouldn't find that," Odom replied.[16] Bradlee felt burned. Nonetheless, when Casey asked Woodward to drop the story, the paper withheld it from publication. The dance between Casey, Odom, Bradlee, and Woodward was particularly perplexing because Ivy Bells had also been described a decade earlier in a 1976 report of the House Select Committee on Intelligence. That report stated, "A highly technical U.S. Navy submarine reconnaissance program, often operating within unfriendly waters, has experienced at least nine collisions with hostile vessels in the last ten years, over 110 possible detections, and at least three press exposures. Most of the submarines carry nuclear weapons. The Navy's own justification of the program as a 'low risk' venture is inaccurate, and has, therefore, not met or resolved the Committee's misgivings."[17]

It seemed as if the secret was already out, but Casey's team was trying to make this a test case for the so-called self-discipline method. On April 9, 1986, at a meeting of the American Society of Newspaper Editors, Casey praised the *Post's* publisher, Katharine Graham, quoting her as telling a London audience the media should cooperate with the authorities wherever possible. She "got it right," Casey said.

Another round of negotiations ensued, this time between Bradlee and the White House. Bradlee then met with Casey, who threatened Bradlee with prosecution of the *Washington Post* under an obscure 1950 communications law. "Lives could conceivably be in danger if that is published," Casey said. Distressed at the possibility of legal action, Bradlee huddled with the *Post's* attorneys, including Boisfeuillet

Jones, who recommended caution. The story was put on hold yet again.

The next move was a phone call from President Reagan to Katharine Graham, asking her to kill the story for reasons of national security. Casey, meanwhile, was threatening *Time, Newsweek,* and the *New York Times* with prosecution. The threats seemed to come out of the blue. Finally, rival reporters publicized the Ivy Bells story. Bradlee had let himself be scooped. Only afterward did he publish Woodward's version. "It had been laundered down to a mere rag." Casey "simply wanted to stop the news media from writing about these matters," Woodward reported later.[18]

A few weeks later, Boisfeuillet Jones was amazed to learn during a phone call from a reporter that the Willard group had concluded that prosecutions of the news media were impractical. "There's a memo on this?" he asked incredulously. "In terms of formal documents, I've never seen such a thing on paper."[19] His ignorance of the Willard report shows just how obscure it remained, even at the most sophisticated of newspapers. This very obscurity enhanced the success of the secrecy program. Had Jones known of the report, he would also have known that Casey's threats were empty. Instead, the bluffs had worked. Members of the press had been made to practice self-discipline, as Casey had wished.

Casey's threats of prosecution against the *Post* and other major periodicals also demonstrated the increase in the CIA's power since 1966, when the Agency had "run down" the left-wing *Ramparts.* The CIA had advanced in a mere twenty years from secretly going after small, alternative publications to publicly and successfully threatening the largest of the mainstream press. And this particular display of strength was especially sweet. Over the years the *Washington Post's* exposures of CIA operations had embarrassed the Agency, and espionage artists disliked the paper. That Casey had bluffed the *Post* into submission was good for morale at CIA headquarters.

It may well be that the Reagan administration's successes with the secrecy program emboldened officials to pursue the Iran-Contra initiative. In January 1986 Reagan signed a presidential finding that authorized Casey to conceal Iranian arms shipments from congressional oversight committees. Vice President Bush witnessed this finding at its presentation to the president, according to a memo from Admiral Poindexter, the national security adviser.[20]

Although by objective measures the secrecy program had expanded successfully beyond the possibilities envisioned in 1982, Willard was depressed. Still new to politics, he had a thin skin. The bad publicity he had personally received for advocating censorship had shocked him. To Willard, it was also a personal defeat that the administration had withdrawn two paragraphs of NSDD 84. He began to turn his back on the whole affair. "After I did the report," he told me later, "I was not much involved in day-to-day operations regarding the investigation of leakers, so I can't tell how effective the program was. I was done in 1984 when the controversial parts were suspended."[21]

Yet the CIA's methods had triumphed. The secrecy contracts had been spread throughout the executive branch. All news media inquiries now had to be referred to an official agency spokesperson, and a public relations officer had to chaperon all employees' conversations with journalists. Though compliance was far from complete, in general these methods were being adopted at many agencies. In the Morison case, the Justice Department had succeeded in obtaining criminal penalties for theft against a government employee whose crime was the publication of a photograph. Most long-term employees were signing Form 189. Agencies had drafted regulations to control media contacts. The FBI was investigating leaks. And the CIA director had persuaded even high-profile journalists to exercise self-discipline.

When I subsequently asked Britt Snider if the intention of the secrecy program all along was to keep information out of the press, he said, "That's right."

ELEVEN

Hiding Political Spying

SOON AFTER REAGAN'S SECOND INAUGURATION, he appointed Bush to chair a cabinet-level Task Force on Combating Terrorism. With this mandate, Bush set out not only to narrow congressional oversight of the CIA and to pass new secrecy laws but also to use terrorism as a justification for domestic spying against left-wing citizen groups that had lobbied Congress to ban Contra funding. That this task force was a cover is clear from its own statistics, which showed domestic terrorism in sharp decline just as Bush was ostensibly cranking up his force to fight it. The number of terrorist incidents reported in the United States fell off sharply from twenty-nine in 1980 to only seven by 1985, with a high of fifty-one in 1982. Nevertheless, the thirty-four-page *Public Report of the Vice President's Task Force on Combating Terrorism* of 1986 recommended that the intelligence agencies involve "conventional human and technical intelligence capabilities that penetrate terrorist groups and their support systems."

In an accompanying cover letter, Bush self-consciously tried to explain away the inconsistency between his orders to "improve America's capability for combating terrorism" and FBI reports that domestic terrorism was virtually nonexistent, arguing that terrorism being waged in foreign countries posed "the potential for future problems . . . here at home."[1] Moreover, the report shifted the ground of the debate by describing terrorism as "political theater designed to undermine or alter governmental authority or behavior." This was a radically new definition. Political theater aimed at altering governmental behavior is an American tradition that started with the Boston Tea Party and has long since been protected by the First Amendment.[2]

Following recommendations from Bush's task force to increase the overall surveillance of terrorists, the FBI conducted 8,450 domestic terrorism investigations in 1986, even though they reported only seventeen actual terrorist incidents that year.[3] Much of the difference between the two figures can be explained by the fact that the FBI was conducting political spying under the "terrorism" label. According to FBI documents later released through FOIA requests, the prime targets of these so-called terrorist investigations were those groups advocating the congressional ban on Contra funding. The CIA used a similar strategy when covering up MHCHAOS: domestic political operations are more easily defended if they are labeled as anti-terrorism.

Some FBI special agents were not willing to pursue wholesale spying against U.S. citizens.[4] In Buffalo, New York, agents took the unprecedented action of refusing to conduct the political investigations ordered by headquarters. In a few instances, the executive assistant director of the FBI, Oliver "Buck" Revell (who was also a member of Bush's terrorism task force), overrode the FBI agents' objections and ordered the investigations to continue.

An even larger problem for Bush's task force was finding a way to keep secrets from journalists. Indeed, there were already problems with exposure. Reporters were beginning to write about some FBI political spying for the White House that had occurred in 1984. Syndicated columnist Jack Anderson reported that the FBI was spying on peace groups.[5] It became known that in 1982 the FBI had conducted an "administrative" probe of the Physicians for Social Responsibility, a worldwide group of doctors whose campaign for a nuclear weapons freeze at the international level was awarded a Nobel Peace Prize in 1985. FBI Assistant Director William Baker admitted to me in the mid-1980s that FBI informants had been used inside the group.

Intent on improving secrecy, Bush's task force attacked the FOIA—particularly the 1974 amendments, which had been a vehicle for exposing Nixon's political intelligence operations. Among the recommendations in the report was the repeal of these post-Watergate reforms on the grounds that terrorists might be using the FOIA. It was a wholly speculative argument, as the recommendation itself showed: "Members of terrorist groups *may have used* the Freedom of Information Act to identify FBI informants, frustrate FBI investigations, and tie up government resources in responding to requests. This *would be a clear abuse* of the Act that should be investigated by the Department of Justice and, *if confirmed,* addressed through legislation to close the loophole" (emphasis added).[6]

The truth was that the task force's concern with the FOIA had little to do with terrorism but much to do with political spying. By the end of 1986, this emphasis on spying was causing a growing rebellion within the FBI's usually well-disciplined ranks. Special Agent John C. Ryan, a twenty-one-year veteran from Peoria, Illinois, flatly and repeatedly had refused FBI orders to conduct a "terrorism" investigation of anti-Contra protesters whom he knew to be religious pacifists. As a result, Ryan was fired for insubordination on August 25, 1987, eighteen months after Bush's task force issued its report.[7] Ryan was the first FBI agent fired for refusing to obey orders as a matter of conscience.

Higher-ups at the FBI now were warned that through FOIA requests the public would begin to learn about bureau activities. In February 1986, a decision in an appellate court made the bureau seem especially vulnerable. Federal prisoner David Ely had requested FBI files connected to the circumstances of his imprisonment, to which the FBI had replied that it would neither confirm nor deny the existence of the files. A trial judge upheld the FBI, but on appeal a higher court ruled that at a minimum the judge must be allowed to review the requested files or to review affidavits that described the files. "Congress made clear that the court, not the agency, is to be the ultimate arbiter of privilege," the appellate judges ruled, underscoring the power of the courts to inspect government files.[8]

A few months after the Ely ruling, and after Bush's task force recommended amending the FOIA, Morton Halperin of the ACLU had two discussions about FOIA changes with Stephen W. Markman, an assistant attorney general in the office of legal policy in the Justice Department.[9] The FBI was proposing that the B-7 exemption be rewritten so law enforcement agencies could have final say over the release of records. The B-7 exemption currently allowed the FBI to withhold records to the extent that their release would interfere with enforcement, deprive a person of a fair trial, constitute an unwarranted invasion of privacy, disclose the identity of an informant, compromise investigative techniques, or endanger the life of an officer.

The desired change would expand this broad scope to virtually unlimited latitude. Large segments of FBI records would simply disappear from FOIA requests and judicial oversight. The proposal would allow the FBI under certain conditions to "treat the records as not subject to the requirements" of the FOIA, particularly when the subject of an investigation did not know of it. Also, the proposal declared FBI records pertaining to foreign intelligence, counterintelligence, or international terrorism "not subject to the requirements" of the FOIA—which would exempt some political spying files from release and judicial review. Further, the proposal would allow the FBI to conceal from FOIA investigations the data supplied by state, local, foreign, and private agencies outside the practical range of congressional oversight, thereby permitting the FBI to use surrogates to gather intelligence while retaining plausible deniability.

Halperin described the proposal as "a codification of court decisions," meaning that Congress would be simply enacting what the courts had already ruled. Either Halperin was not familiar with the Ely decision that had reaffirmed judicial review over FBI files, or he was choosing to ignore the case. In any event, Halperin was signaling that the ACLU would accept this FOIA amendment, just as the organization had accepted the CIA Information Act in 1984, which exempted the CIA from certain provisions of the FOIA.

As the 1986 November elections approached, Senators Orrin G. Hatch of Utah and Robert Dole of Kansas attached the FOIA amendment to a popular piece of antidrug legislation. The Society of Professional Journalists dispatched attorneys Bruce Sanford and Henry Hoberman to try to defeat the amendment. Hoberman described the effort this way:

> We went around to our regular friends who'd stopped this before. They said, we can't stop it now. We were told we had to get somebody on the other side, a Republican. So we went to see Senator Dan Quayle of Indiana, whose grandfather, Eugene Pulliam, founded the Society of Professional Journalists in 1909. Quayle was knowledgeable about the FOIA. We had to brief him on the bill. He listened and was supportive. While Bruce and I were there, Quayle got a phone call and went into the other room to take it. I overheard him address Judge Webster [the FBI director]. That's how good the FBI was. They knew we were there, and had the FBI director phone Quayle during our visit.[10]

A deal was finally negotiated by Senator Edward Kennedy and an attorney working for Halperin, Allan Robert Adler. The deal called for the FOIA amendment to go forward in exchange for a new provision that waived FOIA search fees for the news media. The waiver was of little value, however, since a similar provision already existed. The key to the deal was the willingness of the ACLU to negotiate rather than to fight. Halperin's explanation was similar to the one he gave regarding the CIA Information Act: no greater secrecy would result. Adler, Halperin's deputy, insisted, "We are not in any way expanding authority to withhold information."[11] While no civil libertarian could argue with that sentiment, the reality again was that the Justice Department, not the ACLU, would interpret and execute the new FOIA amendment.

As Congress raced toward adjournment, the FOIA amendment was hurriedly put to a vote. Members of Congress said aye without ever seeing a copy of what they were voting on; there had not been enough time to print an up-to-date version of the legislation. As one staffer for Congressman Glenn English commented in an aside to me, "My boss was over on the floor asking, 'Who's got a copy?'" The bill passed October 17, 1986, and Reagan signed it into law. The fact that the legislation was the handiwork of Bush's task force went essentially unnoticed. And to make matters more confusing, some journalists got it wrong. The *Washington Post,* for instance, reported that the FOIA amendment had not been enacted.[12]

Given this level of misinformation, there was little opportunity to fully assess the political implication. Few journalists understood that the FBI would now be able to withhold files that had nothing to do with the enforcement of laws, such as those dealing with political spying operations. Attorney General Edwin Meese III, whose job it was to implement the new FOIA amendment, reported that it "established important new records exclusions"—a different story than the one told by the ACLU. The amendment shielded "more routine monitoring," said Meese. Under it, the FBI could keep secret all kinds of data, not just "specifically focused law enforcement inquiries." Almost gleefully Meese advised the FOIA supervisors to "be mindful of the greater latitude": documents could be treated "as if they did not exist." Most important, the FBI could now largely exclude secret counterintelligence or international terrorism files from public and judicial review, so long as the operation was so secret that its very existence was classified.[13]

Most journalists missed the significance of the new amendment because they were taking their cues from Halperin, but one who saw through the smoke screen was Scott Armstrong, a former *Washington Post* reporter who had founded the National Security Archive—a privately funded group that collects, indexes, and circulates government documents released under the FOIA. Armstrong tried to make it known that the amendment allowed terrorism and counterintelligence files to be kept secret forever, but his efforts were to little avail.

Another part of the new FOIA amendment permitted the government to seek the dismissal of pending FOIA lawsuits. During the slam-bang passage of the legislation, no one in Congress had thought to remove this ex post facto section, and in equally hasty fashion the Justice Department moved to dismiss FOIA cases just days after the final vote. U.S. District Judge Thomas Flannery subsequently interpreted the law exactly contrary to Halperin's intention. Flannery cited "the newly amended statute, and the broader category of information that is protectable" in blocking the release of documents related to the assassination of President Kennedy.[14]

The Justice Department attorney assigned to take advantage of the new FOIA amendment was Richard Willard. He lost no time in using the amendment to fend off a class action lawsuit brought by, among others, Frank Wilkinson in California. Wilkinson had sued the FBI in 1980 for documents about himself and his organization, the Committee to Abolish the House Un-American Activities Committee, founded in the 1960s. Members of the House Un-American Activities Committee, who had a close relationship with FBI Director J. Edgar Hoover, cited informers who said Wilkinson was a Communist. On that basis the FBI had amassed more than 130,000 pages of documents concerning him and his associates. Wilkinson was asking to see those files under the FOIA, but so far all he had obtained from the FBI were heavily censored copies.

Richard Criley, an elder statesman among California's civil libertarians, had inspected the 130,000 pages, threading his way around the blacked-out words, and had constructed a cross-reference file. He concluded that the documents would prove that the FBI had done the following:

disrupted meetings at which Frank Wilkinson was to speak

manipulated the news media to discredit another organization founded by Wilkinson, the National Committee Against Repressive Legislation (formerly the National Committee to Abolish the House Un-American Activities Committee)

prepared "poison pen" letters against the group

intervened illegally in the legislative process

disrupted the organization through the use of informer/agent provocateurs

sabotaged fund-raising

According to Criley, "the entire operation of the FBI was focused on 'discrediting' and 'disrupting' the organization by illegal means and could not be considered 'law enforcement' by the furthest stretch of the imagination."[15]

Now Wilkinson, represented by attorneys from the Southern California ACLU affiliate, was petitioning the federal courts to compel release of the information that had been blacked out. Three days after Reagan signed the FOIA amendment, however, Willard invoked it to block further release of the files. He argued that the goal of the FOIA amendments was to frustrate the efforts of people like Criley "who have both the incentive and the resources to use the act systematically—to gather, analyze, and piece together segregated bits of information obtained from agency files." He accused Criley of having already put together apparently innocuous information to reveal the identity of at least one FBI informant.[16]

"It's true," Criley said. "I did identify an informant who was dead . . . the guy was an officer of NCARL reporting to the FBI." And by authority of the new amendment, the presiding judge in the *Wilkinson* case ruled that the relationship of an informer to the Bureau can be kept secret in perpetuity, even after the informant's death.

In one hard-fought case, however, the persistence of Ann Marie Buitrago, chairwoman of a group called Freedom of Information and Accountability, together with Michael Ratner of the New York–based Center for Constitutional Rights, led to the release of thousands of pages of the FBI file on the Committee in Solidarity with the People of El Salvador.[17] CISPES had opposed U.S. intervention in Central America. While many portions of the file were censored, the documents revealed that under the heading "terrorism matter," CISPES and more than two hundred other anti-Reagan groups had been targeted by the FBI. Investigations had been carried out by fifty-two of the FBI's fifty-nine field offices (see appendix).

Leaders of CISPES held press conferences simultaneously in five cities to call attention to the FBI's massive political operation. In response to the publicity, FBI Director William S. Sessions denied that the operation was ordered by the White House or was politically motivated. He claimed that it began as a "reasonable examination of a possible terrorist threat." However, Sessions was compelled to concede that the FBI found "no substantial link between CISPES and international terrorism," and in an extraordinary move he disciplined six FBI agents for their role in the scandal, suspending some without pay for two weeks.[18]

In the wake of the CISPES disclosures, Congressman Don Edwards ordered the General Accounting Office to inspect politically motivated FBI "terrorism" investigations into peaceful dissenters opposed to U.S. foreign policy in Central America. But the GAO was stymied by the FBI and not allowed to inspect Bureau files for their political content. Instead, the GAO had to be satisfied with responses to questionnaires, which were filled out by FBI agents themselves. Even so, the GAO did discover that the FBI had obtained information on lawful activities in many of the 18,144 FBI international terrorism cases between January 1982 and June 1988.[19]

"Terrorism incidents are down, and hype is up," said one congressional staffer with FBI oversight responsibilities. "There was a concern that administration policy was undercut by domestic opposition groups. It was necessary to discredit and disrupt those groups. There was interest in the investigation of those groups. It was thought they could be disrupted by arrests. There was at the time a sincere belief that there was a link between political opposition and illegal activity."[20]

A House investigator specializing in the FBI observed, "The only way, the best way, for Congress to learn about FBI political investigations is with the aggressive use of the FOIA. In past years, congressional oversight of the FBI could not function without FOIA. Did the changes in the FOIA adversely affect congressional oversight? Yes. Definitely."

William H. Webster, who had moved laterally from FBI director to CIA director, admitted that the FOIA amendment helped agencies maintain the secrecy of classified covert operations. "[The laws] have been made a little more reasonable in protecting sources and methods," Webster said. "That's what it's all about."[21] With the curbing of the FOIA's application to the FBI and the CIA, the Reagan administration's secrecy program continued to roll along in high gear. At the Pentagon, however, the secrecy program ran into one man who stood up and organized a political counterattack.

TWELVE

One Man Says No

AT AGE FIFTEEN, A. ERNEST FITZGERALD followed his father's foot-steps, working as a pattern maker, an exacting craft in the making of precision tools for mass production, in Birmingham, Alabama. His father taught Fitzgerald to work to the closest possible tolerances, pro-duce his products for a reasonable price, and deliver them on time. "Nothing was wasted at my father's shop," he says. With an American Foundryman's scholarship he obtained a bachelor's degree in indus-trial engineering and took a job as a quality control engineer in an air-craft factory. Later, he started his own consulting business in cost and quality control analysis for the government and for large corporations with military contracts. In 1965 the air force gave Fitzgerald a position in procurement cost control for some of its systems, with a mandate to find savings. His boss, the assistant secretary of the air force, gave him a large office on the fifth floor of the Pentagon. He had taken a large cut in pay to work for the government, but, he says, "I thought I could do some good. I thought—before I wised up—that if the top guys knew about waste, they'd want big changes made."[1]

Within a year, Fitzgerald was ready to suggest specific cuts from the Pentagon budget. At a meeting attended by generals, high civilian officials, and defense contractors, Fitzgerald attacked the Pentagon's unscientific system of estimating costs. Contractors who planned costs to be high, he said, were able to bilk the government because the Pentagon lacked facts about the real costs of weapons systems. He pointed out that reducing waste in the procurement system could free up money to replace old planes then in the air over Vietnam.

Many of Fitzgerald's listeners approved and asked for transcripts of his talk. But before he was permitted to distribute copies, his superiors told him he must submit the speech to a security review. Three weeks passed, and his transcript was not returned. Finally, Director of Security Review Charles Hinckle wrote that Fitzgerald's speech had been "caustic" and "inappropriate," and on September 29, 1966, the Office of the Secretary of Defense suppressed the speech and ordered it to be neither printed nor distributed.[2]

Security review officials told Fitzgerald that his negative comments on procurement practices might undermine public confidence in the Defense Department, which in turn would undermine security. From a security officer, Fitzgerald got a copy of his speech with the reviewers' comments on it. Fitzgerald discovered that among other things the reviewers had objected to his comments on scientific method. Among the material censored were quotes he used from Francis Bacon, the father of the scientific method. "It had become painfully obvious that my stand on cost control was not supported by the powers in the Pentagon," Fitzgerald concluded.[3]

In the interim, as part of his air force duties, Fitzgerald visited the Lockheed plant in Marietta, Georgia, where construction was under way on a fleet of fifty-eight giant C-5A transport planes. Each C-5A was nearly as long as a football field, more a flying freight train than an airplane. They were built to haul two M-1 tanks over the ocean at 552 miles per hour and land on twenty-eight tires.

But the multibillion-dollar project was in serious financial difficulty. On his second visit, after inspecting the partially finished planes encased by scaffolding, Fitzgerald calculated that the cost to the Pentagon would run more than $2 billion over the contract. Two years later, when the matter of C-5A cost overruns reached Congress, Senator William Proxmire of Wisconsin, chairman of a joint economic committee, summoned Fitzgerald to testify. Proxmire planned to dispute testimony by the assistant secretary of the air force for research and development, who had told Congress that costs of the C-5As were normal. Proxmire asked Fitzgerald to submit 100 copies of a prepared statement twenty-four hours in advance of testifying, as is usual for such appearances.

But Fitzgerald appeared without a prepared statement and gave this explanation: "Mr. Chairman, I was directed not to prepare a statement directly by my immediate superior, Mr. [Thomas H.] Nielsen, the assistant secretary of the air force for financial management."

"Well, this is very troublesome to this committee, very disturbing," Proxmire replied. "Here is a man who is well qualified, has information of importance to Congress, nothing classified in it. He is directed by the air force not to prepare a statement for the committee . . . did Secretary of Defense Clark Clifford provide instructions to muzzle this witness?"

An air force officer who accompanied Fitzgerald tried to dodge that question, asserting that Fitzgerald was free to respond to the senator's inquiries. Proxmire then launched into his questions, and Fitzgerald began to make public his findings about the C-5A cost overruns, setting the total at more than $2 billion. "The current Lockheed program . . . could exceed its target cost by 100 percent," he said. He then described fundamental problems with the Pentagon's procurement system. When Fitzgerald finished his testimony, reporters swarmed around him, seeking more answers. Flashbulbs popped. "I knew then that I was in the soup," he recalls.[4]

The Pentagon immediately removed Fitzgerald from any cost-control responsibilities. Then, in January 1969—after Frank Weitzel, the assistant comptroller general of the General Accounting Office, told Proxmire that the air force had refused to provide the General Accounting Office with the current C-5A estimates—Fitzgerald was again called to testify.

Proxmire began, "I understand since your testimony in November you have lost your career tenure, is that true?"

"I certainly do not have it today," Fitzgerald responded.

Proxmire asked Fitzgerald if his job loss was the result of his unauthorized disclosures.

"In a sense, Mr. Chairman, it was. I had not cleared the remarks I made with the secretary of the navy."

Proxmire then asked if all Fitzgerald had done was to respond to congressional questions—a key point in the congressional battle with the executive branch for information about expenditures.

"That is correct, and I would answer again," Fitzgerald said.

"Well, Mr. Fitzgerald . . . you have been an excellent witness, and if there was a computer into which you could put courage and integrity, you certainly would be promoted rather than have your status in such serious and unfortunate jeopardy." Proxmire went on to chew out the air force and issue a warning intended to protect Fitzgerald. "The air force can say, and the armed services can say that their officials are free to speak any time and tell Congress the facts as they see them. But it is going to be very hard for the public and the Congress to accept that if there is any further disciplinary action against you, Mr. Fitzgerald."[5]

Approximately six weeks later, the Pentagon assigned Fitzgerald to a new job. He and his two cost-accounting experts were to review the construction of a bowling alley and mess hall in Thailand. Fitzgerald later recalled, "My civilian assistant found that the bowling alley project was greatly overrun (about 300 percent). . . . [W]e lost that job, too."[6] About two months later, the subject of cost overruns hit the front pages. On December 30, 1969, an Associated Press story ran in the *New York Times:* "Major U.S. Weapons Systems Costing $2 Billion More Than Original Estimates."

Fitzgerald expected to return to making money in the private sector. Although he had sold his interest in his old consulting firm, he contacted the firm's attorney, Alex Keyes, a well-connected New Yorker who had previously helped Fitzgerald by referring many high-powered corporate clients to him. "We had lunch at the Yale Club in New York," Fitzgerald recounted. "He said he'd ask around for me. When I didn't hear from him, I called him. He gave me some advice. 'Open a service station,' he said. 'You're dead on the Street [Wall Street].' " Another old friend, Dick Burtner of Goodyear Aerospace, told Fitzgerald he would loan him money, but " 'if I hire you I'll never get Pentagon business.' "

Unable to find work in his profession, Fitzgerald felt he had little choice but to file a lawsuit demanding to have his old Pentagon job back. At the same time he wrote a book, published in 1972, titled *High Priests of Waste*. It detailed how military contractors plunder the public treasury, how they keep auditors from finding out about high profits and low quality, and how the waste is hidden behind a veil of military secrecy in the name of national security.

In September 1973 a federal judge ordered the air force to reinstate Fitzgerald, but his claims for back salary and damages were to be locked up by legal battles for years. In November 1981, when the case finally went before the U.S. Supreme Court, one of the legal issues was whether the executive branch enjoyed absolute immunity from suits arising from the violation of someone's civil rights.[7]

While Fitzgerald's suit was pending, Morton Halperin was suing former President Nixon for wiretaps illegally placed on his home while Halperin served on the National Security Council staff. Halperin was afraid that the Supreme Court would rule in Fitzgerald's case that Nixon enjoyed absolute immunity, so Halperin intervened. Halperin's lawyer, Mark Lynch, told the court that "civil service employees, such as Fitzgerald, who are fired in alleged retaliation for the exercise of their First Amendment rights, have no cause of action under the First Amendment in view of the special relationship between the federal government and its employees." Lynch also wrote in a motion for Halperin that "the speech for which Fitzgerald was allegedly fired is not protected by the First Amendment."[8] This position by Halperin and Lynch presaged their future stances as civil libertarians: government employees are not protected by the First Amendment.

In May 1984, Secretary of the Air Force Verne Orr assigned Fitzgerald to assist Chairman John D. Dingell, the Michigan Democrat who headed the House Energy and Commerce Committee, to help investigate stock manipulations related to the awarding of multibillion-dollar defense contracts. Resuming his role as a cost-cutting detective, Fitzgerald traveled to the Hughes Aircraft plant in Tucson, Arizona, where he was informed that in a tear-down inspection, made in conjunction with an inspection of the air force's Maverick system, the navy Phoenix missile guidance system had passed all normal quality controls. On probing further, however, he discovered there were 2,578 defects, of which 106 were considered extremely serious. The guidance system is a critical part of the air-launched, radar-guided, solid propellant rocket. But the Pentagon generals did little to fix the problems, and, once again, Fitzgerald decided that his only recourse was to make a public disclosure. As a result, the plant was forced to shut down for six months.

Over the years, Fitzgerald had lost his dark lean look and was now the picture of a bureaucrat, with gray trousers, gray glasses, and gray close-cropped hair. Even his 1985 Toyota GTS, a present from his wife and kids, was gray. On May 13, 1987, he arrived at his office, a much smaller one than he used to command, and walked past the bank of five gray file cabinets containing classified information. Each was secured by a Diebold dial combination lock and had a small paper form affixed to the front of its drawers on which was recorded the times of opening and closing. At 9:20 A.M. Captain David Price walked into Fitzgerald's office. "Mr. Fitzgerald," said Captain Price, "I have a nondisclosure form for you to sign. You must sign it or your security clearance will be revoked." He handed Fitzgerald an envelope, turned, and walked out of the office.

Fitzgerald took a deep breath. His security clearance was necessary for him to do his job: he needed access to the classified papers in his office cabinets. The sheet of paper in Captain Price's envelope was titled "Classified Information Nondisclosure Agreement"—Standard Form 189. The sheet was filled with thirteen paragraphs and at the top was a space for his name: "An agreement between [space] and the United States." Paragraph one defined what was to be kept secret—"information that is classified or is classifiable." It was clear to Fitzgerald that any information is classifi*able,* especially if it is embarrassing to the Pentagon. He might give unclassified information to Congress, and then the generals could classify it.

Fitzgerald came to the third paragraph, an agreement never to divulge any classified information without "written authorization." Instantly, Fitzgerald realized this would mean he could not divulge information to Congress about waste, fraud, and abuse if the Pentagon classified that information as secret. He recalled that his first disclosures about the C-5A cost overruns had been "unauthorized." He had talked to Congress without receiving written permission. That data in his testimony had not been classified. But were they classifi*able?*

Fitzgerald kept reading. The contract forbade "direct or indirect" disclosure. What if he told Congressman Dingell about classified data and Dingell released the information to the public? Under Form 189, Fitzgerald would be liable for this disclosure by the chairman of a House committee. And the scope of the coverage was vast. Paragraph seven said, "I understand that all information to which I may obtain access by signing this agreement is now and will forever remain the property of the United States Government." Fitzgerald's eyebrows shot up. "*All* information?" he thought.

Fitzgerald realized that if he signed the form, he would be greatly restricted from informing Congress about cost overruns. "No way am I going to sign this and be silenced for life," he told his assistant, Betty Dudka. The outlook was bleak. Who would help? The ACLU had capitulated on Form 189. The government worker unions had been all but silent on the issue. Liberals in Congress had been less than effective. The federal courts had bowed to national security claims and long ago ruled that secrecy contracts were binding. The news media had also shown no inclination to fight against Form 189. "I'm alone on this one," Fitzgerald thought, "but I'll be damned if I'm just going to let the Pentagon shut me up without a fight."

Fitzgerald picked up the phone and called one of Capitol Hill's most able investigators, Peter Stockton, an aide to Dingell. Fitzgerald explained that if he signed Form 189, he would be effectively removed from his role as a congressional investigator. On the other hand, if he failed to sign it, he would be terminated from his Pentagon job. Stockton quickly arranged to have the two of them meet with Steven Garfinkel of the Information Security Oversight Office. Garfinkel explained that Form 189 had been drawn up in response to White House irritation over leaks to the press. Fitzgerald made a mental note—Garfinkel was referring to leaks of embarrassing information rather than leaks of classified information.

Stockton and Fitzgerald pressed Garfinkel. "What does the term classifi*able* mean? According to Fitzgerald, Garfinkel responded, "It could mean anything." He tried to clarify his position. Classifi*able* meant any data that would be understood to need classification and hadn't been classified through an oversight. Stockton and Fitzgerald grew more concerned after this vague answer and asked Garfinkel if he would remove the term "classifiable" from the nondisclosure contract before Fitzgerald signed it. Garfinkel replied that he could not.

Fitzgerald felt insulted. He had never been accused of divulging classified information about weapons systems—or anything else.[9] But Garfinkel brushed aside his arguments, boasting that the director of the Washington office of the ACLU had approved Form 189. Why should one man be exempt when so many others had signed?

After Garfinkel left the congressional offices, Stockton and Fitzgerald composed a letter for Dingell to send to William D. Ford, the chairman of the House Committee on Post Office and Civil Service, asking him to investigate. "We wanted to make sure that these agreements . . . would not inhibit the proper and timely flow of information to the Congress," the letter said.[10]

Fitzgerald returned to his Pentagon office, his resolve stronger than ever. "I don't intend to sign it, particularly after talking to Garfinkel. I've talked to my wife and my lawyer and I've prepared for the worst. I can't conceive of any conditions under which I'll sign that damn form," Fitzgerald vowed to Dudka in his Alabama drawl.

While being pestered for his signature on an almost daily basis, Fitzgerald widened his effort to gain congressional support. He phoned and visited the staff of Gerry Sikorski, a young Minnesota Democrat who chaired the House Post Office and Civil Service Subcommittee on Human Resources, which had jurisdiction over government workers. Sikorski agreed to write a letter on Fitzgerald's behalf, which was sent to Frank Carlucci, Reagan's new National Security Adviser. The letter roundly criticized Form 189 for its "ambiguities and inconsistencies, as well as vague and questionable terms which coercively impose inescapable liability on federal employees in violation of their rights." Sikorski's letter also raised a question of whether Form 189 violates laws that prohibit interfering with the rights of federal employees to furnish information to both houses of Congress. "Standard Form 189 tramples on the right of federal employees and the First Amendment" and is "a new thinly veiled attempt to impose prepublication review . . . on federal employees." Sikorski concluded by requesting that Carlucci halt the use of the form.[11]

On July 2 the comptroller of the air force, Lieutenant General Claudius E. Watts III, formally issued written orders telling Fitzgerald to sign Form 189 within thirty days or face the loss of his security clearance and his job. That was followed on July 7 by a policy statement from ACLU attorney Allan Adler announcing that "the ACLU finds no inherent constitutional barrier" to an agreement that "imposes an obligation not to disclose . . . information without authorization." While Adler recommended that Form 189 be rewritten to eliminate vague language, he seemed to undermine Fitzgerald's lobbying effort on Capitol Hill. Adler recommended congressional action only "if administrative solutions are not soon forthcoming."[12] Fitzgerald was displeased, but not surprised, that the ACLU refused to join the growing congressional pressure to suspend the secrecy contracts.

As the deadline neared, however, Fitzgerald gained new and powerful allies. Congressman Les Aspin of Wisconsin, Chairman of the House Armed Services Committee, wrote Carlucci, "Compliance with Standard Form 189 should be suspended."[13]

Fitzgerald next received support from Senator Charles E. Grassley of Iowa, a Republican whose rural constituents were suffering serious financial hardship and were outraged at the chronic squandering of tax money by the Pentagon. As a member of the Senate Appropriations Committee, Grassley asked the Congressional Research Service's legal arm to review the relevant law regarding secrecy and disclosure. The service concluded that Form 189 "is arguably in conflict with the language and intent of" the law protecting whistleblowers.[14]

The same day, Watts repeated his order to Fitzgerald to sign Standard Form 189 by the deadline, now about a week away. Fitzgerald began a series of frantic phone calls to congressional offices. Just one day before the deadline another powerful committee chairman, Congressman Jack Brooks, complained about Standard Form 189 in a letter, "Such a contract is incompatible with the First Amendment to the Constitution, regardless of who is asked to sign it."[15]

In the face of this support, the Pentagon allowed the deadline to pass and permitted Fitzgerald to stay on the job, at least for the time being. On August 17, 1987, the 150,000-member National Federation of Federal Employees, about 40 percent of whom work in the Department of Defense, sued the government to stop implementation of Form 189. The suit was later joined by the 200,000-member American Federation of Government Employees, as well as the American Foreign Service Association, which chiefly represents State Department employees.[16]

On August 21, Garfinkel issued instructions that, as a temporary accommodation to the lawsuit, no employees would have their security clearances revoked solely for refusing to sign Form 189. However, agencies were to continue asking for signed secrecy contracts from their employees.[17] On the same day, the air force suspended Fitzgerald's deadline for signing and set no new one.[18]

With the lines of battle now drawn between the federal employee unions and the Reagan administration, Congressman Sikorski convened a public hearing on October 15, 1987. Sikorski began the hearing by asking, "What waste, what fraud, what incompetence, what malfeasance and misfeasance, what high crimes or misdemeanors would never have seen the healing light of legislative and public scrutiny if federal employees of years past had been forced to contend with such an all-encompassing restriction?" Senator Grassley drove home the point that the administration's intent was to place a blanket of silence over all information generated by the government, and he added that Form 189 would make it easier for the government to "go after" whistle-blowers. Grassley then made a declaration that made the next day's headlines: "Grassley to Civil Servants: Ignore Secrecy Pledge."[19]

Even elected members of Congress had been told to sign secrecy contracts. Brooks reported that the Department of Energy had "recently sent me—and I was probably the wrong one to send it to—a Form 189 nondisclosure contract to sign so that I can have access to a report done by the GAO for the United States Congress." Brooks summed up the lessons he had learned about government secrecy during thirty-four years in Congress. "Most of the classification, in my judgment, is not to keep our enemies from finding out information. It is to keep the American people and the Congress from finding out what in God's world various agencies are doing and how they are throwing away money, wasting it. . . . They throw away money like dirt, and lie and cheat and hide to keep Congress from finding out, and, for God's sake, they don't want the American people to find out," he fumed.[20]

Following the hearing, Congress approved a rider that outlawed the spread of Form 189 (as well as Form 4193, the prepublication review contract) and attached it to an appropriations bill. Reagan had to sign the bill by December 22, 1987, if he wanted the executive branch to have money. Its language was clear: "No funds appropriated in this or any other Act for fiscal year 1988 may be used to implement or enforce the agreements in Standard Form 189 and 4193 of the Government or any other nondisclosure policy, form or agreement . . . that contains the term 'classifiable' [or] . . . obstructs . . . the rights of any individual to petition or communicate with members of Congress in a secure manner." Congress did not want to be kept ignorant. That meant Fitzgerald had prevented his firing—or so it seemed for a time. "Once in a while," Fitzgerald said with a smile, "we get a little bit done. Even a blind hog finds an acorn."

THIRTEEN

Control of Information

THE GOVERNMENT EMPLOYEES' LAWSUIT against the secrecy contracts was heard in federal court in Washington, D.C. Judge Oliver Gasch, a conservative, presided. The plaintiffs, including several members of Congress as well as the federal employee unions, took the position that the executive branch was acting in defiance of a congressional ban on Form 189 and Form 4193. The Reagan administration, in turn, held that the ban was an unconstitutional abridgment of the powers of the commander in chief, arguing on the grounds that the president has sovereign rights to control national security information.

Lawyers for the plaintiffs disputed those grounds. They noted that the Constitution recognizes the occasional need for legislative secrecy and permits Congress to meet in secrecy, but they pointed out that it fails in plain language to mention any secrecy power of the executive. There exists a general legal principle that says, in essence, if a law expressly grants powers to one but not to others, then the omission is presumed as intentional.

Judge Gasch ruled in favor of the Reagan administration, although he could find little constitutional basis for the theory of executive primacy. Indeed, Gasch acknowledged that "[n]either political branch is expressly charged by the Constitution with regulation, accumulation of, or access to, national security information." Nonetheless, relying on English common law, he found that Congress had unconstitutionally violated the president's "sovereign prerogative" to preserve secrets. To posit the existence of a "sovereign prerogative" in a republic such as the United States was strange. The basis of a republic, as distinguished from a monarchy, is that all citizens have equal status before the law, while the notion of sovereignty grants a superlative power to one individual. Nevertheless, Gasch decided that constitutionally the president's secrecy powers were contained, by inference, in his command of the armed forces. Gasch further ruled that the proper role of Congress was to be a supporter of executive secrecy, to "facilitate secrecy with appropriate criminal and civil sanctions."

Gasch did allow that perhaps there was a problem with the excessively broad term "classifiable" used in Form 189. But by the time of Gasch's decision, Steven Garfinkel had written a new definition of "classifiable" as "unmarked *classified* information . . . in the process of a classification determination." This revision seemed to satisfy Gasch.[1] Gasch's decision was appealed directly to the U.S. Supreme Court.

Meanwhile, Congress passed yet another ban on the spread of secrecy contracts as part of another appropriations bill. Reagan, placed in the same political box as before, signed the bill into law on September 23, 1988, even while denouncing the ban. He charged that it "raises profound constitutional concerns" and "interferes with my ability to prevent unauthorized disclosures of our most sensitive diplomatic, military, and intelligence activities." The general impression was that the spread of censorship again had been outlawed. "People will get the impression . . . that it's ended, yes," Garfinkel observed.[2] However, in his signing statement, Reagan ordered: "In accordance with my sworn obligation to preserve, protect and defend the Constitution, [the ban] will be considered of no force or effect unless and until the ruling of the district court is reversed by the Supreme Court."[3]

Seven days later, Garfinkel replaced Standard Form 189 with Standard Form 312, from which he had removed the catchall term "classifiable." He sent the new form to more than fifty agency chiefs for circulation to employees. Fitzgerald waited on edge, expecting the worst. If the Supreme Court upheld the Gasch decision, Fitzgerald might be fired.

———————

On November 5, 1988, George Bush won the presidential election. As CIA director in 1976, he had been a strong advocate of spreading secrecy agreements, and he became the first president-elect in history to require his transition team to sign secrecy contracts.[4]

On April 18, 1989, Chief Justice William H. Rehnquist delivered the Supreme Court's ruling on the Gasch decision. Gasch was ordered to reconsider the case. Rehnquist stated, "We emphasize that the District Court should not pronounce upon the relative constitutional authority of Congress and the Executive Branch unless it finds it imperative to do so." Rehnquist was sidestepping the issue, preferring to keep the courts out of a fight that might never be settled permanently.

In the fall of 1989, Congress again legislated limits on the secrecy contracts with a rider to another appropriations measure. President Bush signed it on November 3, 1989, but, as Reagan had done, he instructed his subordinates to ignore the law. Bush's signing statement, which received little notice, read:

> I am compelled to note my strong objection to section 618, . . . which purports to forbid the implementation or enforcement of certain nondisclosure agreements required of government employees with access to classified information. This provision . . . raises profound constitutional concerns. . . . Article II of the Constitution confers responsibility on me as President and Commander in Chief to conduct the national defense and foreign affairs of the United States. In this capacity, I have the constitutional duty to ensure the secrecy of information whose disclosure would threaten our national security. . . . Furthermore, section 618 could suggest that I am prohibited from establishing and enforcing appropriate procedures to control the dissemination of classified information by executive branch employees to Members of Congress.

Here was the crux of the matter—the executive branch sought the control of information going to Congress.

"I believe," Bush continued, "that section 618, thus construed, would jeopardize the nation's security by unconstitutionally interfering with my ability to prevent the unauthorized disclosure of information concerning our most sensitive diplomatic, military, and intelligence activities." Thus he "direct[ed] that executive branch officials implement the provisions of section 618 in a manner consistent with the Constitution."[5] In essence, Bush was ordering that the law be disobeyed.

"We're still in business," Garfinkel said. He kept pressuring agencies to distribute the new Form 312. With Bush as president, Garfinkel's Information Security Oversight Office headquarters was moved out of the sixth floor of the General Services building to a fancier address closer to the White House. According to Garfinkel, this move was intended to signal the increased importance of information security.

In his Pentagon office, meanwhile, Fitzgerald kept refusing to sign the new secrecy contract. No one, however, cared to press Fitzgerald any longer, for he had achieved celebrity status in Washington. During an interview Garfinkel threw up his hands at a question about Fitzgerald, as if to say, "I don't ever want to hear about Ernie Fitzgerald again, and I don't want to know if he does not sign a secrecy contract."

With Gasch's decision remanded back to his court, lawyers began trying to negotiate a settlement between Congress and the Bush administration over the secrecy oaths. From the point of view of the congressional lawyers, it was one thing for the executive to say to a civil servant, "You can't disclose to the public," but quite another to say, "You can't disclose to Congress." Bush's lawyers were also willing to make the same distinction. Garfinkel would amend the secrecy contracts to protect government employees who inform Congress. In January 1991, he added to Form 312 the sections from the Whistleblower Protection Act that protect those who disclose waste, fraud, and abuse to Congress.

The congressional right to know had been steadily eroded during the previous two decades, and, given a political climate in which the executive branch was still in the ascendancy, Congress was satisfied with this small victory. The compromise essentially ended congressional resistance to the secrecy contracts.

Congress has many arcane rules designed to control information, many in conflict with one another. Historically, Congress could and did release information, classified or not, as a branch of government equal to the executive. Up until 1976, even the CIA recognized the power of Congress to declassify information, according to an internal Agency memorandum that has never been made public. The turning point came when the House Select Committee on Intelligence (usually referred to as the Pike Committee for its chairman, Congressman Otis Pike of New York) issued a report on the CIA so scathing that the House voted to seal it. In January 1976, John D. Morrison Jr., the CIA deputy general counsel, analyzed the report and discovered to his delight a crucial assertion: "no one in Congress can declassify."[6] To the CIA, this was news. In a memo, Morrison pointedly remarked, "We shall cherish this latter statement against interest and use it as precedent, so do not say anything to make them [the committee] reconsider it."[7] It is a particular irony that the Pike Committee, while it criticized the CIA and fought for access to CIA documents, inadvertently contributed to surrendering the congressional right to disclose secrets of the executive branch.

From that point on, Congress continued to lose control of executive information. The next setback was in the traditional right for each and every member of Congress to have complete and equal access to all information in the custody of any congressional committee.[8] In practical terms, this meant when a member was concerned with, say, the overthrow of a government in Chile, the member could inspect the classified testimony of the CIA director delivered in executive session of the intelligence committee and engage in political debate, through correspondence with fellow members about it. However, on July 14, 1977, when Stansfield Turner was CIA director, the House consolidated CIA oversight in the House Permanent Select Committee on Intelligence and set up a special House rule creating a five-day waiting period before classified information can be disclosed to the public. The rule gave the president time to indulge in arm-twisting, thus preventing the vast majority of secrets from ever being released. Another rule restricted the sharing of such information with another member of Congress. By limiting debate among members of Congress, these rules amounted to an erosion of the basic autonomy of Congress in favor of executive power.[9]

In 1982 Congress imposed upon itself the requirement that the House and Senate, in consultation with the CIA director, "shall each establish, by rule or resolution, procedures to protect from unauthorized disclosure all classified information and all information relating to intelligence sources and methods furnished to the intelligence committees." Thus, Congress accepted the president's right to determine unilaterally what must be kept secret from the public.[10]

The congressional acceptance of secrecy soon became of particular importance. President Reagan, trying to get Congress to appropriate money to support the Contras, claimed that Nicaragua's Sandinistas were shipping arms to communist guerrillas in El Salvador. Members of the House Permanent Select Intelligence Committee knew from their access to classified reports that Reagan's claims were not truthful. "But we were unable to respond to the president's assertions because the information was classified," Congressman Lee Hamilton later wrote in the *Washington Post*. Likewise, Senator Daniel Patrick Moynihan later expressed his chagrin. "I knew the president's claim could not be substantiated," he said. "But I knew this from classified briefings which a chairman or vice chairman of such a committee is sworn not to discuss in public."[11] His assessment of the secrecy system was blunt: its "effect is to hide things from the American people that they need to know."

By the early 1990s, the CIA was trying more aggressively than ever to force censorship contracts upon congressional members and their staffs. An eleven-year CIA career officer, Thomas R. Smeeton, had become the minority counsel to the House Permanent Select Committee on Intelligence, under Representative E. G. ("Bud") Shuster of Pennsylvania, the ranking Republican on the committee. Beginning in 1990, Smeeton—with Shuster's support—made repeated attempts to convince members of Congress to take oaths to uphold executive secrecy classifications.[12] Initially, Intelligence Chairman Dave McCurdy of Oklahoma was able to stop Smeeton and Shuster. "We get it rejected each time we bring it up," Smeeton said. "But we ought to continue to offer it, even though they always shoot us down."

On June 11, 1991, Shuster offered Smeeton's secrecy oath amendment to the Intelligence Authorization Bill for the fourth time. Written by Smeeton, it read as follows: "I do solemnly swear that I will not directly or indirectly disclose to any unauthorized person any classified information received in the course of my duties on the Permanent Select Committee on Intelligence, except with the formal approval of the committee or of the House." Shuster said the primary purpose was to increase the readiness of the CIA to provide secrets to the committee necessary for it to carry out its legislative oversight, by stopping leaks of classified information from the committee.[13] McCurdy, tired of spending time endlessly debating the oath, grudgingly accepted Smeeton's amendment.

The oath gave the CIA yet another hold on the congressional oversight committee. It was reminiscent of Richard Ober's old method of getting CIA officers to sign secrecy contracts before briefing them on the MHCHAOS domestic operations. Once sworn to secrecy, they could no longer object to any illegalities about which they learned during a briefing. However, the entanglements of the secrecy contract could be dense and seemingly endless, as Michael Pillsbury, a highly regarded official, discovered.

A balding man with a patrician nose, Pillsbury had served in the 1980s as an aide to Senator Orrin Hatch, a Republican from Utah. By virtue of Hatch's conservative senatorial sponsorship, Pillsbury became what is called a "player" inside U.S. covert operations, even though he had a somewhat controversial background. Wealthy and outspoken, he was born into the Pillsbury flour family. He graduated from Stanford University and pursued his study of China at Columbia University; he learned to speak Mandarin. While working at the Rand Corporation, he advocated the establishment of relations with China before the idea became a popular Republican policy.

Pillsbury enjoyed a kind of filial relationship in his job with Senator Hatch, who was a senior member of the Senate intelligence committee. Pillsbury believes he was, in 1983, the first Senate staffer to volunteer for a CIA polygraph test. Hatch asked him to take the test as a concession to CIA director William Casey, who wanted to implement a system of polygraphs for all staffers on the intelligence committee. Pillsbury said, "Casey was told to use me [as a precedent] to have the Senate staff polygraphed." CIA examiners tested and approved him. "I was pro-polygraph. Passing makes you pro-polygraph," he recalled later.

As part of his duties for Hatch, Pillsbury began to attend secret interagency meetings between the White House, the Pentagon, the CIA, and Congress to discuss supplying weapons to nations engaged in superpower proxy wars. These supply operations were among the nation's most closely guarded secrets, known only to Pillsbury and perhaps a dozen other people. He was admitted into the limited-access compartment of special activities code-named "Veil," which held a higher classification than "top secret." Pillsbury saw himself as a hero in a business suit, lobbying to get anti-Communist guerrillas the best possible weaponry. He pushed to send the high-tech anti-aircraft Stinger missile to anti-Communists in Angola, Afghanistan, and Nicaragua.

With Hatch's blessing, Pillsbury then moved to a full-time position at the Pentagon, as the assistant under secretary of defense for policy planning (one of the civilians who run covert Pentagon operations). But while in pursuit of his Stinger policy, Pillsbury made a powerful enemy in Admiral John Poindexter, who was then National Security Adviser to President Reagan. Poindexter was opposed to putting Stingers in the hands of third world guerrillas, reasoning that the weapons could be sold on the black market to terrorists who might shoot down civilian airliners. Also, as a rule, the CIA supplied only weapons of Eastern Bloc manufacture to anti-Communists involved in insurgencies in order to maintain a "plausible deniability" that the United States was involved. The shipments of Stingers, manufactured in the United States, would end any pretense of noninvolvement.

Pillsbury's single-mindedness appealed to President Reagan, however, and in March 1986 the decision was made to supply Stingers to the rebels in Afghanistan and to UNITA rebels in Angola. Pillsbury was to coordinate the shipments. On March 27, the intelligence committees of Congress were briefed about the new development. Two days later, Pillsbury received a phone call from *Washington Post* reporter Patrick E. Tyler, who had learned about the deployment of Stingers to Afghanistan. Pillsbury tried to lie to Tyler, saying the missiles had not yet been sent.[14] Tyler and another *Post* reporter, David B. Ottaway, subsequently reported that the shipments of Stingers were taking place and an escalation of the Afghan war could be expected.[15]

President Reagan was furious with Poindexter over the leak. (What Pillsbury did not know, he said later, was that the Veil compartment also contained the Iranian arms-for-hostage operations.) The day after the Stinger story appeared, an FBI investigation was launched to try to determine the identity of the leaker. Officially titled "Unauthorized Disclosure of Classified Information" and labeled on FBI documents as "Espionage (Media Leak)," the investigation lasted one year and focused on Pillsbury. Poindexter marked Pillsbury as the main suspect by instructing CIA officer Vincent Cannistraro, who was posted to the Planning Coordination Group for covert operations at the National Security Council, to take Pillsbury's name off the access list. "I was the gatekeeper and I did it," Cannistraro later said. "He was blacklisted from the White House."[16]

As the reality of his predicament dawned on Pillsbury, he came to believe that Poindexter and Cannistraro were using the leak investigation as a weapon in a bureaucratic policy dispute. Cannistraro, like Poindexter, had been against the Stinger shipments. "Cannistraro was opposed to Stingers [because] as a CIA career officer on loan to the NSC he was obliged to defend the traditional CIA view that no weapons from the United States could be used in covert actions for plausible deniability reasons," Pillsbury said later.[17]

Within days Pillsbury heard through the grapevine that agents of the Defense Investigative Service (DIS) were also investigating him. By process of elimination, Pillsbury had come to their attention. "They find out the number of people with access to the covert operation. In this case, it was under ten at the Pentagon, two or three at the National Security Council, and four or five at State. They try to discover who talked to a reporter, and what was said," he said. He was singled out because he had talked to a *Post* reporter. Within a few days, DIS agents knocked on Pillsbury's Pentagon office door. Agent Larry Dubrowsky asked Pillsbury questions typical of a leak investigation.

"Did you have access [to the leaked information]?"

Pillsbury answered, "Yes."

"Did you leak?"

"No," Pillsbury said.

"Did you talk to reporters?"

"Yes," Pillsbury answered.

Pillsbury explained that he tried to mislead the reporter. Because false information cannot be classified as secret, Pillsbury thought he was free to lie to the *Post*. Pillsbury had followed regulations, he said, by calling his Pentagon supervisor, Fred C. Ikle, at home to report his contact with the journalist.

While the leak investigations progressed, the shipment of Stingers to Afghanistan was delayed, as Poindexter and Cannistraro wished. As he recalled the events, his frustration was still clear: "With the slow pace of the investigation, my program was in trouble. The Stinger decision had not been implemented." It is Pillsbury's belief that by casting suspicion on him and by keeping him out of the White House meetings while he was being investigated, Poindexter and Cannistraro were able to negate the Stinger decision.

To get the Stinger project back on track, Pillsbury volunteered to take a polygraph test to prove he had not leaked secrets to reporters. Poindexter's staff arranged for a Navy Investigative Service polygraph operator named Deborah Baughman to administer the test at a site an hour and a half out of Washington, D.C. "That's when I first thought something is wrong," Pillsbury said. "Usually, polygraphs are given at the Pentagon." The polygraph operator acted in a hostile manner and questioned him for hours, he said.

The key question was, "Did you tell [reporters] Tyler or Ottaway of Stinger decisions?" Pillsbury told her, "Well, I had talked to Tyler about the Stinger issue to make him think there had been no decision. I did not disclose the decision. I tried to mislead the reporter."[18] The Navy examiner flunked Pillsbury and concluded that he had lied about disclosure. The consequences were immediate: Pillsbury's security clearances were revoked, and he was terminated from his position in the Pentagon.

He was able to land a job back on Capitol Hill, working for the conservative bloc of Republican Senators Jesse Helms of North Carolina, Gordon J. Humphrey of New Hampshire, and Jacob C. Hecht of Nevada. But Pillsbury was convinced that he was a victim of the Iran-Contra scandal. "With hindsight, we can now see [Poindexter's] fear was that I'm going to get into what Ollie [Lt. Col. Oliver North] and Vince [Cannistraro] were up to—the off-the-shelf enterprise that was the Iran-Contra affair," Pillsbury said later. "The essence of these guys is contemptuous: to lie to the Senate. I'm a Senate staffer, so I'd never have gone along [with the Iran-Contra cover-up]."[19]

In its investigation, the FBI made no determination as to whether the information provided by Pillsbury to the *Washington Post* was classified. The Justice Department considered the Pillsbury affair "closed" as of April 1989. Assistant Attorney General Markman wrote Senator Humphrey that he hoped the affair could be "seen in the context of the fact that the Department of Defense has now restored [Pillsbury's] Top Secret Security clearance."[20]

Later, after Pillsbury learned about the Willard group's secrecy program, he said, "I was the first example of the implementation of the Willard report regarding investigation of leakers." Others agreed that Pillsbury's rights were abused. Pillsbury's former boss at the Pentagon, Fred Ikle, an under secretary of defense, said that the Pillsbury case "showed the bureaucratic system for protecting government secrets at its worst."[21]

In an effort to find out more about the secrecy program, Pillsbury undertook his own investigation. As an aide to conservative senators, he was able to get some answers. He discovered that Casey's staff in 1984 had organized the Unauthorized Disclosures Analysis Center (UDAC) to monitor the news media and to stop leaks. Commanded by Dell Bragan, UDAC was housed in a large building in downtown Washington and staffed by full-time intelligence officers. UDAC's findings were forwarded to the Justice Department for potential prosecutions under theft and espionage laws and under the Intelligence Identities Protection Act. UDAC received reports from other intelligence agencies such as the DIS, and UDAC's own reports were also sent to Steven Garfinkel at ISOO.

CIA officers around the nation were called upon by UDAC to keep track of reporters who obtained news stories through leaks. Official CIA spokesperson Sherry Mauck explained, "UDAC takes calls from other employees that know of [leaks'] existence, alerting them to certain leaks." The purpose of the monitoring, Mauck stated, was "to combat the unauthorized disclosure of intelligence." Another spokesperson, Mark Mansfield, said UDAC was the coordinating center to combat disclosures.[22] The CIA's use of the word "combat" implied a domestic counterintelligence role—taking action to prevent certain information from reaching the public—a role forbidden to the Agency under the 1947 National Security Act. By figuring out the names of leakers, UDAC agents were able to make unofficial approaches to discourage them from further contact with journalists.

It was clear to Pillsbury that any intelligence analyst who gathers evidence over a period of years about a reporter's sources will develop a great deal of background information on individuals in the media. He explained,

> When I was interviewed by the FBI and DIS agents in my own case, they openly asked me, and demanded as part of my cooperation, a great deal of background about the reporters. That leak investigation was not confined to "Did you leak or not?" I was intimidated into describing all I knew about the reporter, his sources, his interest, and how the newspaper works. I described to the agents a great deal about reporters Tyler and Ottaway and their relations to managing editor Ben Bradlee. When I saw the record of my interview, they had marked "secret" my statement of the reporters'

opinions of their editor. All of this will be filed under the name Pat Tyler. They have all the articles he has ever written that have undisclosed classified information in them. An analyst can see a very clear picture of Tyler's sources.

Pillsbury discovered that journalists were analyzed in terms of how many unauthorized disclosures they had printed per year. Columnist Jack Anderson, *Washington Post* reporter Bob Woodward, and Bill Gertz of the *Washington Times* were often near the top of the list. His own analysis was acute:

> The prosecution of Mr. Morison put the legal framework in place to arrest and prosecute journalists for receiving stolen property in prosecutions presented by the government that would go like this: This gentleman has a pattern of many years of damaging national security, he is essentially a thief. The presentation to the jury could be highly persuasive in the same way a criminal is indicted on twenty counts of burglary—even if some counts are dismissed, there are enough counts to send him away for many years in prison. The Morison prosecution laid the foundation for successful prosecution of U.S. journalists who have, in the opinion of the government, gone too far.[23]

In addition to UDAC, the CIA has an even more secretive unit that investigates leaks, performs damage assessments, and investigates journalists. Located in the Office of Security and called the Special Security Office, this unit reports to UDAC. It has the special responsibility of investigating leaks made from within the CIA. Polygraph operators who work for the unit are known as the SY boys, after the first and last letter of security, and are feared throughout the Agency.

But even as a tighter system for prosecuting investigative journalists was put in place, rapidly shifting international political relations were forcing new approaches to secrecy and, ostensibly, to openness.

FOURTEEN

The CIA Openness Task Force

WITH THE DISSOLUTION OF THE SOVIET EMPIRE into its constituent republics in the early 1990s, the old rationale for U.S. government secrecy began to disappear as well. Maynard Anderson, the Pentagon's assistant deputy under secretary for counterintelligence and security, was among the Bush administration officials who tried to find a new threat to replace communism.[1]

Anderson's idea was to make a sophisticated change in the government's classification system. Previously, following the 1982 Executive Order 12356 written by Richard Willard, information was classified according to the damage that its release would cause to national security. *Top secret* would cause grave damage, *secret* would cause serious damage, and *confidential* was presumed to cause identifiable damage.[2] Anderson proposed that classification instead be done according to the value of the information.

"Certainly on the basis of money," Anderson said, "you could ascribe a new concept of national security, which I would rename 'national interest.' We are faced with a threat from foreign intelligence collectors of economic information. If it is in our national interest to protect technology, industrial production, and our competitive position in world markets, does not the national interest have a significant impact on national security? Look at classification in terms of its value—value of this information to our economy." Anderson's reasoning was that theft of intellectual property would weaken the economy and affect military capability. "You could prosecute under those kind of situations if you can quantify loss. You can get a writ of mandamus and retrieve the leaked information, yes, you can prosecute for theft. It would be much easier," argued Anderson, "to convince a judge of something's value than to convince a judge that serious damage has been done to the national security."[3]

On February 22, 1990, under the jurisdiction of Anderson's office, Steven Garfinkel chaired the first meeting of the new Information Security Committee (ISC) of the Advisory Group for Security Countermeasures—formed to bring secrets under better control. Garfinkel's ISC was a successor to the Willard group of the 1980s and Richard Ober's group of the 1960s. Garfinkel's committee, meeting every six weeks or so, included representatives of the secretary of defense, army, navy, marines, air force, coast guard, Defense Intelligence Agency, CIA, NSA, National Security Council, FBI, Justice, Commerce, State, Energy, Treasury, and the Office of Personnel Management. Garfinkel's ISC differed from its predecessors in that it was not organized out of the Justice Department, with sub-rosa guidance from the CIA representative, but rather was under the direct command of the CIA via Anderson's office. CIA participation that in Ober's day was potentially scandalous had by 1992 become routine.

The ISC discussed the need for security education and training and reviewed outstanding problems that required action. Garfinkel said that he aimed to reduce the quantity of classified information because when everything was classified, classification became meaningless. From a managerial viewpoint, it also was costly to protect mountains of unimportant secrets from release. Garfinkel wished to tighten the system. Some of his plans, he admitted, were "pie in the sky." For example, he wanted a computerized system to track all official information.

"I'd love to achieve a database of what information has been declassified," Garfinkel said. "This would be the same thing as the CIA operates, but on a broader scale. We would want to know what every agency has put out there. We could center something like that in the National Archives. It is a massive undertaking [and we are] talking about whether it's feasible. One of the major problems is that not every agency is operating with computer systems that can read each other."[4] This vision of information control via gigantic, interagency computer systems was intended to take the government into the twenty-first century.

———

On January 17, 1991, Senator Moynihan made a metaphorical point about the ending of the cold war by introducing a bill that would have abolished the CIA and transferred its functions to the Department of State. Before the collapse of the Soviet Union, only the former editor of *CounterSpy* magazine had dared to suggest such an idea. Moynihan's bill, S. 236, also proposed that intelligence budgets be published. While the abolition of the CIA was not taken as a serious threat, the prospect that budgets might be drastically cut back struck terror into the heart of the bureaucracy. The leadership of the CIA was put on notice that they had to find new reasons to justify the Agency's rarefied governmental powers.

In May 1991, President Bush nominated Robert M. Gates to replace William Webster as CIA director. Gates had specialized in Soviet affairs as a career intelligence analyst. In September, during Gates's contentious confirmation hearings before the Senate Select Committee on Intelligence, Melvin A. Goodman appeared as a witness. Goodman, a former CIA division chief in Soviet foreign policy, testified that Gates had, over a period of years as deputy director of the CIA, given Congress and the president misleading and politicized intelligence. "Gates's role," he said, "was to corrupt the process and the ethics of intelligence . . . [and] to ignore and suppress signs of the Soviet strategic retreat."[5] Other witnesses at the hearings accused Gates of having shaped intelligence reports during 1986 in a manner that supported the U.S. sale of arms to Iran.

This damning testimony undercut Gates's chances of confirmation. Fighting to gain favor and to show that he understood the changing times, Gates pledged to the committee that if approved as director he would run a more open CIA. The committee was persuaded by his promise and voted in favor of his confirmation.

After Gates was sworn in, he sent a memorandum on November 18, 1991, to his director of public affairs, Joseph DeTrani, setting up the CIA Openness Task Force. Its purpose was to continue "improving accessibility to information about [the] CIA by the public and overall openness to the extent possible" (the operative words being "to the extent possible"). DeTrani was ordered to explore how the CIA could improve "openness" and "accessibility" through use of the news media and by expanding relations with universities. A report was due in a month.[6]

DeTrani's task force came up with twenty-one recommendations to counter the growing impression that the CIA and secrecy itself had become anachronisms. The principal recommendation called for a public relations campaign directed at members of the general public. Rather than take any substantive steps toward reform, the idea was to do a better job of selling the mystique of the CIA. "There was substantial agreement," the report said, "that we need to make the institution and the process more visible and understandable rather than strive for openness on specific substantive issues."

For Gates, the point was to use the so-called openness public relations campaign to answer critics who wanted big reductions in the congressional intelligence community appropriation (estimated to be about $30 billion annually). For DeTrani, the point was the same, except on a smaller scale. He was facing a cut of 33 percent in the CIA public affairs office. In his report DeTrani stressed, "We recognize that a program of increased openness will require commitment of additional resources, not only for [the public affairs office] but for other parts of the Agency."[7] Gates and DeTrani proved the Washington cliché: the first concern of a bureaucrat is to preserve his budget.

DeTrani recommended that the CIA engage in a broad program to influence U.S. academia, forgetting the scandal over the CIA use of the National Student Association in the 1960s. The CIA Editorial Board had identified hundreds of CIA-authored articles, and DeTrani suggested that scholars connected with journals and editors at university presses could be pushed to publish them. In addition, he noted that the Agency had a wide range of contacts with academics through recruiting, professional societies, and contractual arrangements, which he thought could be expanded. The CIA, he proposed, could become an institutional member of scientific and professional societies and could sponsor more academic conferences and seminars, even bringing scholars to study at Langley. Furthermore, DeTrani wished to expand the CIA officer-in-residence program, which currently had thirteen CIA officers at universities, each provided with about $100,000. This entire recommendation, of course, flew in the face of the lessons supposedly learned after the Pike Committee severely criticized the CIA in the 1970s for trying to manipulate public opinion through academia.

The Pike Committee also had rebuked the Agency for manipulating the U.S. media. News organizations, domestic and international, had been scandalized to discover that the CIA employed more than four hundred journalists as spies. Now DeTrani was recommending "a strategy for expanding our work with the media as a means of reaching an even broader audience." It was a suggestion remarkable in its brazenness—and clever as well. DeTrani wanted the CIA to declassify certain files about historical events in order to put the Agency in a more positive light. By assisting journalists, "intelligence failure" stories could be turned into "intelligence success" stories, he argued, and he boasted about past triumphs with the news media: "In many instances, we have persuaded reporters to postpone, change, hold, or even scrap stories that could have adversely affected national security interests or jeopardized sources and methods."

DeTrani also wanted to work with filmmakers on "accuracy" and "authenticity" and to help friendly Hollywood directors by allowing them to shoot movies at CIA headquarters. Along the same lines he wanted to cooperate with feature writers to "personalize the world of intelligence in broad circulation newspapers or magazines." Other propaganda could be aimed directly at the public. Unclassified versions of the Agency's *Studies in Intelligence* could be sold, and CIA officers could step up their number of speeches to civic and service clubs, mainly Rotary and Kiwanis. A CIA speakers bureau already had been established in 1990.

In addition, DeTrani had a full set of recommendations for working more closely with new members of Congress, as well as staffers on Capitol Hill and at congressional agencies, such as the Congressional Research Service and the Office of Technological Assessment. Basically, the plan was to take them into the Agency's confidence in attempts to convince them of the CIA's worth, a rather cynical process of co-optation in which spies befriend and manipulate their targets. This technique is a specialty of espionage agents. For the average outsider, being taken into the CIA's confidence can be breathtaking.

The public release of the Openness Task Force report was scheduled for April Fool's Day 1992—with the last four inches of DeTrani's report to be blacked out. But the report was made public after its secrecy had become an embarrassment to the CIA. A *New York Times* reporter, Elaine Sciolino, revealed its existence on January 12, 1992. During the following week, DeTrani called it an "internal advisory document that [could not] go outside the Agency," classified secret. On January 14, DeTrani said he would keep the Openness Task Force report secret until Gates issued his orders based upon it.[8] However, Director Gates had already dispatched those orders for the domestic propaganda operation ten days earlier, on January 6, to his deputy directors: they covered five pages.[9]

Gates accepted DeTrani's primary recommendation—the CIA should improve and update its image without changing its fundamental character. Gates stated, "I believe that CIA, whatever the level of its public affairs effort, will find it difficult to win recognition as an 'open' institution." In other words, the Agency should give out information that makes it look good and, as usual, keep the rest secret. While ordering new cooperation with the news media, Gates cautioned that the CIA would not be pressured into changing its approach to secrets. The only incentive for cooperating with journalists, Gates said, was to enhance "the broader Agency programs."

Gates wanted the CIA to conduct carefully controlled background briefings of selected reporters who could be relied upon to deliver the CIA message without the public being able to discern precisely the source. Gates also took up DeTrani on his suggestion to persuade friendly journalists to write profiles of CIA officers, although he insisted that meticulous records be kept of such contacts. Such records would, of course, assist the Agency's Unauthorized Disclosures Analysis Center agents in combating news leaks. Gates refused DeTrani permission to appear more often on television but instead assigned extra television time for himself. He was to be the CIA's premier salesman, and everyone else was to fall in behind him. "All of us in the Agency simply should keep our eyes and ears open for feedback, from whatever quarter, on the success of our efforts," Gates directed.

In addition to media operations, Gates approved direct CIA propagandizing of the general population through the circulation of press releases detailing the Agency's history, mission, and functions in light of the new world order. "The Agency's briefing program for the full range of potential audiences should be expanded as opportunities arise," Gates ordered. He approved CIA officers joining scientific and professional societies and urged that operations on American college campuses be expanded by setting up intelligence studies programs and finding universities to publish CIA material. Scholars would also be encouraged to publish CIA-subsidized articles in the United States. Gates also established a program to bring chief executive officers of corporations to Langley for a day, beginning with CEOs already cooperating with the Agency. Under a similar program, members of the media with influential voices—including even Norman Mailer—were to be invited to speak with CIA groups.

Regarding the release of documents, Gates ordered a review of historical and FOIA records, "with a view to accelerating the process [of release]." However, Gates's orders made it plain that CIA "openness" did not mean the lessening of secrecy. "Openness" meant adopting a well-crafted public relations scheme aimed at the most important opinion makers in the nation.

Gates's assessment that the CIA had a public relations problem was proved later in January. The news commentator with the largest audience in the United States, *60 Minutes* sage Andy Rooney, blasted the CIA in his syndicated newspaper column printed January 26, 1992. It was headlined by the San Francisco Sunday newspaper "A Lack of

Intelligence: Fire the Spies." Rooney wrote, "If they cut the $30 billion [*sic*] Central Intelligence Agency budget tomorrow by 75 percent, it wouldn't be a month too soon." He said, "When the CIA is questioned about anything, they have a standard answer: 'That's a secret that would compromise the security of the United States.'"[10]

EPILOGUE

The Cold War Ends and Secrecy Spreads

FOR NEARLY TEN YEARS ALDRICH AMES SPENT MONEY in lavish fashion on cars, real estate, and the good things in life.[1] A longtime CIA agent, Ames often purchased his extravagances with cash. Unbeknownst to his superiors at Langley, the KGB was regularly paying him large sums of cash, eventually totaling more than $2.5 million.[2] In return, Ames was stealing documents from Agency files and supplying the Soviets with the names of U.S. agents working behind the Iron Curtain. As far as can be ascertained, the information passed on by Ames led to the deaths or disappearances of at least twelve members of the U.S. intelligence community in Europe and the former Soviet Union.[3] After sustaining a career of thirty-one years with the CIA, Ames was finally caught in February 1994. He immediately made Agency history as the most senior officer ever found spying for the other side in the cold war.[4] He was also by far the best-paid KGB mole inside America—so well paid, in fact, as to raise a question about how he was able to elude detection for so long.

On accepting a plea bargain that sentenced him to life in prison without parole, Ames himself suggested an answer in an extraordinary confession at the U.S. District Court in Alexandria, Virginia. First Ames described how a culture of cynicism had taken over at the CIA.

"I had come to believe," he told the judge, "that the espionage business as carried out by the CIA and a few other American agencies was and is a self-serving sham, carried out by careerist bureaucrats who have managed to deceive several generations of American policymakers and the public about both the necessity and the value of their work." In order to protect their own bureaucratic interests, he said, CIA officials set up a system that keeps every detail from the American people. The "sham" of the U.S. intelligence community, he said, is "immeasurably aided by secrecy."[5] The revelation of Ames's duplicitous life and the publicity from his courtroom statement sent shock waves across Capitol Hill. Senator John Warner, a Republican from Virginia, spoke grimly about the need to set up an outside, independent group to issue recommendations for a major restructuring of U.S. intelligence.[6]

The new CIA director, R. James Woolsey, who had been appointed by the first Democratic president in twelve years, William Jefferson Clinton, felt obliged to try to counter Ames's allegations during a speech on July 18, 1994, at the Center for Strategic and International Studies in Washington. Woolsey compared Ames to Benedict Arnold and sarcastically noted that while there were a few differences between the two traitors, "they are all in Benedict Arnold's favor." Clearly no one in Woolsey's audience of journalists and intelligence experts held any brief for someone as mercenary as Ames, and yet the criticisms leveled by Ames had struck a chord with the Washington insiders. Since 1947 they had promoted the premise of large-scale secrecy as a necessary element of the cold war. With the cold war over and arguably won, wasn't it time to take a hard look to see if the CIA had become too self-righteous and secretive, too antagonistic to a society based on democratic precepts?

Woolsey tried to deflect the criticisms by accepting some of them as valid. "The camaraderie within the [CIA] fraternity can smack of elitism and arrogance," he admitted. Then, in a Reaganesque tactic, Woolsey straightened up at the lectern and aimed his remarks over the heads of his audience to the public at large. "The American people have the right to ask where the CIA is going after the cold war and after, for that matter, Aldrich Ames," he said. "For us to assume your continued support or your willingness to give us the benefit of the doubt will not do. We have the obligation to provide you with answers through the deliberative process with the members of Congress and through speaking directly to you. Problems that have arisen will be addressed fully, openly and honestly, warts and all. Programs that are no longer relevant will be abolished."[7]

No CIA director had ever sounded so defensive about the Agency in a public speech, nor had a CIA director ever come so close to a mea culpa for the abuses inherent in the secrecy program. Nonetheless, the reforms promised by Woolsey—more openness, more accountability—had been promised before, most recently by Robert Gates. Given the record of past directors and past presidents, was it realistic to believe the Clinton administration would usher in a new era?

The answer lay in a struggle between two forces. One was the historical and political force created by the end of the cold war. In America, land of the free, it had usually been assumed that secrecy was an aberration, something to be tolerated only in the extreme circumstances of wartime. Now, without a security rationale for secrecy, the guardians of open government would presumably be able to rally most of the American people to their side. On the opposite side was the countervailing force of the intelligence bureaucracy, whose leaders for nearly half a century had operated with secrecy uppermost in mind. Although many of the old cold war warriors were now dead or retired, their younger protégés still occupied positions of power. Even if Woolsey could be taken at his word, he would have to overcome active resistance from within his own ranks, as well as the inertia present in any bureaucracy.

The key would be the new president. Clinton's election in 1992 had brought into office the first president since Herbert Hoover who had no association with World War II and who had not lived through the Japanese attack on Pearl Harbor. Shortly after his inauguration, Clinton pledged to usher in an era of candor, and he set into motion various efforts to liberalize the rules governing secrecy.

The era of candor began with a presidential memo issued on October 3, 1993, addressed to the heads of all government agencies, which directed them to stop their routine resistance to FOIA requests.[8] Clinton's attorney general, Janet Reno, explained the rationale for openness by saying that it was essential to government accountability and that the FOIA "has become an integral part of that process." According to Reno, the Justice Department would scrap a 1981 rule promulgated by the Reagan administration that allowed agencies to withhold information if they had any conceivable legal excuse.[9] Justice would no longer provide legal counsel as a matter of routine when federal agencies denied FOIA requests. In an even more radical departure from the past, Clinton took the position that the public should not have to rely just on the FOIA to obtain information about the inner workings of the federal government. Rather, he wrote in his memo, it is up to the government to keep the citizens informed: "Each agency has a responsibility to distribute information on its own initiative."

Within a month, however, Clinton's enthusiasm for an open, accountable government began to fade, and so did the hope that he would institute a major overhaul of the secrecy program. Like Presidents Johnson and Nixon before him, Clinton found the sticking point to be not concern about national security but rather his own sensitivity about activities at the White House. In essence, Clinton decided that White House affairs would not be subject to his policy of openness. Clinton's friend and associate attorney general, Webster Hubbell, reminded all federal FOIA officers to return to the White House any document found in the course of FOIA searches if it had originated at the White House; under no circumstances were the documents to be released to the public. In addition, Hubbell increased the number of White House departments that could be exempt from the FOIA, including such working groups as the Clinton health care task force, which was then facing a legal challenge for holding meetings in secret under the supervision of Hillary Rodham Clinton.[10]

Although actions of the president and his staff had always been exempt from the FOIA, the Clinton administration soon made it clear that the ring of secrecy around the White House would become even tighter. When a request by Knight-Ridder Newspapers for the salaries of presidential staffers was denied, Richard Oppel, on behalf of the

American Society of Newspaper Editors, fired off a letter to Clinton: "There may be no specific law commanding the release of the salaries," he wrote, "but there is certainly no law authorizing the withholding of the information. In the absence of such authorization, the information should be public without discussion. The people's business, we submit, is the people's business."[11] Despite the scant possible justification for refusing to disclose as innocuous a piece of information as someone's salary, the Clinton administration held firm.

In addition, the Clinton administration became the first to argue in court in favor of a more restrictive interpretation of the FOIA with respect to National Security Council (NSC) documents. Previous administrations had agreed that the NSC generated two kinds of records—presidential records and agency records—and that the latter were subject to the FOIA. Departing from precedent, the Clinton Justice Department took the position that all NSC records fell into the presidential category and could not be obtained through the FOIA.[12]

A rare opportunity for reforming the intelligence bureaucracy seemed to be slipping away from an embattled Clinton. At the beginning of his presidency, Clinton did not boldly challenge the bureaucracy and relied on others—often the bureaucrats themselves—to carry out reforms. In the case of the CIA, he relied on Woolsey, a Yale lawyer whose background and sensibilities were similar to those of many career officers under him. In light of Ames, that reliance on Woolsey and the Agency good old boys for reform was now seen as questionable. [13]

Clinton showed how far he was willing to go with the new policy of openness in the summer of 1994. The issue at hand was whether the total amount of the intelligence community's annual budget would remain a secret. For some time there had been no plausible reason for the American people not to know how much the intelligence community spends. The full Senate had passed resolutions in 1991, 1992, and 1993 favoring disclosure of the figure. Robert Gates had testified in 1991 that he had no problem with disclosure. Besides, almost everyone who frequented the corridors of Capitol Hill or the nearby watering holes (including any foreign agents worth their salt) already knew the number. And, to make the secrecy even more of a joke, a Senate committee had inadvertently published enough figures to allow easy calculation of the intelligence community budget for fiscal year 1994 ($28 billion).[14] However, when it came time for Woolsey to release the budget figure formally, he refused. Instead, he and Clinton's other national security officials lobbied Congress to prevent formal disclosure. When Dan Glickman of Kansas, chair of the House Permanent Select Committee on Intelligence, and Robert Torricelli of New Jersey introduced an amendment to make the disclosure mandatory, the Clinton team managed to defeat it by a 221–194 vote.[15]

What Woolsey wanted to protect was obviously not the budget number, open secret that it was, but rather the principle of secrecy. As for Clinton, he could have ordered his CIA director to begin unilateral disclosure of many secrets, consequential or not; but such a move would no doubt have involved the White House in a political battle with an entrenched, secretive, and politically wily bureaucracy. So Clinton left the CIA alone for as long as he could.

After Ames was caught, the clamor in Congress for change at the CIA forced Clinton to intervene. On the Hill, Woolsey's continuing defensiveness was found to be irritating, at best. He resigned in December 1994 and Clinton found his replacement at the Pentagon. John Deutch was working there as under secretary of defense with his long-term associate in government and business, Defense Secretary William J. Perry. Clinton persuaded Deutch to move to Langley by making the CIA job a cabinet post.[16]

The pattern of maintaining secrecy was repeated when it came to reforming the system whereby government documents are classified and declassified. Clinton had moved in 1993 to replace the 1982 classification/declassification model inherited from the Reagan administration.[17] But it became obvious that he did not intend much change when he gave the job to none other than Steven Garfinkel, who had been director of the Information Security Oversight Office (ISOO) for more than a decade.

Although Garfinkel's operation, with an annual budget of about $1.2 million and a staff of a dozen people, has always been tiny by Washington standards, his role in secrecy as a classification expert has been disproportionately large because classification management is central in a security system.[18] During the Bush administration, ISOO was transferred from the General Services Administration to the Office of Management and Budget. ISOO was transferred again in 1995, this time to the National Archives and Records Administration, with which Garfinkel had been working closely on declassification.[19]

Whereas Richard Willard, exhausted from the controversies over secrecy, had left government to join a Washington law firm that represents defense contractors, Garfinkel had continued his efforts to implement National Security Decision Directive (NSDD) 84, which included the secrecy contract and prepublication review. To a large degree, he had succeeded. "Willard took it on the chin because he chaired the group that wrote NSDD 84," Garfinkel said. But, Garfinkel added, he himself still believed in NSDD 84, and he felt it was his duty to hold the line for secrecy. "I take it on the chin, too. If you are dealing in the subject of government secrecy, which is my responsibility, I'm going to get hit by the media and by certain members of Congress. That's the way things are. If you can't take it, you don't belong in the job."[20]

In the first spring of the Clinton administration, the most urgent task for Garfinkel was declassification of the mountain of obsolete secrets that had accumulated since the end of World War II. Not only were the millions of documents expensive and inconvenient to house, they were costly and enormously time-consuming to declassify under the existing system of page-by-page review. Until declassified, they remained inaccessible to historians, reporters, students, and the public.

While Garfinkel explored new classification methods, documents were continuing to pile up. During Clinton's first year in office, ISOO later reported, his administration had stamped "secret" on 60,000 more documents than the Bush administration had the previous year. At the same time, the Clinton administration had declassified far fewer documents in 1993 than the Bush administration had in 1992. The outcome, according to Garfinkel, was a net increase of "many more millions of classified pages." Steven Aftergood, a public interest policy advocate with the Federation of American Scientists (FAS), ridiculed the lack of progress under Clinton. "This means," he said, "that unless you are a Russian spy, there is more and more information becoming inaccessible. The situation is basically out of control; more information is classified today than there was when the Berlin Wall was torn down."[21]

Even before the 1992 elections, a group of openness advocates from the ACLU, the National Security Archive, and the Center for National Security Studies (formerly affiliated with the ACLU), together with Aftergood from the FAS, proposed principles for a new classification system.[22] These principles would curb the prevailing practice of classifying everything in sight and keeping it classified for decades. Specifically, they proposed limiting the universe of classifiable information, mandating the automatic downgrading and declassifying of information, reducing the number of people authorized to classify information, and eliminating Special Access Programs (SAPs)—supersecret programs designed to minimize oversight and provide for an exotic level of secrecy.[23]

Early in 1995 Garfinkel completed Clinton's Executive Order (EO) 12958, "Classified National Security Information," which disregarded most of the proposed classification principles. Of the principles, the new executive order incorporated only automatic declassification, applying it to all records more than twenty-five years old. (Garfinkel bragged that this was "a radical departure.")[24] The proposals to prevent the accumulation of masses of classified materials were ignored, and instead of eliminating SAPs, the EO specified ways to start up new ones. In addition, it also institutionalized two of the most extreme and far-reaching features of the cold war: a classification system without recourse to judicial review and the long-standing lifetime "secrecy contract." Clinton signed EO 12958 on April 17, 1995. Aftergood commented on a leaked draft of the EO, "While it is an improvement over the status quo, it does not go far enough. Somebody needs to decide whether the Cold War is over or not."[25]

This secrecy contract meant that government employees still had to sign away their constitutional right to free speech in exchange for employment. In an interview before Clinton's election, Garfinkel had predicted that reformers would find their going tough: "Once you get outside [Washington], very few people are concerned about this issue. There are no more than three to four people in this country who would go into a voting booth and vote because of it."[26]

─────────

Garfinkel's estimate was a bit low: At least three to four of these people were living in Nevada in the 1980s. Outcries against the secrecy contracts came from employees whose health was threatened by the burning of hazardous waste at a secret 85,000-acre air force base set on the sun-dried bottom of Groom Lake near Las Vegas, Nevada. The workers were allowed to bring in their own gloves, but "base security policy" barred any other protective clothing. Because it was classified as an "unacknowledged Special Access Program (SAP)," no information about the base, not even its name (Area 51), could be disclosed. Sheet metal workers Robert Frost and Walter Kasza were in a bind when they became seriously ill, because they had signed secrecy contracts. Local air force security officers warned them they faced ten-year prison terms if they told doctors where they worked or what chemicals might be involved.

In August 1994, George Washington University law professor Jonathan Turley filed two lawsuits on behalf of Frost and Kasza (who have since died of their illnesses), their wives, and a small group of fellow workers challenging the secrecy system. One suit targeted leaders of the air force, the Defense Department, and the National Security Agency, the other the Environmental Protection Agency (EPA). The suits alleged that environmental crimes had been concealed by secrecy and that workers' health and safety had been damaged. The EPA was specifically charged with failing to exercise its inspection and oversight responsibilities. The workers, who were employees of government contractors, were seeking not damages but information and money to help with medical diagnoses and treatment for skin lesions, cancer, and other illnesses.[27]

The government fought back hard. One of the suits had been filed in Washington, D.C.—for maximum media coverage, among other reasons. The air force promptly asked that the suits be consolidated and moved to the federal district court in Las Vegas, in air force country. The court agreed. The court also sealed plaintiff attorney Turley's office and his briefcase, retroactively agreed to classify an Area 51 manual that the plaintiffs wanted to use in evidence, and placed gag orders on almost everyone who had any connection with the case.

Leslie Stahl, *60 Minutes* cohost and reporter, stated on the March 17 broadcast about Area 51, "The Environmental Protection Agency inspected Area 51 last year [1996] for the first time."[28] At that time the EPA prepared a hazardous waste inventory, which was evidence that toxic materials were indeed present at the base, a fact the air force had previously refused to admit. In court Turley asked to see the inventory, since by law it must be made public, unless the president of the United States personally exempts it. The air force requested the exemption—and Clinton gave it to them.

On March 6, 1996, the federal judge dismissed the suit, saying it risked "significant harm to the national security." Turley is appealing the decision. The plaintiffs and Turley believe they stand a better chance in the appeals court than they did before the district court in Las Vegas.[29]

The use of secrecy—this time to hide crime and corruption in the defense industry—also became a major legal issue in 1995 in a closely watched whistle-blower suit brought against the top U.S. military contractor, Lockheed Martin. In 1988 software configuration expert Margaret Newsham and associate technician Martin Bloem, coworkers at Lockheed's Sunnyvale, California, missile and space equipment plant, filed a suit against the corporation under the federal False Claims Act. In effect, they accused Lockheed of overcharging the government hundreds of millions of dollars by billing for wages on work never done.[30] Newsham had noticed that while she was always busy on the job, there were many people apparently without work, "just walking around," but getting paid. They were "in the ice box," she learned, waiting for clearances before they could work on Special Access Programs or other supersecret jobs. She reported the situation to a government auditing office; hearing nothing, she took her story to Saperstein, Goldstein, Demchak, and Baller, a large employment and false-claims law firm in Oakland, California.[31]

In 1995 accounting methods became a contentious issue in the Lockheed suit. Corporations use ten-digit codes to track wage costs on contracts, and Lockheed had responded earlier to the plaintiffs' request for the codes by turning over some of them. But suddenly Lockheed said that that had been a mistake; the company claimed that an enemy power could deduce Lockheed's product mix from the codes and previously released information. Therefore the codes could not be revealed. The plaintiffs, on the other hand, insisted there was no way an outsider could determine whether there had been an overcharge without the codes. The lawyers worked out a solution to the code problem, although by the spring of 1996 the plaintiffs' access to the codes had apparently not been restored.[32]

Meanwhile security had become a more general problem, with Lockheed refusing to produce virtually any documents. According to Guy T. Saperstein, the lead attorney for the plaintiffs, there was no substantive security content to the case: Lockheed was giving documents to their own lawyers but refusing them to Saperstein on the grounds that his attorneys did not have clearance. Saperstein went so far as to arrange to have delivery taken by Maynard Anderson, a former assistant deputy under secretary for counterintelligence and security at the Pentagon, but that didn't satisfy Lockheed.

A chilly police-state atmosphere invaded the courtroom. Though the Justice Department had no status in the litigation, a U.S. attorney was present in the courtroom to guard against breaches of security. And there were references in the courtroom and the press to high-level reviews of security policy going on in Washington. Those reviews and the outcome of this case may have a profound effect on openness in government and the near-term survival of constitutional freedoms.

The lifetime secrecy contracts had emerged from the Operation MHCHAOS offices, spreading throughout the CIA and the National

Security Agency. Then, at ISOO and CIA insistence, the contract moved into the ranks of government and civilian workers at the State Department and in the Pentagon and to some 1.5 million employees of government contractors.[33] The use of the contract expanded pervasively through the executive branch; as opposition from the defenders of constitutional rights evaporated, it gradually moved into Congress. In 1991 Garfinkel made some small changes in the secrecy contract and added whistle-blower protection for congressional witnesses. That seemed to silence the last outspoken opposition in the House. A few senators, including Charles E. Grassley, Republican of Iowa, continued to be wary of White House intrusions on traditional congressional independence.[34]

By the 1990s, reflecting the general conservative shift in Congress, many House members were actively welcoming a secrecy oath. Consideration of the oath, less comprehensive than the standard contract, first came up in the House Select Committee on Intelligence during a discussion of the fiscal year (FY) 1992 Intelligence Authorization Act. That led to a House rule requiring the intelligence committee members and staff to sign the oath. Interest in broadening the use of the oath did not stop there, especially for committee member Porter J. Goss of Florida. Goss's ties to the CIA dated from 1962 and his ten-year stint as a clandestine service officer at the Agency. He and his fellow enthusiast, Henry J. Hyde of Illinois, offered amendments to the FY 1993 and 1994 authorization acts that would require secrecy oaths from every member of the House. The amendments did not prosper, but when the 104th Congress convened on January 4, 1995, backers of the oath changed tactics. This time the oath requirement for every House member was included in the packet of rules from the House Conference of the Majority. It became a new rule without debate.

In the mid-1980s, Jeane Kirkpatrick sounded the alarm about government censorship. Although a member of the Reagan administration's inner foreign policy circle, Kirkpatrick had had a personal encounter with government censors over her refusal to sign the lifetime secrecy contract. Upon returning to her political science chair at Georgetown University from her post as U.S. United Nations ambassador, Kirkpatrick reexamined John Stuart Mill's classic essay *On Liberty* and delivered a lecture on censorship. "Societies are not made stronger by the process of repression that accompanies censorship," she warned. "Censorship requires an assumption of infallibility, and that seems to Mill invariably negative. Repression of an opinion is thus bad for the censor, who inevitably acts from a conviction of his own infallibility," she told her students, "and bad for the opinion itself, which can neither be corrected nor held with conviction equal to the strength of an opinion submitted to challenge."

As the twentieth century draws to a close, the 1947 National Security Act has become the Pandora's box that Ambassador Kirkpatrick and Congressman Hoffman had feared. Placing a legal barrier between foreign intelligence operations and domestic politics in the National Security Act has proved ineffectual. In the decades that followed 1947, the CIA not only became increasingly involved in domestic politics but abridged First Amendment guarantees of free speech and free press in a conspiracy to keep this intrusion from the American people. The intelligence and military secrecy of the 1940s had broadened in the 1960s to covering up the suppression of domestic dissent. The 1980s registered a further, more fundamental change, as the suppression of unpopular opinions was supplemented by systematic and institutionalized peacetime censorship for the first time in U.S. history. The repressive machinery developed by the CIA has spread secrecy like oil on water.

The U.S. government has always danced with the devil of secrecy during wartime. By attaching the word "war" to the economic and ideological race for world supremacy between the Soviet Union and the United States, a string of administrations continued this dance uninterrupted for fifty years. The cold war provided the foreign threat to justify the pervasive Washington belief that secrecy should have the greatest possible latitude and openness should be restricted as much as possible—constitutional liberties be damned.

With the collapse of the Soviet Union as a world power in 1990, even the pseudo-war rationale evaporated. But the partisans of secrecy have not been willing to accept the usual terms of peacetime. They have made clear their intentions to preserve and extend the wartime system. They will find a rationalization: if not the threat of the Soviet Union, then the goal of economic hegemony. Thus the U.S. government now needs to keep secrets to give an advantage to American corporate interests. Yet it is entrepreneurs who have been making the most use of FOIA—not journalists, not lawyers. As of 1994, the great preponderance of all FOIA requests have been for business purposes.[35] As the framers of the Constitution understood, the free exchange of ideas is good for commerce, but this idea has been widely forgotten in the years since the passage of the 1947 National Security Act.

Only recently in the history of the world's oldest republic has secrecy functioned principally to keep the American people in the dark about the nefarious activities of their government. The United States is no longer the nation its citizens once thought: a place, unlike most others in the world, free from censorship and thought police, where people can say what they want, when they want to, about their government. Almost a decade after the end of the cold war, espionage is not the issue, if it ever really was. The issue is freedom, as it was for the Minute Men at Compo Hill. The issue is principle, as it was for Ernest Fitzgerald, who never signed a secrecy contract but retained his Pentagon job because he made his stand for the First Amendment resonate in Congress.[36] Until the citizens of this land aggressively defend their First Amendment rights of free speech, there is little hope that the march to censorship will be reversed. The survival of the cornerstone of the Bill of Rights is at stake.

APPENDIX

TARGETS OF DOMESTIC SPYING

An Annotated List of Some FBI
Surveillance Targets during the 1980s

I WROTE TO THE FBI IN FEBRUARY 1987 asking for files on 127 political groups, most of which were opposed to the U.S. government's arming of the Contras. The Bureau's response was dragged out over five years. The vast majority of the files were denied under the 1986 FOIA amendment, but the FBI did release some information about the size of the files, the number of pages kept secret, and the reasons for that secrecy. The FBI also released a few heavily blacked-out pages, enough to give a glimpse of the Bureau's investigations into a number of highly visible political groups.

The unwanted and unwarranted attention to these politically active citizen organizations shows both the FBI's institutionalized disregard for constitutionally guaranteed rights and the use of FOIA exemptions to hide this abuse of power. Many of the groups have a long history of lobbying Congress and publishing newsletters—activities well within the scope of the First Amendment. None of the FBI investigations resulted in criminal indictments. Rather the purpose of the investigations, as is evident from the documents, was to monitor their political activities. The following is a digested version of information concerning these FBI investigations.

American Committee on Africa/Africa Fund was a New York–based organization opposed to apartheid in South Africa. The FBI withheld 425 of 615 pages "in the interest of national defense or foreign policy." On July 18, 1979, the FBI searched for all subversive and nonsubversive information on this group, on which the FBI kept a domestic security file and a Registration Act investigative file.

Arms Control Computer Network, Christic Institute, and the Committee Against Registration and the Draft. The FBI kept all records on these groups secret for "national defense" and to protect "confidential sources."

Black Student Communications Organizing Network is based in Jamaica, New York, and unifies black student groups. FBI files have been withheld in their entirety to protect "national defense or foreign policy."

The Center for Defense Information, based in Washington, D.C., opposes excessive spending for weapons and policies that increase the danger of war. The FBI Director, in an administrative matter involving no alleged violation of laws, searched FBI files for data on the group for reasons the FBI kept secret. The FBI withheld fifty-seven pages of documents to protect national defense, privacy, and confidential sources in a "foreign counterintelligence matter." Other FBI reports profiled the head of the group, Gene Robert LaRocque, citing *Who's Who:* "[He] is a retired naval officer, commander Task Group in Sixth Fleet, member of faculty of Naval War College." Another FBI document said the Center for Defense Information "functions as a 'gadfly' to the U.S. military establishment and is staffed with very liberal, anti-establishment, anti-FBI/CIA academics." A memo from the Special Agent in Charge to the FBI Director was stamped "SECRET" and said that LaRocque published *The Defense Monitor,* which reports timely information regarding military establishments. On August 13, 1986, FBI headquarters requested that information on the group be forwarded to the FBI agent attached to the U.S. Embassy in Bonn.

Central American Solidarity Association was a group opposed to Contra funding. Of the seventeen pages in this foreign counterintelligence–terrorism file, fifteen were kept secret.

Children's Campaign for Nuclear Disarmament and the Environmental Policy Center is based in Plainfield, Vermont. The FBI has kept one reference secret to protect "confidential sources."

Citizens Against Nuclear War. The FBI has kept six cross-references secret for reasons of "national defense."

Institute for Defense and Disarmament Studies, headquartered in Cambridge, Massachusetts, conducts public education and research and advocates lowering defense spending. In June 1983, the Naval Investigative Service asked the FBI to check on this group because of a counterintelligence interest.

Interfaith Center to Reverse the Arms Race. The FBI has kept six cross-references classified secret to "protect the national defense, privacy, and confidential sources."

Lawyers Committee for Human Rights. The FBI kept two cross-references exempt from disclosure to protect "confidential sources."

Lutheran World Ministries was based on Park Avenue South in Manhattan, New York. FBI documents containing cross-references were determined to be exempt from disclosure to "protect confidential sources."

Medical Aid for El Salvador. The FBI kept secret one file of an investigation that was pending on November 30, 1988, to protect "confidential" sources and the "national defense."

National Network in Solidarity with the People of Guatemala is a Washington group advocating an end to U.S. military aid in Guatemala. All FBI counterintelligence-terrorism records on it are kept secret under the 1986 FOIA amendment.

National Network in Solidarity with the People of Nicaragua was a Washington group opposed to arming the Contras. Of the forty-six pages in this file, the FBI kept secret forty-one pages.

National Peace Academy Campaign, Sojourners Peace Ministry and World Peacemakers. Four cross-references were withheld to protect "national defense."

Nuclear Control Institute has worked since 1981 in Washington to oppose nuclear proliferation. Of the FBI file on this group, the FBI has kept nine pages secret "to protect privacy and confidential sources."

The Nuclear Weapons Freeze Campaign was a major opponent of Reagan-Bush arms policies. Of its file, the FBI kept secret thirty pages and released eight, which revealed that in 1985, an FBI agent got a leaflet in Burlington, Vermont, about the organization of a nationwide contingency plan by the *Resistance Pledge Network* to block U.S. intervention in Central America. The agent reported the contents of the leaflet, which advocated a nonviolent, no drugs, no-property-damage demonstration against U.S. intervention, and on March 6, 1985, forwarded the report to the CIA, the Naval Investigative Service, the Air Force Office of Special Investigations, the United States Secret Service, and the Army Intelligence Command at Fort Meade.

Patrice Lumumba Coalition/Unity in Action Network was based in Harlem, New York. Of the FBI's file of 105 pages, it kept secret 78. At least one FBI document in the file had been sent to the CIA, the Defense Intelligence Agency, and the State Department Bureau of Intelligence and Research. The subjects of the documents were the African National Congress, the Pan African Congress, and the identities of individuals who attended the International Conference on Islam during October 1986. The contents of the memo were withheld to protect "foreign policy" and "privacy."

Peace Child Foundation. The FBI has kept twenty-two pages secret concerning a June 1986 foreign counterintelligence investigation by FBI Squad 14, San Francisco.

Peace Links: Women Against Nuclear War. An FBI agent in Detroit wrote headquarters on November 6, 1986, that a Peace Links chapter was part of a national organization of women to promote nuclear disarmament and peace between East and West. The rest of the memo was censored to protect "defense, foreign policy and confidential sources."

Student/Teacher Organization to Prevent Nuclear War of Boston. The FBI Special Agent in Charge of the New Haven, Connecticut, Field Office sent documents to the FBI director that had been provided by a confidential source, including a state, local, or foreign agency or authority, under the 1986 amendment. The New Haven FBI office placed this file in closed status March 11, 1985.

Union of Concerned Scientists. The FBI has kept 296 pages secret to protect foreign policy, privacy, and confidential informants. According to a December 16, 1986, FBI summary, "The central files of this Bureau reveal the following information. . . . The Union of Concerned Scientists is composed of senior and junior faculty members and graduate students at the Massachusetts Institute of Technology . . . organized for the expressed purpose of a one-day strike aimed at turning scientific research applications away from military technology and toward the solution of environmental and social problems. The UCS maintained no formal membership rolls. . . . As of this date, the UCS is under investigation due to the fact that its activities meet the criteria that fall within the Attorney General's guidelines."

United Nations Center Against Apartheid, established by the General Assembly of the United Nations in 1962, was opposed to South African racial policies. The FBI files contain a secret report from the CIA dated April 1984. The CIA withheld the document in entirety to protect the "national defense."

U.S. Out of Central America. The FBI has kept twenty pages secret to protect confidential sources.

Washington Office on Latin America was a Washington group with thirteen employees and an annual budget of $500,000 that opposed the Reagan policies in Central America. The FBI's file contained seventy-nine pages, of which the FBI kept secret seventy-three pages under the FOIA amendment's provisions for hiding foreign counter-intelligence matters. Parts of this file were distributed to the FBI San Antonio office and to the Defense Intelligence Agency.

Witness for Peace is a Washington group with an annual budget in excess of $1 million that characterizes itself as a grassroots, faith-based, nonviolent group opposed to U.S. intervention in Central America. The FBI kept secret eleven pages on this group under the 1986 amendment because they could "reasonably be expected to interfere with enforcement proceedings."

NOTES

PROLOGUE

1. Donald E. Walker, "Congressional Career of Clare E. Hoffman, 1935–63" (Ph.D. diss., Michigan State University, 1982), 12.

2. House Permanent Select Committee on Intelligence, *Compilation of Intelligence Laws and Related Laws and Executive Orders of Interest to the National Intelligence Community, National Security Act of 1947, Title 1, Sec. 102 (3)(d)(5)*, 98th Cong., 1st sess., 1983.

3. House Committee on Expenditures in the Executive Departments, *Hearings on National Security Act of 1947*, 80th Cong., 1st sess., April 2–July 1, 1947, 125, 127.

4. Ibid., 172, 102.

5. *Cong. Rec.,* 80th Cong., 1st sess., 1947, 93, pt. 7:9396.

6. John E. Moss, interview by author, undated.

7. For an earlier history of the FOIA, see Senate Committee on the Judiciary, Subcommittee on Administrative Practice and Procedure, *Freedom of Information Act Source Book: Legislative Materials, Cases, Articles*, 93d Cong., 2d sess., 1974.

CHAPTER I

1. Stanley K. Sheinbaum, letter to Center for Investigative Reporting, June 7, 1994.

2. Sheinbaum, interview by author, August 9, 1990.

3. Sheinbaum, introduction to "Michigan State: University on the Make," *Ramparts,* April 1966, 11.

4. Sheinbaum, letter, June 7, 1994.

5. Warren Hinckle, with research editor Sol Stern and foreign editor Robert Scheer, "Michigan State: University on the Make," *Ramparts,* April 1966, 13. Also, Sheinbaum, interview by author, April 26, 1991.

6. *Mackenzie v. CIA,* Dube, doc. 603. The identifying document numbers appeared in the Vaughn index prepared by the CIA for *Mackenzie v. Central Intelligence Agency,* No. 82–1676 (D.D.C. 1982). As divulged to me, the documents were untitled. In FOIA cases, the burden of proof for the need for secrecy is on the government agency. This index is part of the CIA's item-by-item justification for withholding (or releasing), entirely or in part, the documentation requested by the plaintiff, me. Although the contents of the documents from which Dube read were divulged to me—at least in part—the CIA in some cases refused to release the material indexed. For instance, doc. 603, the directive to the CIA unit to prepare a brief on *Ramparts* for the director, is still classified in its entirety.

7. Deputy Director of Security, memorandum to Director of Security, on "Ramparts Magazine Article on CIA," April 18, 1966.

8. Memorandum from Richard Helms, Office of Deputy Director of Central Intelligence, to Mr. Bill D. Moyers, the White House, and S. Douglass Cater Jr., the White House, May 19, 1966, 2, [item] "3. *Ramparts* . . . Donald Duncan is a former Special Forces enlisted man who has written earlier attacks against the CIA in *Ramparts,* and who has publicly stated, 'We will continue to be in danger as long as CIA is deciding policy and manipulating nations.'" (The memo is signed "Dick" on p. 3 over typed "Richard Helms, Deputy Secretary.")

9. Mackenzie v. CIA, Dube, doc. 421, Secret routing slip from director of security, June 16, 1966.

10. Warren Hinckle, *If You Have a Lemon, Make Lemonade* (New York: Bantam, 1976), 183–90; quotation on 190.

11. Ibid., 185.

12. Much of the information on Ober comes from his top secret testimony before the Rockefeller Commission; I obtained a transcript. (Some transcript page numbers failed to survive hurried photocopying.)

On January 5, 1975, President Ford appointed Vice President Nelson Rockefeller to head an eight-member commission to investigate allegations of illegal domestic spying by the CIA. Officially known as the Commission on CIA Activities within the United States, its members were David Belin, executive director, and Commissioners John T. Connor, C. Douglas Dillon, Erwin N. Griswold, Lane Kirkland, Lyman T. Lemnitzer, Ronald Reagan, and Edgar F. Shannon Jr. The commission took Ober's testimony early in 1975 during its whitewash of the Agency. Other data on Ober were released to the author under the FOIA. Additional information was supplied by sources who wish to remain anonymous.

13. Hinckle, *Make Lemonade*, 190.
14. Ibid.
15. "*Ramparts*—Tax Returns," CIA memorandum, February 15, 1967.
16. Carl T. Rowan, "Miasma of Political Distrust Grows," *Washington Star*, February 24, 1967, 4.
17. *Mackenzie v. CIA*, Dube, doc. 463.
18. Ibid., Dube, doc. 468.
19. Ibid., Dube, doc. 452.
20. Ibid., Dube, doc. 483.
21. Ibid., Dube, doc. 352.
22. Ibid., Dube, doc. 325.
23. Ober, secret testimony before the Rockefeller Commission, 434 (see n. 12 above).
24. The CIA maintains an active presence on many of the nation's campuses to gather intelligence on foreign students it might recruit.

CHAPTER 2

1. Testimony of Thomas Karamessines, *United States v. Marchetti*, No. 179–72A (E.D. Va., May 15, 1972), transcript.
2. Karamessines "originated" MHCHAOS with a memorandum to "chief of Counterintelligence Staff [James Jesus Angleton], 15 August 1967," according to Ober's testimony before the Rockefeller Commission, transcript, 411 (see chapter 1, n. 12).

   A few days later, Angleton replied: "Interim Progress Report, August 31, 1967, memorandum for: Deputy Director for Plans [Karamessines]." Angleton's report covered August 5–31, beginning the day after the kickoff telegram to field stations mentioned by Ober, and included "actions . . . taken in compliance with initial instructions from the DDP to Chief CI Staff . . . under memorandum dated 15 August 1967." Heading the list of actions: "Designation of Dick Ober as focal point and coordinator of operational activity" (photocopy, 4).

   Ober's working relationship to Angleton is unclear. Although Angleton was at least nominally his boss, Ober insisted that his own operation was "highly compartmentalized and essentially self-contained" (Rockefeller Commission transcript, 416). He told the commission he reported directly to Karamessines or Helms, not to Angleton. In his biography of Helms (*The Man Who Kept the Secrets* [New York: Knopf, 1979], 247), Thomas Powers states that in May 1969, Helms "ordered" Ober not to discuss his work with Angleton. Helms, however, told the Rockefeller Commission he did not remember giving any order to change the Ober-Angleton-Karamessines-Helms chain of command. By mid-1969 Ober was chief of SOG.
3. MHCHAOS, memorandum for the record, on meeting with Dick Ober, May 23, 1969, from Acting Chief, Division.

4. Ober, testimony before the Rockefeller Commission, 411.

5. Ibid., 434.

6. Ibid., 429.

7. Army intelligence units were dispatched across the nation to spy on and disrupt antiwar groups and publications.

8. William Blum later wrote *The CIA: A Forgotten History* (London: Zed Books, 1986).

9. *Mackenzie v. Central Intelligence Agency,* No. 82–1676 (D.D.C. 1982), Dube. Included in the material Dube read to the author were reports from informants inside *Quicksilver Times.* Dube identified them only by code names, but by checking with witnesses, the author determined that many of the reports were Ferrera's. It is possible that some of these might be attributed to another CIA agent in the same location at the same time as Ferrera.

10. Salvatore J. Ferrera, "Regis Debray and Revolution" (master's thesis, Loyola University, 1969).

11. "COINTELPRO—NEW LEFT, SAC WFO Report to Director, FBI [J. Edgar Hoover], June 26, 1970, file 100–449698–53–45." This was a standard report that under usual circumstances would not contain many details of the operations referenced.

12. The document quoted was in the possession of the author, but the original cannot be located.

13. "J. S.," meeting with Domestic Contact Service officers, memorandum for the record: subject case, May 20, 1970. Participants, in addition to Ober and his deputy, included a CIA officer and representatives from Counterintelligence/Special Operations and Domestic Contact Service.

14. A photocopy of this contract bears the handwritten date. It is headed "MHCHAOS INDOCTRINATION." The information called for, in addition to the date (CIA telephone "extension" number, "name," and "office"), has evidently been eradicated and replaced by handwritten 3s.

   A photocopy of a later contract form, dated "19 Jan 72," carries Ober's signature in the bottom left-hand corner, under "Clearance Approval" and over "chief, CI/SO." This version of the contract (stamped "SENSITIVE") has been tightened to limit disclosure of MHCHAOS information, even to authorized persons, by the "need-to-know principle."

15. *Mackenzie v. CIA,* Dube, docs. 255, 261.

16. Ibid., docs. 277, 266, are the principal sources for Mayday plans and Davis's role.

17. Ibid., docs. 279, 280.

18. Chip Berlet, interview with author (facts confirmed with Berlet, June 1996).

19. "OMB visit to CIA offices," memorandum, Richard Ober, Chief, CI/SO to Chief (deleted), 5 August 1971.

20. Based on investigative reporting by Neil Sheehan, *Pentagon Papers: The Secret History of the Vietnam War as Published by the "New York Times"* (New York: Bantam, 1971).

21. White House, Intelligence Evaluation Committee, "The Unauthorized Disclosure of Classified Information," ed. Richard Ober, November 1971.

CHAPTER 3

1. See Victor Marchetti, *The Rope-Dancer* (New York: Grosset and Dunlap, 1971), 303.
2. Summary of Office of Security Domestic Surveillances and Other Operations, CIA document marked "OS-11 Count 1," title redacted, n.d.
3. Victor Marchetti, "CIA: The President's Loyal Tool," *Nation*, April 3, 1972, 430.
4. *United States v. Marchetti*, No. 179–72A (E.D. Va., May 15, 1972), transcript.
5. Melvin L. Wulf, introduction to *The CIA and the Cult of Intelligence*, by Victor Marchetti and John D. Marks (New York: Alfred A. Knopf, 1974), xxvii.
6. John S. Warner with CIA attorneys John K. Greaney and Lawrence R. Houston, "The Marchetti Case: New Case Law," unpublished and undated typescript, 7.
7. *United States v. Marchetti*, transcript, 147.
8. Victor Marchetti, interview by author, June 13, 1991.
9. Meeting with the director on CHAOS, December 5, 1972, Richard Ober, memorandum for the record. Participants: The director (Helms), executive director (Colby), deputy director for plans (Karamessines), assistant deputy director for plans, and Richard Ober.
10. Ibid.
11. Summary of December 5, 1972, meeting on MHCHAOS, W. E. Colby, executive director–comptroller, memorandum to deputy director for plans [Karamessines], December 20, "EYES ONLY."
12. Victor Marchetti and John D. Marks, *The CIA and the Cult of Intelligence* (New York: Dell Publishing, a Laurel Book, 1983), 16. This edition includes passages previously deleted and classified by the CIA.
13. *Knopf v. Colby*, No. 540–73A (E.D. Va., March 29, 1974), memorandum opinion, 471.
14. Victor Marchetti and John D. Marks, *The CIA and the Cult of Intelligence* (New York: Dell Publishing, a Laurel Book, 1975). This edition shows the location and length of CIA deletions.
15. Marchetti, interview by author.
16. *Knopf v. Colby*, 509 F.2d 1362 (4th Cir. 1975).
17. Albert V. Bryan Jr., letter to Philip J. Hirschkop, June 23, 1975.
18. Charles Wilson, interview by author, November 5, 1990.
19. Warner, "The Marchetti Case," 10.
20. Alfred W. McCoy, *The Politics of Heroin in Southeast Asia* (New York: Harper and Row, Colophon, 1973), 14.
21. Senate Committee on Appropriations, *Hearings on Foreign Assistance and Related Programs, Appropriations for Fiscal Year 1973*, 92d Cong., 2d sess., 1972, 702.

22.   Brooks Thomas, interview by author, October 18, 1990. Thomas, a Harper and Row attorney, left the publisher in 1987.

23.   Ibid.; Alfred McCoy, interview by author, February 8, 1990.

24.   Seymour M. Hersh, "CIA Assails Asian Drug Charge," *New York Times,* July 22, 1972, 1.

25.   McCoy, interview by author. McCoy became a professor of Southeast Asian history at the University of Wisconsin. A revised and expanded version of his 1973 book was published as *Politics of Heroin: CIA Complicity in the Global Drug Trade* (Brooklyn, N.Y.: Lawrence Hill Books, 1991).

26.   Ober was also linked to Dean by membership on the top secret interagency Intelligence Evaluation Committee, which reported directly to Dean. The committee itself, however, was usually ascribed to the Justice Department. Ober told the Rockefeller Commission that it was "unclear" whether Dean or Justice's Robert C. Mardian was chairman.

      The Watergate burglary had been conducted by several former CIA officers, at least one of whom, James McCord, was previously associated with Karamessines. CIA agents were caught placing phone taps and bugs inside Democratic National Committee headquarters in the Watergate office building.

27.   This account relies on two books by Philip Agee: *On the Run* (Secaucus, N.J.: Lyle Stuart, 1987) and *Inside the Company: CIA Diary* (New York: Stonehill, 1975).

28.   Agee, *On the Run,* 55.

CHAPTER 4

1.   Sally Quinn, "Norman Mailer Turns 50," *Washington Post,* February 7, 1973, B1; Mel Gussow, "Mailer's Guests ($50 a Couple) Hear His Plan on 'Secret Police,' " *New York Times,* February 6, 1973, 23.

2.   John Leonard, "Happy Birthday, Norman Mailer!" *New York Times Book Review,* February 18, 1973, 35; Frank Crowther, "Who's Paranoid Now?" *Village Voice,* July 12, 1973, A1.

3.   Nat Hentoff, "After Ellsberg: CounterSpy," *Village Voice,* July 19, 1973, 28.

4.   Tim Butz, interview by author, March 12, 1992.

5.   "Why CARIC? [Committee for Action/Research on the Intelligence Community]," *CounterSpy* 1, no. 1 (March 1973), n.p.

6.   Winslow Peck, "The Symbionese Connections," *CounterSpy* 1, nos. 4–5 (May 20, 1974), 5.

7.   *Environmental Protection Agency v. Mink,* 410 U.S. 73 (1973).

8.   Despite the FOIA amendment, the CIA years later tried to use high fees to block my request for documents. On August 1, 1980, the CIA demanded $61,348 to cover search and review of the documents, boosting the price on September 15 to $61,501. The CIA demanded a deposit of $30,000 before it would begin processing the request and wrote that after the $30,000 was paid, it might not find any information "releasable" (see the introduction, above).

The Washington, D.C.–based Reporters' Committee for Freedom of the Press arranged for me to have the pro bono services of Kevin Brosch at Steptoe and Johnson. Brosch soon discovered that the CIA had no legal justification for its demand for such fees.

9. Senate, *FOIA Conference Report, 93–1200,* to accompany H.R. 12471, 93d Cong., 2d sess., October 1, 1974.

10. Seymour M. Hersh, "Helms Disavows 'Illegal' Spying by CIA in U.S.," *New York Times,* December 25, 1974, 1.

11. For discussion of the commission and the roster of commissioners, see chapter 1, n. 12.

12. William Colby and Peter Forbath, *Honorable Men: My Life in the CIA* (New York: Simon and Schuster, 1978), 400.

13. George Bush with Victor Gold, *Looking Forward* (New York: Doubleday, 1987), 160.

14. Senate Committee on Armed Services, *Nomination of George Bush to be Director of Central Intelligence: Hearings,* 94th Cong., 1st sess., December 15 and 16, 1975.

15. "Remark [*sic*] on the Swearing in of George H. W. Bush as Director of Central Intelligence, January 30, 1976," in *Public Papers of the Presidents of the United States, Gerald R.. Ford, 1976–77* (Washington, D.C.: GPO, 1979), book 1, doc. 44, 112.

16. Victor Marchetti, interview by author, June 13, 1991.

17. Ibid.

18. "Criminal Prosecution Resulting from Richard Welch's Murder," CIA memorandum to John K. Greaney, associate general counsel, January 15, 1976, OGC (Office of General Counsel), 76–0186.

19. Butz, interview by author.

20. John Ranelagh, *The Agency: The Rise and Decline of the CIA,* rev. ed. (New York: Simon and Schuster, Touchstone, 1987), 628 n. The most notable exception to this silence about Bush and the CIA was provided by Scott Armstrong, reporter and founder of the National Security Archive, and Jeff Nason: see their "Company Man," *Mother Jones,* October 1988, 20–25, 42–47.

21. Senate Committee on Rules and Administration, *Hearing on S. Res. 400 to Establish a Standing Committee of the Senate on Intelligence Activities,* 94th Cong., 2d sess., March 31, 1976.

22. George Bush, "Address" (presented at the 1976 convention of the American Society of Newspaper Editors, Shoreham Americana Hotel, Washington, D.C., April 15, 1976), 207–15.

23. House Committee on Government Operations, Subcommittee on Government Information and Individual Rights, *Central Intelligence Agency Exemption in the Privacy Act of 1974: Hearing,* 94th Cong., 2d sess., April 28 and May 11, 1976.

24. House Committee on Armed Services, *Hearings on Full Committee Consideration of the Inquiry into Matters Regarding Classified Testimony Taken on April*

22, 1974, concerning the CIA and Chile, 94–13, 94th Cong., 1st sess., June 16, 1975, 7.

25. House Committee on Government Operations, Subcommittee on Government Information and Individual Rights, *Hearings on Notification to Victims of Improper Intelligence Agency Activities,* 94th Cong., 2d sess., April 28 and May 11, 1976, 1–3.

26. Ibid., 50. According to material that Bush submitted to the Abzug committee, "Of the approximate 200,000 names in the CHAOS index, about 96 percent represent only name entries with no further identifying information."

27. Ibid., 31–32, 35.

28. Ibid., 37–38.

29. Ibid., 46.

30. Bush spoke at Cleveland's City Club on June 6, 1976; his remarks were released by the CIA on June 9.

31. Those familiar with the Senate Select Committee on Intelligence report that it is heavily influenced by the agency it oversees. One old CIA hand, in a position to know, remarked to me about the consolidated intelligence committees' interest in any particular CIA scandal: "We brief 'em for about ten minutes and that's all they want to know."

32. Anthony A. Lapham, interview by author, April 22, 1991.

33. House Permanent Select Committee on Intelligence, Subcommittee on Oversight, *Prepublication Review and Secrecy Agreements, Hearings: Testimony by CIA Director of Public Affairs Herbert E. Hetu,* 96th Cong., 2d sess., March 6, 1980.

34. John Greaney, interview by author, April 13, 1991.

CHAPTER 5

1. John Ranelagh, *The Agency: The Rise and Decline of the CIA,* rev. ed. (New York: Simon and Schuster, Touchstone, 1987), 633 n.

2. "Frank Warren Snepp III—Threatened Violation of Secrecy Agreement," Anthony A. Lapham, memorandum to Director of Central Intelligence, January 13, 1977, OGC (Office of General Counsel), 77–0305.

3. Deposition of William A. Christison, *United States v. Snepp,* 456 F. Supp. 176 (E.D. Va. 1978), 12.

4. Ibid., deposition of Frank Snepp, April 16, 1976, 121.

5. Ibid., deposition of Paul V. Walsh, May 1, 1978, 14.

6. Ibid., deposition of William Parmenter, May 2, 1978, 31.

7. John Greaney, interview by author, April 13, 1991.

8. *United States v. Snepp,* transcript of hearing before Judge Lewis.

9. Stansfield Turner, *Secrecy and Democracy: The CIA in Transition* (Boston: Houghton Mifflin, 1985).

10. Stansfield Turner, interview by author, April 17, 1991.

11. Charles Wilson, interview by author, November 5, 1990.

12. Greg Kaza, "Ex-CIA Official Speaks Out," *Full Disclosure* (Ann Arbor), August–October 1985, 14.

13. Charles Wilson, interview by Center for Investigative Reporting, October 12, 1995.

14. Turner, interview by author.

15. George Bush with Victor Gold, *Looking Forward* (New York: Doubleday, 1987).

16. "Protection of Sources and Methods in Disclosure Law Requests," Anthony A. Lapham, general counsel, memorandum to deputy director for operations, January 20, 1979, signed by Mayerfeld over Lapham's typed name.

17. House Permanent Select Committee on Intelligence, Subcommittee on Legislation, *Impact of the Freedom of Information Act and the Privacy Act on Intelligence Activities: Hearing*, 96th Cong., 1st sess., April 5, 1979, 7, 8.

18. Ibid., 162.

19. Mayerfeld also faced my 1979 FOIA request for MHCHAOS files on hundreds of anti–Vietnam War tabloids (see chapter 4, n. 8).

20. House Committee on Government Operations, *The Freedom of Information Act: Central Intelligence Agency Exemptions: Hearings*, 96th Cong., 2d sess., May 29, 1980, 102.

21. Ibid., 95.

CHAPTER 6

1. *To Improve the Intelligence System of the United States and for Other Purposes*, 96th Cong., 2d sess., 1980, S.R. 2216; House version 96th Cong., 1st sess., 1979, H.R. 5615.

2. This identical language is found in H.R. 5615, 2, 3 [Report No. 96–1219, Parts I and II] and S.R. 2216, 6 [Reports No. 96–896, 96–990].

3. Joseph E. Persico, *Casey* (New York: Viking, 1990), 103.

4. House Permanent Select Committee on Intelligence, Subcommittee on Legislation, *Intelligence Identities Protection Act: Hearings on H.R. 4*, 97th Cong., 1st sess., "Statement for the Record," by William J. Casey, director of Central Intelligence, April 7, 1981, 13.

5. Richard K. Willard, interview by author, November 1, 1989.

6. House Subcommittee, *Intelligence Identities Protection Act: Hearings*, testimony, Richard K. Willard, 30.

7. *Cong. Rec.*, 97th Cong., 1st sess., 1981, 127, pt. 16:21730. Remarks of Rep. John M. Ashbrook.

8. "Spy Bill Wrapped in Flag," editorial, *New York Times*, March 4, 1982, 22.

9. See n. 7 above.

10. Column by Cord Meyer dated June 7, 1980 (otherwise unidentified), quoted by Rep. Edward J. Derwinski, *Cong. Rec.*, 97th Cong., 1st sess., 1981, 127, pt. 16:21739.

11. Ibid.

12. Ibid., 21732–33.

13. John M. Crewdson, "CIA: Secret Shaper of Public Opinion," *New York Times,* December 25, 1977, 1; December 26, 1; December 27, 1.

14. *Cong. Rec.,* 97th Cong, 2d sess., 1982, 128, pt. 2:2580, questions concerning David Binder and Robert Woodward; concerning Robert Pear, 2579.

15. Ibid., 1237, 1247.

16. *Cong. Rec.,* 97th Cong, 2d sess., 1982, 128, pt. 4:4281, 4284.

17. Ibid., 4502.

18. Ibid., 4682

CHAPTER 7

1. "President's News Conference on Foreign and Domestic Matters," November 10, 1981, transcript, *New York Times,* November 11, 1981, 14. For Haig's attack on Britain's foreign secretary, see Bob Woodword, "Staff Notes Convey Haig's Candid Views," *Washington Post,* February 19, 1982, 1; on Allen, see Jack Nelson, "Haig Feud with Allen Flares into the Open," *Los Angeles Times,* November 4, 1981, 1.

2. William Greider, "The Education of David Stockman," *Atlantic Monthly,* December 1981, 27.

3. Jack Nelson, "Reagan Issue: How Long to Back Problem Aides?" *Los Angeles Times,* November 19, 1981, 1.

4. Richard K. Willard, interview by author, November 1, 1989. This long retrospective interview is the source of Willard's comments in this chapter on the work of his secrecy group.

5. President Carter, Executive Order 12065, "To Balance Public Interest in Access to Government Information with Need to Protect National Security Information," *Federal Register* 43, June 28, 1978:28949.

6. L. Britt Snider, interview by author, October 24, 1989.

7. House Committee on Government Operations, *Hearings on Executive Order on Security Classification,* 97th Cong., 2d sess., March 10 and May 5, 1982, 146.

8. Ronald Reagan, quoted in John Weisman, "TV and the Presidency," *TV Guide,* March 20, 1982, 4.

9. Snider, interview by author.

10. Interdepartmental Group on Unauthorized Disclosures of Classified Information, Chairman Richard K. Willard, *Summary of Recommendations,* March 31, 1982; hereafter referred to as the Willard report.

11. *U.S.C.* 12 § 105 (1988).

12. *U.S.C.* 18 § 641 (1988).

13. House Committee on the Judiciary, Subcommittee on Civil and Constitutional Rights, *Hearings on Presidential Directive on the Use of Polygraphs and Prepublication Review,* 98th Cong., 1st sess., April 21 and 28, 1983, and 2d sess., February 7, 1984, appendix 2, "The Willard Report," 169.

14. Richard Willard, briefing reporters, March 11, 1983: "As far as I know, NSA and CIA are the only agencies that have formal regulations on prepublication disclosure."

CHAPTER 8

1. House Committee on Government Operations, Subcommittee on Government Information and Individual Rights, *Hearings on Executive Order on Security Classification,* 97th Cong., 2d sess., March 10 and May 5, 1982, 132.
2. Ibid., 201.
3. Richard K. Willard, interview by author, November 1, 1989.
4. Text of agreement between the CIA and ACLU on CIA exemption from FOIA, June 28, 1982; Ernest Mayerfeld, letter to Mark Lynch, July 2, 1982.
   This and subsequent correspondence between Mayerfeld and Lynch, released to James Lesar under the FOIA, are the basis of this account, combined with interviews of the principals. Halperin confirmed to me that the CIA documents released to Lesar are accurate. Lesar, an attorney and an investigator of the assassination of President Kennedy, resisted the ACLU deal because it would lead to the dismissal of legal efforts to obtain secret documents pertaining to JFK's assassination.
5. Morton Halperin, interview by author, May 1, 1992.
6. Thus my lawsuit seeking MHCHAOS files, which Kevin Brosch had filed several weeks earlier, would be dismissed under the Halperin-Lynch-CIA agreement.
7. Meanwhile, on September 9, 1982, Brosch negotiated an agreement with the Justice Department and the CIA. The CIA was to release documents on thirty-eight newspapers during the next year and granted a full fee waiver.
8. Mark Lynch, interview by author, July 15, 1991.
9. Presidential Directive on National Security Decision Directive 84 on Safeguarding National Security Information (NSDD 84), internal directive distributed on White House stationery, March 11, 1983.
10. Willard, interview by author.
11. Steven Garfinkel, interview by author, August 3, 1983.
12. Ralph W. McGehee, *Deadly Deceits: My 25 Years in the CIA* (New York: Sheridan Square Publications, 1983).
13. Based on investigative reporting by Neil Sheehan, *Pentagon Papers: The Secret History of the Vietnam War as Published by the "New York Times"* (New York: Bantam, 1971).
14. Ralph McGehee, interview by author, May 18, 1983.
15. House Committee on the Judiciary, Subcommittee on Civil and Constitutional Rights, *Hearings on Presidential Directive on the Use of Polygraphs and Prepublication Review,* 98th Cong., 1st sess., April 21 and 28, 1983; 2d sess., February 7, 1984, 1, 3.
16. Ibid., 30.

NOTES TO PAGES 102–12   219

17. William A. Donahue, *Politics of the American Civil Liberties Union* (New Brunswick, N.J.: Transaction Press, 1985).
18. Text of agreement between the CIA and ACLU on CIA exemption from the FOIA, June 28, 1982; Ernest Mayerfeld, letter to Mark Lynch, July 2, 1982.
19. Henry Hurt, interview by author, early 1980s.
20. Editorial, "The Plot Thickens," *Nation*, June 18, 1983, 1; "Clarification," *Nation*, July 2, 1983, 2.
21. Angus Mackenzie, "CIA Admits Study of Domestic Group Despite 1975 Ban," *Washington Post*, July 16, 1983, A10. This article was also distributed nationally by Pacific News Service.
22. Angus Mackenzie, "The Operational Files Exemption," *Nation*, September 24, 1983, 231.
23. *Mackenzie v. Central Intelligence Agency*, No. 82–1676 (D.D.C., January 19, 1984), Memorandum, 8.
24. House Permanent Select Committee on Intelligence, Subcommittee on Legislation, *Hearing on H.R. 5164, CIA Information Act, Legislation to Modify the Application of the Freedom of Information Act to the CIA*, 98th Cong., 2d sess., February 8, 1984, 2. This legislation was known as the Mazzoli bill.
25. "Notes from the Hill: Shielding CIA Files," *Washington Post*, September 20, 1984, A3.
26. 50 *U.S.C.* § 431 (1984).
27. Ira Glasser, ACLU executive director, letter to ACLU Director John Shattuck, on ACLU letterhead, June 18, 1984.
28. "Southern California's Questions on H.R. 5164," Mort Halperin, memorandum to Ira Glasser, June 15, 1984.
29. House Permanent Select Committee on Intelligence, *Compilation of Intelligence Laws and Related Laws and Executive Orders of Interest to the National Intelligence Community, As Amended through March 1, 1981*, 97th Cong., 1st sess., March 1, 1981, 150.
30. National Security Council, "National Security Planning Group Meeting, June 25, 1984; 2:00–3:00 P.M., Situation Room," minutes, document marked System IV NSC/ICS 400615; *The Iran-Contra Affair: The Making of a Scandal, 1983–1988*, ed. Malcolm Byrne and Peter Kornbluh (Alexandria, Va.: Chadwyck-Healey; Washington, D.C.: National Security Archive, 1992).
31. *60 Minutes*, CBS News, vol. 19, no. 26, March 15, 1987, 1, 2. Transcript provided by CBS, Inc.

CHAPTER 9

1. House Committee on Government Operations, Subcommittee on Legislation and National Security, 98th Cong., 1st sess., Frank C. Conahan, director, U.S. General Accounting Office, to Jack Brooks, letter B-206067, October 18, 1983. Enclosure I, *Responses to Questions of the Legislation and National Security Subcommittee;* Enclosure II, *Executive Branch Agencies and Offices That Handle*

Classified Information; Enclosure III, *Information Obtained from Executive Branch Agencies That Handle Classified Information,* 8.

2. House Committee on Government Operations, Subcommittee on Legislation and National Security, *Review of the President's National Security Decision Directive 84 and the Proposed Department of Defense Directive on Polygraph Use,* 98th Cong., 1st sess., October 19, 1983, 272.

3. *Cong. Rec.,* 98th Cong., 1st sess., 1983, 129, pt. 20:28704.

4. Ibid., 28704, 28715.

5. Associated Press, "Senate Shelves Plan to Censor Federal Workers," *San Francisco Chronicle,* October 21, 1983, 13; Stuart Taylor Jr., "Senate Would Bar Strict Censorship Urged by Reagan," *New York Times,* October 21, 1983, 1; William Safire, "The Right to Say 'No,' " *New York Times,* January 19, 1984, A23; Anthony Lewis, "Meese and Secrecy," *New York Times,* January 30, 1984, A17.

6. Hedrick Smith, "A Public Call for Secrecy," *New York Times,* December 20, 1984, A1.

7. Richard K. Willard, interview by author, November 1, 1989.

8. Steven Garfinkel, interview by author, October 24, 1983.

9. House Committee on the Judiciary, Subcommittee on Civil and Constitutional Rights, *Hearings on Presidential Directive on the Use of Polygraphs and Prepublication Review,* 98th Cong., 1st sess., April 21 and 28, 1983; 2d sess., February 7, 1984, 155.

10. Robert C. McFarlane, national security adviser to the president, letter to Patricia Schroeder, House Committee on the Post Office and Civil Service, chairwoman of Subcommittee on Civil Service, March 20, 1984.

11. Norman Dorsen, president of the American Civil Liberties Union, letter to Kenneth W. Dam, acting Secretary of State, Department of State, April 13, 1983, copy to Morton Halperin of the ACLU Washington, D.C., office. Dorsen's letter stated clearly that the ACLU had focused on obtaining the best possible implementation of the censorship operation. The bankruptcy of this approach, however, may be gleaned from the reply of Dam to Dorsen, dated May 11, 1983. "I was particularly interested in your discussion of partial as opposed to total review of manuscripts which you included in your letter and the concern you express over the possibility of the officials of one administration censoring the work of senior officials from previous administrations. In fact, the Department has in the past reviewed manuscripts which were voluntarily submitted for review and the Department's experience to date is that such reviews need not become adversarial."

12. Garfinkel, interview by author.

13. Allan Robert Adler, interview by author, May 10, 1985.

14. Willard, interview by author.

15. *From Official Files: Abstracts of Documents on National Security and Civil Liberties,* Center for National Security Studies Library, CNSS Report No. 102–5, March 1985.

16. Steven Garfinkel, interview by author, August 3, 1983.

17. Andrew A. Feinstein, interview by author, May 1985.

18. The account of Wilbur Crane Eveland is based on interviews by the author and letters from Eveland to the author beginning in 1983.

19. Wilbur Crane Eveland, *Ropes of Sand: America's Failure in the Middle East* (New York: Norton, 1980).

20. This policy was stated in a letter from Robert A. McConnell, assistant attorney general, to William V. Roth Jr., chairman, Senate Committee on Governmental Affairs, October 28, 1983. Paragraph seven specifically responded to senatorial questions concerning the Eveland affair: "In any event, it is our view that the obligation to submit materials for prepublication review may be imposed by express agreement or by agency regulations interpreting the fiduciary obligations of employees." Eveland was correct when he believed that the government could not sue him on the basis of any contracts he might have signed during his employment by the CIA. DOJ order 2620.8 (paragraph 5.c) required an expressly provided prepublication review agreement before Justice Department action could be undertaken to enforce censorship obligations.

21. CIA, memorandum to Donald B. Lakely (one of Eveland's aliases), August 19, 1959, under paragraph eight, "Secrecy": "You will be required to keep forever secret this contract and all information which you may obtain by [unintelligible] unless released in writing by the United States Government from such obligation, with full knowledge that violations of such secrecy may subject you to criminal prosecution under applicable laws and regulations." This document bears a stamp "Approved for release 9.4.80," and another, "Released 2 Mar 1983." The document was provided to me by Eveland.

22. In other words, Mayerfeld got Lynch to convince his client Eveland to sign a prepublication review agreement where one did not previously exist. Small wonder that Eveland was upset that he went along with the plan.

23. This might seem insignificant, but it pointed to larger issues that would plague the United States. CIA officer William Buckley was abducted while traveling to work at the Phalangist headquarters in Beirut. He was tortured and told his captors much of his knowledge. Learning of Buckley's torture provided George Bush and Ronald Reagan the motivation for getting Iran to help release the hostages in exchange for weapons. This plan became the Iran-Contra scandal.

24. William P. Clark at the White House, letter to Wilbur C. Eveland, August 13, 1983. In this letter, Clark verifies the date of Eveland's earlier letter to him as July 14.

25. Benis M. Frank, *U.S. Marines in Lebanon, 1982–1984* (Washington, D.C.: History and Museums Division, Headquarters, U.S. Marine Corps., G.P.O., 1987), 152.

CHAPTER 10

1. L. Britt Snider, interview by author, October 24, 1989.

2. Steven Garfinkel, interview by author, May 9, 1985.

3. House Permanent Select Committee on Intelligence, Subcommittee on Oversight, *Hearings on Prepublication Review and Secrecy Agreements,* 96th Cong., 2d sess., May 1, 1980, 114, 123–24.

4. Nat Hentoff, "How Samuel Morison Frightened the Free Press," *Village Voice,* December 17, 1985, 40.

5. The document quoted was in the possession of the author, but the original cannot be located.

6. Jeffrey T. Richelson, *The U.S. Intelligence Community* (Cambridge, Mass.: Ballinger, 1989).

7. Mark Lynch, direct examination of Prof. Jeffrey Richelson, 38, *United States v. Morison,* 604 F. Supp. 655 (D. Md. 1985).

8. *United States v. Morison,* transcript, 868.

9. Snider, interview by author.

10. Garfinkel, interview by author.

11. Lucille Manko, interviews by author, May [no date] 1985 and May 10, 1985.

12. Jeane J. Kirkpatrick, *Legitimacy and Force* (New Brunswick, N.J.: Transaction Books, 1988), vol. 1, 454; "Dictatorships and Double Standards," *Commentary,* November 1979, 34.

13. Jeane Kirkpatrick, interview by author, May 1985.

14. Angus Mackenzie, "Fit to Be Tied," *The Quill,* July/August 1985, 13; "Saying No to the Censors," editorial, *Washington Post,* July 12, 1985, A24.

15. Steven Garfinkel, interview by author, November 2, 1989.

16. Bob Woodward, *Veil: Secret Wars of the CIA, 1981–1987* (New York: Simon and Schuster, Pocket Books, 1987), 520–31.

17. House Select Committee on Intelligence, *CIA: The Pike Report* (Nottingham, England: Spokesman Books for the Bertrand Russell Peace Foundation, 1977), 219. Woodward showed the *Pike Report* to Bradlee as evidence, along with a *New York Times* clip, in an effort to push the story (*Veil,* 451).

18. Woodward, *Veil,* 600.

19. Boisfeuillet Jones, interview by author, June 3, 1986.

20. National Security Archive, *Chronology: The Documented Day-by-Day Account of the Secret Military Assistance to Iran and the Contras* (New York: Warner Books, 1987), 261.

21. Richard K. Willard, interview by author, November 1, 1989.

CHAPTER 11

1. Cover letter signed by Vice President George Bush that accompanied the *Public Report of the Vice President's Task Force on Combating Terrorism* (Washington, D.C.: G.P.O, February 1986), 1.

2. Bush's terrorism task force created a full-time position on the National Security Council staff to deal with terrorism and promoted Lt. Col. Oliver North to fill that position. North was later made the scapegoat for the Iran-Contra initiative.

3. Jonathan Dann and Dan Noyes, "So You Didn't Believe in Domestic Spying," *Current* (San Antonio), June 23–29, 1988, 1.

4. Angus Mackenzie, "Conversion: The Cost of Fired FBI Agent's Journey to Catholic Nonviolence," *National Catholic Reporter,* November 27, 1987, 1.

5. Anderson's report, acquired from me, was based upon documents received from the FBI under the FOIA and on interviews; see Jack Anderson and Dale Van Atta, "FBI Spied on Peace Groups, Papers Show," *Washington Post,* February 26, 1986, E23.

6. *Task Force on Combating Terrorism,* 26. The speculation is Bush's.

7. FBI Acting Director John E. Otto, letter to John C. Ryan, October 30, 1987, making final his firing. Additional sources: FBI files, correspondence, and interviews of Ryan by author.

8. *Ely v. FBI,* 610 F. Supp. 942 (N.D. Ill. 1985), *aff'd,* 792 F.2d 132 (11th Cir. 1986).

9. Morton Halperin, interview by author, May 15, 1986.

10. The document quoted was in the possession of the author, but the original cannot be located.

11. Allan Robert Adler, interview by author, October 1986.

12. Editorial, "A Blow to the Death Penalty," *Washington Post,* October 18, 1986, A22: "Changes in the exclusionary rule, restrictions on the Freedom of Information Act, limitations on habeas corpus, the use of the military for law enforcement and the death penalty were all considered. Not a single one is in the final bill."

13. Edwin Meese III, Department of Justice, "Attorney General's Memorandum on the 1986 Amendments to the Freedom of Information Act, for the Executive Departments and Agencies concerning the law enforcement amendments to the FOIA, U.S.C. 5 § 552," December 1987, iii, 6, 25.

14. *Allen v. Department of Defense,* 658 F. Supp. 15, 23 (D.D.C. 1986). Justice Department attorneys also went into court with their claim that the new amendment allowed the FBI to withhold secret documents from a political scientist who was researching FBI surveillance of gay and lesbian organizations.

15. Exhibit A, Richard Criley, Analysis of Documents Relating to NCARL at 1, 2, *Wilkinson v. FBI,* 111 F. Supp. 432 (C.D. Cal. 1986).

16. Richard K. Willard, Supplemental Memorandum on the Effect of Recent Amendments to the Freedom of Information Act, *Wilkinson v. FBI.*

17. Center for Constitutional Rights, "Political Spying and the Central America Movement," *Movement Support Network News* 4, no. 1 (Spring 1988), 3.

18. Ronald J. Ostrow, "6 FBI Officials Disciplined for Broad Terrorism Probe," *Los Angeles Times,* September 15, 1988, 26.

19. House Committee on the Judiciary, Subcommittee on Civil and Constitutional Rights, report by the Government Accounting Office to the chairman, *International Terrorism: FBI Investigates Domestic Activities to Identify Terrorists,* September 1990, GAO/GGD–90 112, 41.

20. Eugene Pugliese, interview by author, January 14, 1991.

21. Director of Central Intelligence Webster visited San Francisco in October 1988, giving what was—despite its billing—a subtle campaign speech for President Bush. I spoke with him briefly there.

CHAPTER 12

1. The quotations from A. Ernest Fitzgerald in this chapter are taken from a series of interviews with the author and from Fitzgerald's writing in *High Priests of Waste* (New York: Norton, 1972) and *The Pentagonists: An Insider's View of Waste Management and Fraud in Defense Spending* (Boston: Houghton Mifflin, 1989).

2. Charles Hinckle, letter to Air Force Office of Security Review, quoted in Fitzgerald, *High Priests of Waste*, 91, 92.

3. Fitzgerald, *High Priests of Waste*, 93.

4. Joint Economic Committee, Subcommittee on Economy in Government, *Hearings on Economics of Military Procurement*, 90th Cong., 2d sess., November 11–13, 1968, and January 16, 1969, 199–201; Fitzgerald, *High Priests of Waste*, 223.

5. Joint Economic Committee, Subcommittee on Economy in Government, hearings, 91st Cong., 2d sess., November 17, 1969.

6. Fitzgerald, *High Priests of Waste*, 252.

7. *Nixon v. Fitzgerald*, 457 U.S. 731 (1982); argued November 30, 1981.

8. Mark H. Lynch, Alan B. Morrison, and John Cary Sims, Motion of Morton, Ina, David, Mark, and Gary Halperin to Intervene and for Other Relief, *Nixon v. Fitzgerald*.

9. Fitzgerald, *The Pentagonists*, 263–66.

10. Congressman John D. Dingell, letter to Congressman William D. Ford, May 18, 1987.

11. Gerry Sikorski, letter to Frank Carlucci, June 24, 1987.

12. "Re SF 189 Classified Information Non-Disclosure Agreement," Allan Adler, legislative counsel, ACLU, memorandum to All Interested Parties, July 7, 1987.

13. Les Aspin and Barbara Boxer, letter to Frank Carlucci, July 14, 1987.

14. "Effect of Secrecy Agreements on Whistleblowing Protections," Congressional Research Service, Library of Congress, American Law Division, memorandum to Charles Grassley, July 28, 1987, 6.

15. Jack Brooks, letter to John Herrington, secretary of energy, October 14, 1987, quoted in Fitzgerald, *The Pentagonists*, 275.

16. *National Federation of Federal Employees v. United States*, 695 F. Supp. 1196 (D.D.C. 1988).

17. "No employees' clearances to be revoked for refusing to sign Form 189," Information Security Oversight Office Director Steven Garfinkel, letter to agency heads, August 21, 1987. But employees continue to sign.

18. Department of the Air Force, Office of the Judge Advocate General, Lt. Col. Russell Carparelli, letter to John Bodner Jr., Fitzgerald's attorney, August 21, 1987. Fitzgerald's suspension had already been pushed back to August 24, 1987.

19. House Committee on Post Office and Civil Service, Subcommittee on Human Resources, *Hearings on Classified Information Nondisclosure Agreements*, 100th Cong., 1st sess., October 15, 1987, 2, 4; Michael Isikoff, "Grassley to Civil Servants: Ignore Secrecy Pledge," *Washington Post,* October 16, 1987, A2.

20. House Subcommittee, *Hearings on Classified Information Nondisclosure Agreements*, 23, 26.

CHAPTER 13

1. *National Federation of Federal Employees v. United States,* 695 F. Supp 1196 (D.D.C. 1988).

2. Steven Garfinkel, interview by author, November 2, 1989.

3. Office of Federal Register, National Archives and Records Service, General Services Administration, *Weekly Compilation of Presidential Documents* (Washington, D.C.: G.P.O., 1988), 1189.

4. Maureen Dowd, "Bush Narrowing Field for Top Cabinet Posts," *New York Times,* November 17, 1988, B12.

5. "President's Statement on Signing the Treasury, Postal Service and General Government Appropriations Act, 1990" (Public Law 101–136), November 3, 1989.

6. House Select Committee on Intelligence, *CIA: The Pike Report* (Nottingham, England: Spokesman Books for the Bertrand Russell Peace Foundation, 1977). The Pike Committee (House Select Committee on Intelligence) report contains a detailed discussion of the fight between Congress and the CIA over access to documents. Morrison's joy came from the first sentence in a paragraph that read, in full:

   The difficulty is that no one in Congress can declassify. The Executive Branch claims exclusive and sole jurisdiction. This gives an administration the power to use the classification system in a manner that can result in manipulation of news by declassifying information that can be used to justify policy, while maintaining classification of information that may lead to contrary conclusions. Another aspect to be recognized is that classification can hide conduct from the American people that is well-known to the foreign country involved. Castro knew of the assassination attempts, the Cambodians knew they were being bombed, but the American people, whose government was engaging in these practices, were not aware of the activities because of the classification system.

7. "Comments on House Select Committee Draft Final Report," John D. Morrison Jr. (CIA deputy general counsel), Memorandum for: [blacked out], January 20, 1976, sanitized version released July 22, 1983, Re: *Center for National*

Security Studies v. CIA (Court IV—157 Pike Committee Documents—C.A. No. 80–1235 [D.D.C.], Doc. 113).

8. Frederick M. Kaiser, Congressional Research Service, "Congressional Rules and Conflict Resolution: Access to Information in the House Select Committee on Intelligence," *Congress and the Presidency* (The Center for Congressional and Presidential Studies at American University) 15, no. 1 (Spring 1988), 49–73.

9. Senate autonomy over executive classifications is slightly different, following its own rules. Senate Intelligence Committee rules allow it to release classified information upon its own vote, without the vote of the whole Senate.

10. Kaiser, "Congressional Rules and Conflict Resolution," 60.

11. Lee Hamilton, "Costs of Too Much Secrecy," letter, *Washington Post*, April 13, 1992, 21. Daniel P. Moynihan, quoted in *Albany Times Union*, May 3, 1992; reprinted in Center for National Security Studies, *First Principles* 17, no. 2 (July 1992), back cover (outside).

12. Thomas R. Smeeton, interview by author, June 10, 1991.

13. *Cong. Rec.,* 102d Cong., 1st sess., 1991, 137, pt. 89:4250.

14. Michael Pillsbury, interview by author, January 25, 1991.

15. D. B. Ottaway and Patrick Tyler, "U.S. Sends New Arms to Rebels: Afghans, Angolans Get Stinger Missiles in Change of Policy," *Washington Post*, March 30, 1986, A1.

16. Vincent Cannistraro, interview by author, undated.

17. The deeply felt disagreements between Pillsbury and Cannistraro are difficult to untangle. For instance, Cannistraro says he was in support of sending Stingers to Afghanistan. They disagreed, however, on Stinger policy regarding Central America. Both men concur that Pillsbury wanted to ship Stingers to the Contras while Cannistraro and the administration were dead set against it. When asked why Pillsbury was blacklisted, Cannistraro says, "It may have been part of the decision that he was a leaker, but there was great anger that he was undercutting the White House policy."

18. Michael Pillsbury, interview by author, April 20, 1990.

19. Pillsbury, interview by author, January 25, 1991.

20. Assistant Attorney General Stephen J. Markman, Department of Justice, Office of Legal Policy, letter to Senator Gordon Humphrey, April 10, 1989, 4.

21. Fred C. Ikle, letter to Senator Gordon Humphrey, September 22, 1989.

22. Sherry Mauck, interview by author, May 4, 1992; Mark Mansfield, interview by author, May 4, 1992.

23. Michael Pillsbury, interview by author, April 24, 1992.

CHAPTER 14

1. After eliminating the Interagency Groups and Special Interagency Groups (IGs and SIGs) that were exposed in the Iran-Contra scandal, President Bush replaced them with National Advisory Groups, or NAGs, one of which Anderson chaired.

2. The Reagan executive order mandated the same three classification categories that had been specified in Carter's Executive Order 12065.

3. Maynard Anderson, interview by author, June 12, 1991.

4. Steven Garfinkel, interview by author, June 14, 1991.

5. Senate Select Committee on Intelligence, *Hearings on Nomination of Robert M. Gates to be Director Central Intelligence,* 102d Cong., 1st sess., September 24, 1991, vol. 2, 143.

6. "Greater CIA Openness," Robert M. Gates, memorandum to Joseph De-Trani, November 18, 1991.

7. "Task Force Report on Greater CIA Openness," Task Force on Greater CIA Openness, to Director of Central Intelligence, December 20, 1991, 2.

8. Joseph DeTrani, interview by author, January 14, 1992.

9. "Task Force Report on Greater CIA Openness," Robert M. Gates, memorandum to CIA deputy director of administration et al., January 6, 1992. All of the following quotations are taken from this document.

10. Andy Rooney, "A Lack of Intelligence: Fire the Spies," *This World, San Francisco Examiner/Chronicle,* January 26, 1992, 5.

EPILOGUE

1. The epilogue was finished after Angus Mackenzie's death by Howard Kohn, Anna DeCormis Mackenzie, Jim Mackenzie, and Mary Wommack.

2. David Johnston, "CIA Officer Takes Deal for Life Term in Spy Case," *New York Times,* April 27, 1994, A12.

3. Walter Pincus, "CIA: Ames Betrayed 55 Operations," *Washington Post,* September 24, 1994, A1.

4. Michael Kilian, "Sentenced to Life, Spy Labels CIA a 'Sham'", *Chicago Tribune,* April 29, 1994, 3.

5. Lar-Erik Nelson, "Spy vs. Spy Leaves US in the Cold," *Newsday,* May 1, 1994, A40.

6. James A. Finefrock, "'Sham' Intelligence: The Ames Case Is Not the Only Place US Spies Are Stumbling," *San Francisco Examiner,* May 6, 1994, A22.

7. Tim Weiner, "Agency Chief Pledges to Overhaul Fraternity Atmosphere at CIA," *New York Times,* July 19, 1994, A1.

8. "The Freedom of Information Act," President Bill Clinton, memorandum to Heads of Departments and Agencies, October 3, 1993.

9. "The Freedom of Information Act," Attorney General Janet Reno, memorandum to Heads of Departments and Agencies, October 4, 1993.

10. Kathleen Kerr, "White House Trims Access; Memo Widens Freedom of Information Act Exemptions," *Newsday,* Nassau Edition, January 10, 1994, 15.

11. Richard Oppel, quoted in Debra Gersh Hernandez, "The FoIA and the White House: Freedom of Information Act," *Editor and Publisher,* November 20, 1993, 22.

12. Jim McGee, "Clinton Tries to Limit Access to NSC Data," *Washington Post,* March 26, 1994, A7.

13. Mark Thompson, "The Trouble Within," *Time,* August 1, 1994, 22.

14. Stephen Aftergood, "Intelligence Budget Disclosed by Mistake," *Secrecy and Government Bulletin,* May 1994.

 The monthly bulletin, written by Aftergood and published by the Federation of American Scientists (FAS), usually consists of a single legal-size sheet. FAS was organized in 1945 by scientists from the Manhattan Project concerned about the nuclear weapons they helped to create. It has 3,000 members, including many scientists who have won the Nobel Prize, and focuses on arms control, disarmament, and other national security issues, including secrecy.

15. Glickman Amendment for Disclosure of Budget FY 1994, "Almanac: 103rd Congress, 2nd Session . . . 1994," vol. L, *Congressional Quarterly,* 460.

16. Senate Select Committee on Intelligence, *Hearing on Nomination of John M. Deutch, of Massachusetts, to Director of Central Intelligence,* 104th Cong., 1st sess., May 8, 1995; Douglas Waller, "Master of the Game, the Formidable John Deutch is Becoming the Most Powerful CIA Chief Ever," *Time,* May 6, 1996, 41.

17. President Reagan, The White House, "National Security Information," Executive Order No. 12356, April 2, 1982.

18. Joint Security Commission (CIA Director R. James Woolsey and Secretary of Defense William J. Perry), Chairman Jeffrey H. Smith, "Redefining Security," Washington, D.C., February 28, 1994.

19. Steven Garfinkel, interview by Anna DeCormis Mackenzie, October 16, 1995.

20. Steven Garfinkel, interview by author, June 14, 1991.

21. Steven Garfinkel and Stephen Aftergood, quoted in R. Jeffrey Smith, "32,400 Workers Stockpiling U.S. Secrets," *Washington Post,* May 15, 1994, A1.

22. Stephen Aftergood, "Towards a New Classification System," *Secrecy and Government Bulletin,* September 1992.

23. The current total of SAPS, if known, is inaccessible. In 1985 the General Accounting Office esitmated that there were "about 5,000 or 6,000" SAP contracts with industry. Stephen Aftergood, *Secrecy and Government Bulletin,* December 1991.) The largest is the National Reconnaissance Office (NRO). The NRO is responsible for procuring and operating intelligence satellites for the Department of Defense. With an annual budget of more than $6.2 billion, it is larger by far than any of the intelligence agencies: the National Security Agency has a budget of around $3.7 billion and the CIA's budget is about $3.1 billion. (Aftergood, cited by R. Jeffrey Smith, "Making Connections with Dots to Decipher U.S. Spy Spending," *Washington Post,* March 12, 1996, 11.)

 In 1994, NRO was caught building a huge new $310 million facility in Virginia without bothering to fully advise Congress of its size, scope, or cost and sitting on a $3.8 billion buildup of appropriated but unspent funds. (Stephen Aftergood, "Get Smarter, Deystify the NRO," *Secrecy and Government Bulletin,* August/September 1994; Tim Weiner, "Senate Angered over Cost of Spy Agency's New Offices," *New York Times,* August 9, 1994.)

24. Steven Garfinkel, interview by Anna DeCormis Mackenzie, October 16, 1995.

25. Ralph Vartabedian, "When Is a Secret No Longer a Secret? Debate Rages on," *Los Angeles Times,* January 25, 1994, A5.

26. Steven Garfinkel, interview by author, April 30, 1992.

27. Margaret A. Jacobs, "Secret Air Base Broke Hazardous-Waste Act, Workers Suit Alleges," *Wall Street Journal,* February 8, 1996, A1.

28. *60 Minutes,* CBS News, March 17, 1996. Transcript by Burrelle's Information Services.

29. Michael Cavallo, president of the Cavallo Foundation, Inc., makes annual awards for "acts of moral courage in business and government" and is a supporter of the Area 51 plaintiffs. Michael Cavallo, interview by Anna DeCormis Mackenzie, May 23, 1996.

30. *Newsham v. Lockheed Missiles and Space Company, Inc.,* 907 F. Supp. 1349 (ND Cal 1988). This is a *qui tam* case, that is, a case in which individuals sue on behalf of themselves and taxpayers, with or without the government a party to the suit. Any monetary settlement is divided between those who bring the suit and the U.S. Treasury, in this case perhaps a ⅓ to ⅔ split.

31. Susan Guberman-Garcia, staff lawyer with Saperstein, Goldstein, Demchak, and Bakker, interviews by Anna DeCormis Mackenzie, February 3, 1996; April 26, 1996.

32. Andy Pasztor and Jeff Cole, "Lockheed Martin Whistle-Blower Suit Becomes a Test of U.S. Security Rules," *Wall Street Journal,* June 5, 1995, B4; Susan Guberman-Garcia, interviews by Anna DeCormis Mackenzie.

33. Stephen Aftergood, *Secrecy and Government Bulletin,* November 1991.

34. At least as recently as 1995, Congress, led by Grassley, has renewed the ban on using failure to sign the secrecy contract as the sole reason for firing a government employee. Since 1987 this ban, in the form of a rider to an appropriations bill, has made it possible for Ernest Fitzgerald to continue working as an analyst in the Air Force Comptroller's Office (see chapter 12).

35. Daniel J. Metcalfe, codirector, Information and Privacy, Department of Justice, interview by Anna DeCormis Mackenzie, November 20, 1996.

36. A. Ernest Fitzgerald, interviews by Anna DeCormis Mackenzie, December 7, 1995; January 8, 1996.

INDEX

Chapworth, Perry M. (pseud.), 129
"Chicago Eight" trial, 3, 32–33
Children's Campaign for Nuclear
    Disarmament, 205
Chile: 1973 coup in, 64, 69; 1970 elections
    in, 50
Christic Institute, 204
Christison, William A., 74
Church, Frank, 62, 64
CIA. *See* Central Intelligence Agency
CIA and the Cult of Intelligence, The
    (Marchetti and Marks), 42, 43–48,
    49–51
CIA Covert Action Division No. Five, 19
CIA Directorate of Plans, 20
CIA Domestic Contact Service (DCS), 27,
    34–35
CIA Information Act of 1984, 117, 150
CIA International Terrorism Group, 49
CIA Openness Task Force, 184–88
CIA Special Operations Group (SOG),
    26–27, 54–55
CIA Special Security Office, 180
CIR. *See* Center for Investigative
    Reporting
CISPES. *See* Committee in Solidarity with
    the People of El Salvador
Citizens Against Nuclear War, 205
Civil Service Commission, 11–12
Clark, William P., 91–93, 132
Classifiable information, definition of, 164,
    169
Classified information: categories of, 93,
    181; reforming system of, 194–97;
    selectivity of, 96; value of, 181–82
Clifford, Clark, 159
Clinton, Hillary Rodham, 192
Clinton, William Jefferson, 190, 191–94
COINTELPRO. *See* Operation
    COINTELPRO (FBI)
Colby, William E., 43–44, 49, 61, 62, 63,
    69, 137
Cold war era: atmosphere of secrecy
    during, 12–13, 201; counterspying
    during, 189; end of, 181, 201–2
College Press Service collective, 39, 55, 70
Commission on CIA Activities within the
    United States (Rockefeller
    Commission), 62, 210n12

Committee Against Registration and the
    Draft, 204
Committee in Solidarity with the People
    of El Salvador (CISPES), 154–55
"Committee of Greeks and Greek
    Americans to Prevent Their Country,
    Their Fatherland, from Being Perverted
    to the Uses of the CIA," 65
Committee to Abolish the House Un-
    American Activities Committee, 153
Communist Party, U.S., 17, 23
Conahan, Frank C., 122
Confidential, definition of, 93, 181
Congress, U.S.: attempts to control
    reporters by, 83–89, 91, 98; creation of
    CIA by, 9–11; declassification of
    information by, 172–73; FOIA
    exemptions approved by, 105, 116–18,
    151–52; and Intelligence Identities
    Protection Act, 83–89; investigation of
    CIA by, 62–71, 79–80; openness
    encouraged by, 60; oversight of CIA by,
    12, 67, 172–74; secrecy contracts banned
    by, 167, 168, 169, 170, 171–72; student
    lobbying of, 25; support for civil liberties
    in, 111–13; support for Contras in, 121.
    See also House Select Committee on
    Intelligence; House Subcommittee on
    Government Information and
    Individual Rights; Senate Permanent
    Select Committee on Intelligence
Congressional Research Service, 165, 186
Connor, John T., 210n12
Conyers, John, Jr., 21, 69
Copyright law, 100
Counterintelligence, 5, 20–21, 27, 105
Counterspying, 189
CounterSpy magazine, 59–60, 65, 89–90
Covert Action Information Bulletin, 84
Crewdson, John, 87
Criley, Richard, 153–54
Culpepper, James W., 95

Dam, Kenneth W., 127
Davis, Rennie, 37–38
DCS. *See* CIA Domestic Contact Service
Deadly Deceits (McGehee), 110–11
Dean, John, 30, 40, 55, 126
Debray, Regis, 32

Compositor:	Impressions Book and Journal Services, Inc.
Text:	Adobe Garamond
Display:	Perpetua and Adobe Garamond
Printer and Binder:	Edwards Bros., Inc.

DATE DUE	
MAR 1 3 2002	
APR 2 8 2006	
MAY 1 8 2006	
MAY 0 2 2006	